STRIVE FOR A 5
Preparing for the AP® European History Exam

Based on the 2017 AP® European History redesigned curriculum.

Authored by

Louise Forsyth

Brooklyn College, CUNY, Department of Education
Former Head, History Department, Poly Prep Country Day School

This product was developed to accompany

A History of Western Society for the AP® Course

Twelfth Edition

John P. McKay | Clare Haru Crowston | Merry E. Wiesner-Hanks | Joe Perry

AP® is a trademark registered by the College Board®, which was not involved in the production of, and does not endorse, this product.

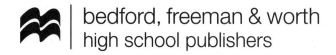

bedford, freeman & worth
high school publishers

Manufactured in the United States of America.

1 2 3 4 5 6   21 20 19 18 17

For information, write:
Bedford/St. Martin's
Attn: High School Department
1 New York Plaza
New York, NY 10004

Or email:
socialstudies@bfwpub.com

ISBN 978-1-319-03668-3

AP® is a trademark registered by the College Board®, which was not involved in the production of, and does not endorse, this product.

Contents

Preface   1

SECTION 1: Study Guide

A Review of AP® European History & *A History of Western Society for the AP® Course,* Twelfth Edition

AP® Period One/Part One c. 1450–c. 1648

AP® Period Two/Part Two c. 1648–c. 1815

AP® Period Three/Part Three c. 1815–c. 1914

AP® Period Four/Part Four c. 1914–Present

SECTION 2: Prep Guide

Preface for Students

By the time you open this book to help prepare you for the AP® European History Exam, you are likely already immersed in the study of European history. Your AP® European History course can be a deep and rewarding experience, demanding a high level of understanding and analysis as you read your textbook and consider other materials included in your course. If you work hard, you will find that this experience will hold great value beyond the AP® course or the AP® exam; you will have the intellectual tools to wrestle with complex ideas, to see connections between the past and the present, to write thoughtfully, and to know how to justify your thoughts as you prepare for college and adult life.

This book is designed to ease your way into a high score on the AP® European History Exam. Many students feel overwhelmed by the amount of material that the exam covers. Do not be daunted—you can master this vast amount of knowledge and walk into the exam confident that you have the knowledge and skills not only to do well, but to strive for a 5!

What's in This Book?

While this study guide is designed to accompany McKay's *A History of Western Society for the AP® Course*, Twelfth Edition, it can be used with almost any European history text. The guide follows the organization of the McKay text and is divided into the four time periods of European history as described in the AP® European History Course and Exam Description, effective Fall 2017. It follows a thematic narrative, making it an easy addition to any test review regimen. Dividing the content of this guide into four chronological periods helps structure the main themes of the course and puts the details of events and ideas into an overall context.

Each chapter in the study guide begins with a brief overview of the main events and key figures, followed by a succinct summary of the chapter in *A History of Western Society*. Each chapter is summarized using the six themes of AP® European History:

- Interaction of Europe and the World
- Poverty and Prosperity
- Objective Knowledge and Subjective Visions
- States and Other Institutions of Power
- Individual and Society
- National and European Identity

Following the thematic summaries are Focus Questions that allow you to answer questions as you study the chapters to build your knowledge and understanding of European history.

After the Study Guide Unit, the Prep Guide explores how to prepare for the AP® exam and includes two complete practice exams in the redesigned AP® format and style—with multiple-choice questions, a Short Answer Questions (SAQ) section (in which the first two questions are required, but you will be able to choose between questions 3 or 4), a Document Based Question (DBQ), and a Long Essay Question (LEQ) section (in which you may choose one of the three questions provided).

Notice this guide does not include answers to the exam questions. This is because some teachers like to use these practice exams for credit. Your teacher has access to the practice exam answers (for essays: what good answers will include), and can provide them to you, depending on his or her plans for utilizing this book in class.

Preface for Teachers

Strive for a 5: Preparing for the AP® European History Exam is a student prep guide, designed to provide your students with a thorough review of the course material while practicing AP® test-taking skills that will help them on the AP® European History Exam.

Designed to pair seamlessly with *A History of Western Society for the AP® Course*, Twelfth Edition, by John P. McKay et al., *Strive for a 5* applies a strong AP®-specific framework to the text's narrative and offers extended attention to the exam format and test-taking strategies. Either assigned as a core component of your test preparation coursework or recommended to students as an independently navigable review and practice tool, *Strive for a 5* is designed to familiarize students with the exam format, thematically organize and review key concepts, and provide cumulative practice exams. For students who are striving for a 5, there is no better preparation guide.

Features of this Prep Guide

Unit 1: Study Guide follows the textbook's structure and groups course material into four chronological periods; these four parts closely correspond with the historical periodization of the AP® European History Exam. Within each part, **thematic chapter reviews** organize and summarize the major developments of each era using the six themes in European history and the key concepts relevant to that time period. Using this format allows students to review information in the categories that are often used in AP® European History Exam questions, especially the essay questions.

Unit 2: Prep Guide serves as an introduction to the AP® European History Exam and includes an overview of the exam, strategies for success, and essay-writing instructions. **AP®-style practice exams** conclude the Prep Guide portion of this book. Each practice exam includes multiple-choice questions, short-answer questions, a document-based question, and long-essay questions—in the same "redesign" style* that students will encounter on the AP® exam. The practice exams can be assigned as assessment, or students can independently measure their progress and areas in need of further review.

Note: Model answers are available on our Teacher's Resource Flash Drive or the Instructor's Companion site; contact your local rep for access. This allows you to decide how to use the practice exams in this text.

*Based on the 2017 AP® European History Curriculum Framework.

About the Author

Louise Forsyth holds a B.A. and an M.A. in European history and taught AP® European History at Poly Prep Country Day School in Brooklyn, New York, for more than twenty-five years, including one year teaching the course via Skype from London. She has been an AP® European History Exam reader and table leader for nearly as long, and she served as question leader for the document-based essay when core scoring was introduced. In addition to publishing several scholarly articles and several other textbook manuals, she has made numerous presentations on European and world history at the AHA and NCSS, as well as other conferences here and abroad. She taught AP® Comparative Government and Politics as well as AP® European History and served as head of the history department at Poly Prep for seven years. Most recently she was the curriculum specialist for the NEH Summer Institutes on Bach in 2008, 2010, and 2012, and she also recently participated in a Fulbright-Hays seminar abroad in Turkey and the Balkans. Currently, Louise Forsyth is an adjunct lecturer at Brooklyn College, CUNY, Department of Education.

Preface

The story before our story begins:

Europe, located on the western part of the huge Eurasian landmass, is bordered on three sides by water–the North Sea, the Atlantic, and the Mediterranean. Its eastern frontier, stretching from the Ural Mountains in Russia to the Bosporus in Turkey, is amorphous. Europe's heartland–where most of the history related in this book took place–is England, France, Italy, and Germany. The periphery–Iberia, Russia, Scandinavia, Eastern Europe, and the Balkans–took center stage at crucial moments but rarely held it for long. Most Europeans belong to one of three language groups–Germanic (Germany, Austria, England, Scandinavia), Slavic (Russia, most of Eastern Europe) and Latin (Italy, France, Spain, Portugal, Romania).

Ancient Greece and Rome

Europa was the name of a princess abducted by the Greek god Zeus. It's proper that the continent's name be of Greek origin, for Greek culture is the foundation of Western civilization. Like everyone in the ancient world except for the Hebrews, the Greeks were polytheists. Their gods were human-like, capricious and passionate, unlike the stern gods worshipped elsewhere. Greece, with its many islands and mountainous terrain, was divided into small self-governing city-states. One of these, Athens, laid the foundation of Western culture. It was the world's first (and only) democracy, limited as that was to free-born Athenian males, and during its heyday, the 5th century BCE, philosophy (Socrates, Plato, Aristotle), theatre (Aeschylus, Euripides), and the essential principles of Western art and architecture (proportionality, mathematical perspective, realism) developed. A vibrant civic life promoted individualism and openness to other cultures. Other Greeks created the disciplines of history (Herodotus), science (Thales), medicine (Hippocrates) and mathematics (Pythagoras). Athens became dominant after leading the Greeks in defeating the Persian invasion of 490 BCE, but was weakened by a long war with the Spartans, famed for their militarism. Philip of Macedonia conquered the Greek city-states a century later. His son, Alexander, was an extraordinary general who conquered most of the "known" world, from Egypt to western India, in his short life and in doing so spread Greek civilization far and wide. After his death in 323 BCE, Greece ceased to play a significant role in European affairs.

At the center of the Italian peninsula in the 6th century BCE, the Latin-speaking Romans established a strong state with a new political form, a republic, a partially representative government with an appointed Senate, popular assemblies, and two elected consuls as executives. With their highly effective army of foot soldiers, Rome conquered first the Italian peninsula and then the entire Mediterranean basin. By the early first century CE, Caesar and Augustus had replaced the Republic with rule by hereditary emperors. The Romans incorporated much of Greek culture into their own but their greatest achievements were in engineering and architecture. Europe below the Danube is dotted with Roman aqueducts, roads, bridges, baths, temples, and theatres. The second century CE was the *Pax Romana,* a time of prosperity, stability, and peace from Spain to Syria. Five good emperors in a row ruled from a splendid capital.

But within a century, it all fell apart. Inflation became constant and nomadic Germanic tribes, never part of the Empire, regularly invaded its northern borders. During this difficult third century, many people converted to Christianity, created in Roman Palestine in the first century. Late in the fourth century, it became Rome's official religion. The empire's situation was so dire that it was divided in half. The Western Roman Empire fell to one of the Germanic tribes in 476 CE; the Eastern Roman Empire (Byzantium), centered in Constantinople, lasted nearly another thousand years more.

The Early Middle Ages (ca. 500–1000 CE)

Within Italy, as the Empire broke up, stability was provided by the Papacy. The Bishop of Rome asserted his authority to be Pope, the leader of all Christians, and organized an effective hierarchy and bureaucracy, defined doctrine, and ruled as a temporal power. Economically, the large slave plantations of the Empire morphed into manors ruled by heritary nobles and worked by serfs, tenant-farmers bound to the soil. Manorialism was the basis of the European economy for hundreds of years. Instead of the internationalism and easy movement among various peoples of the Empire, life became local. Trade declined to the point that there was very little coinage of gold, used for international trade, or silver. By the sixth century, there were no large cities in western and central Europe, people rarely traveled, and literacy virtually disappeared. Politically, centralized Roman rule gave way to a decentralized feudal system in which titular kings gave nobles territory in exchange for military service. Wars, fought by armored knights, were typically brief. While the Western Empire declined, its counterpart in the East flourished. Orthodox Christianity, which uses vernacular languages in liturgy rather than Latin, took root there and spread throughout the Balkans and to Russia.

Isolated, Europe in the five centuries of the Early Middle Ages was relatively static. Islam, the newest monotheistic religion founded in the early 7th century CE, helped spark change. Within a century, Moslem Arabs had conquered all of North Africa, the Middle East, and parts of Europe itself (Spain and Sicily) until their advance was stopped in 732. They developed a sophisticated civilization centered in Damascus and later Baghdad, and translated into Arabic the Greek and Latin texts found in their conquests, thus preserving them for us. Hoping to create a strong Christian state independent of the Eastern Roman Empire, the Pope crowned the Germanic king Charlemagne Holy Roman Emperor in 800.

The High Middle Ages (ca. 1000–1300)

In the next few centuries, agricultural production began to increase and consequently population grew, allowing the recreation of urban life. Cities were small, often self-governing communes, and dynamic economic centers. Organized by trade guilds, manufacturing, most importantly of textiles, and trading both international and national, created a new class of wealthy burghers. Resurgent Europe waged a series of wars (the Crusades) against Muslim control over the Holy Land, which although ultimately unsuccessful, spurred international trade. Intellectual life also reawakened. Universities were created, specializing in law, theology, or medicine, and scholars flocked to Muslim Spain where Greek manuscripts, particularly Aristotle's scientific works, were translated from Arabic into Latin, sparking the "12th century Renaissance." Theologians (Aquinas) incorporated this pagan knowledge into university curricula. New artistic styles (Romanesque, Gothic), new literary styles (vernacular love poetry), new secular ideals (chivalry), and highly popular new preaching orders (Franciscans, Dominicans), were hallmarks of a distinct medieval culture. Slowly, some rulers began to centralize power. In England and France, kings established effective monarchies. England was territorially unified centuries before most other European states when the Normans conquered it in 1066. The *Magna Carta* of 1215, foundational to Western democracy, limited the king's power. France's Capetian and Valois kings increased royal authority and crushed Christian dissidents. Germany and Italy remained divided into many small states, a few of them republics where nobles (aristocrats) were excluded from power. The Holy Roman Empire proved unwieldy and ineffective while the Papacy grew in power and wealth. On the periphery, Christian Spaniards fought *La Reconquista* for centuries to overthrow Muslim rule, while Eastern European faced marauding Mongols. By 1300, heartland Europe had laid the foundations for many modern institutions and asserted itself on the international stage.

CHAPTER 11
The Later Middle Ages, 1300–1450

Areas of Focus: England, France, Italy, and Holland/Flanders

Main Events: the Black Death, the Hundred Years' War, and the Babylonian Captivity/Great Schism

Key Figures:

- Giovanni Boccaccio: Florentine writer; described the Black Death
- Henry V: king of England; won the Battle of Agincourt
- Joan of Arc: religious mystic who led French troops to victory; tried and executed for heresy
- William of Occam: philosopher who challenged temporal power of the Papacy
- John Wyclif: English theologian who challenged key tenets of Catholicism
- Jan Hus: Czech theologian; brought Wyclif's ideas to Bohemia
- Christine de Pizan: first female professional writer
- Dante Alighieri: Florentine poet; wrote the *Divine Comedy,* the first major work in Italian
- Geoffrey Chaucer: English poet; wrote *The Canterbury Tales,* a pivitol work in the development of English vernacular literature
- Edward III: king of England who accepted Parliamentary approval of new taxes

AP® Themes
Interaction of Europe and the World

> The Black Death came to Europe from southwestern China where it originated. This fast-spreading plague was brought into Europe on trading ships, reflecting the role of international trade for the Italian city-states in the late medieval era.

Poverty and Prosperity

> The "Little Ice Age" (1300–1450) brought wetter and colder climates, severely reducing agricultural output. A terrible famine across Europe (1315–1322) increased vulnerability to diseases. A decline in English wood exports in 1318 caused unemployment in Flanders and the Hanseatic and Italian city-states.

> As a result of the plague known as the Black Death (first reported in mainland Europe in 1347) and the resulting labor shortage, urban craft guilds opened their doors to "new men" and tried efficient methods of production. Laborers could demand higher wages and the prices of goods rose.

> The Hundred Years' War devastated France's lands and disrupted its trade; high taxes to finance the war angered the peasants who bore the brunt of costs. The war was also very costly for England.

> These economic dislocations led to the end of serfdom in western Europe as landlords switched to cash rents and payments.

Objective Knowledge and Subjective Visions

> Many people were convinced that the Black Death was a punishment from God; flagellants went from town to town whipping themselves in repentance.

> Popular Christianity expressed itself in confraternities, voluntary associations of men devoted to particular Christian tasks, and in the spread of lay mysticism, inspired by such figures as Meister Eckhart and Bridget of Sweden. The Brethren and Sisters of the Common Life, founded in Holland in the late fourteenth century, lived simple lives devoted to Christian charity. Their ideas were developed by Thomas à Kempis in the fifteenth century in his hugely popular work, *The Imitation of Christ.*

> The fourteenth century saw the growth of vernacular literature, with two literary masterpieces bracketing the century. Dante's *The Divine Comedy* described in poetic cantos the author's journey through hell, purgatory and heaven; in hell, the great Roman poet Virgil accompanied him. Dante is considered a pivotal figure between the Medieval and Renaissance periods, and due to his work, the Florentine vernacular became the basis of the modern Italian language. Geoffrey Chaucer's *Canterbury Tales* related ribald stories told by a group of pilgrims, reflecting the secularism and materialism of late medieval England.

> The Dance of Death became a common artistic motif, reflecting the impact of the plague.

> New colleges and universities were established that, unlike their early medieval counterparts, tended to be more national (rather than international) in focus. Schools also spread, as did literacy.

> Several intellectuals, philosophers, and theologians in the first half of the fourteenth century challenged the legitimacy of the Papacy as an institution. William of Occam argued for separation of church and state, and said that governments must be limited and accountable to those they govern. Marsiglio of Padua argued that the church ought to be subordinate to the state and that the church should be run not by the pope, and a hierarchical structure subservient to him, but by a council of laymen and priests. The Church declared both men's works heretical, but a movement arose in support of their ideas. John Wyclif denied a scriptural basis for the Church's secular powers and insisted that Scripture alone should be the basis of Christian belief and practice, and that it should be read by the laity. He was the first person to translate the Bible into English

States and Other Institutions of Power

> The Papacy became subject to the French kings when it moved to Avignon in 1309. The 67 years of the Avignon residency, known as the Babylonian Captivity (1309–1376), were famously extravagant and hurt the prestige of the Church.

> When the Papacy returned to Rome in 1377, political disputes divided Europe into factions supporting one of the two, and later three, popes, in what became known as the Great Schism. The Schism ended in 1417 with the selection of a new pope at the ecumenical Council of Constance.

> In England (but not in France) the war led to the strengthening of Parliament, the national representative body. Kings called Parliament into session many times to get funds for the war. In France there were many provincial assemblies, not one.

Individual and Society

> The event with the greatest impact on every aspect of society in the fourteenth century was the Black Death, the epidemic of bubonic plague that killed at least one–third of the population of Europe and upwards of 60 percent of the population in cities like Florence. Cities were crowded, filthy, and filled with rats bearing the disease; medical science was limited in its ability to cure. Wealthier people fled the cities but remained vulnerable to the plague, which returned with decreasingly intensity until 1721.

> The clergy generally tended the sick and dying at great risk. Contemporaries like the Florentine Boccaccio described a decline in moral standards and family feelings.

> The plague loosened social class strictures and briefly allowed greater social mobility.

> Angered by high taxes and their poor quality of life and resenting the privileges and demands of nobility and church, peasants rose up in several rebellions. First, in Flanders in the 1320s, then in a large-scale uprising in France—the Jacquerie—in 1358. In 1381, the English Peasants' Revolt exploded in resentment over the replacement of labor services by cash rents and a statute freezing wages and binding workers to their manors. Manors were attacked, nobles killed or assaulted, manorial records destroyed. The rebellions were brutally suppressed.

> Demands for greater opportunity for journeymen [day laborers] in the guild system generally failed. Similarly, the guilds excluded women more and more over the course of the fourteenth century.

> Men and women married later, usually in their 20s, or even older for wealthier men. To deal with the problem of unwed young men, city governments in various parts of Europe set up brothels and regulated the women workers. Some young men also took sex by force. Same-sex relations, at that time called 'sodomy,' had become a capital crime in most of Europe by the end of the fourteenth century.

> Suffering from inflation and reduced income, some nobles became bandits and demanded protection money. This "fur-collar crime" aggravated peasants' lives.

National and European Identity

> England and France became more nationalistic during the intermittently fought Hundred Years' War (1337–1453), which began as a feudal war over disputed claims of kingship and vassalage. The English won most of the important battles due to their use of new technologies like the longbow and cannon, but lost the crucial siege of Orléans because of the extraordinary political and military leadership of the young Joan d'Arc, later captured, tried and executed as a witch.

> Jan Hus brought Wyclif's ideas to Bohemia around 1400, where they were extremely popular among nationalistic Czechs. Hus was condemned as a heretic by the Council of Constance and burned at the stake. The Hussite Wars that followed (1419–1430s) were caused by a fusion of Czech nationalism and Hus's religious ideas. In the 1430s, the emperor recognized the Hussite church in Bohemia.

> Economic hardship and then the plague increased ethnic group tensions, leading to violence against outsiders like Jews and lepers. Minorities were increasingly excluded from positions in church or government, and laws against intermarriage were instituted. New ideas about the importance of "blood" were particularly strong in Spain where "purity of blood"—meaning no Jewish or Muslim ancestors—became a national obsession. In Ireland, the English issued statutes denying the Irish the same rights as Englishmen.

McKay Chapter 11 Focus Questions

1. How did climate change shape the late Middle Ages?

2. How did the plague reshape European society?

3. What were the causes, course, and consequences of the Hundred Years' War?

4. Why did the church come under increasing criticism?

5. What explains the social unrest of the late Middle Ages?

NOTES:

CHAPTER 12
European Society in the Age of the Renaissance, 1350–1550

Areas of Focus: England, France, Italy, and Spain

Main Events: the Renaissance, nation-state development in France and England

Main Figures:

- Francesco Petrarch: poet; "father of humanism"
- Lorenzo de' Medici: "Il Magnifico," *de facto* ruler of Florence, great patron of the arts and letters
- Michelangelo: sculptor of the David, architect, painter of the ceiling of the Sistine Chapel
- Leonardo da Vinci: universal genius, inventor, engineer, painter of the Mona Lisa
- Leonardo Bruni: historian, civic humanist, chancellor of Florence
- Niccolò Machiavelli: author of *The Prince,* political scientist, Florentine Chancellor
- Pico della Mirandola: author of *Oration on the Dignity of Man*
- Marsilio Ficino: founded the Platonic Academy in Florence
- Giorgio Vasari: art historian and artist
- Baldassare Castiglione: author of *The Courtier, a* guide to aristocratic behavior
- Francois I: king of France; negotiated the Concordat of Bologna with the pope
- Ferdinand of Aragon and Isabella of Castille: rulers of Spain; completed the Reconquista, expelled the Jews
- Thomas More: English humanist, author of *Utopia*
- Desiderius Erasmus: Dutch humanist, author of *In Praise of Folly*
- Johann Gutenberg: inventor of the printing press
- Sofonisba Anguissola: Italian court painter in Spain
- Henry VII: first Tudor king of England
- Cassandra Fedele: Venetian woman scholar and humanist
- Savonarola: Dominican friar, briefly head of Florentine government; critic of materialism and secularism

AP® Themes
Interaction of Europe and the World

> The Renaissance was, to some degree, an intensely localized phenomenon; particularly in Florence, but was stimulated by contacts with the fading Byzantine Empire that brought the knowledge of ancient Greek to humanists. The Renaissance spread from Florence to the other Italian city-states and then to France and elsewhere in Europe.

> The Europeans had many contacts with the Ottoman Empire, which was established when the Ottoman Turks took Constantinople (renaming it Istanbul) in 1453. The Ottoman Empire would expand to rule most of the eastern Mediterranean and the Middle East. France's King Francois I had diplomatic relations with Sultan Suleiman the Magnificent.

> After Ferdinand and Isabella defeated the last Moorish kingdom of Granada, they expelled the Jews who refused to convert to Christianity from Spain. Many of them were welcomed in the Ottoman Empire.

Poverty and Prosperity

> Prosperous trade and thriving manufacturing created a great deal of disposable wealth in the northern Italian communes. The wealthy medieval ports of Venice and Genoa were soon rivaled by Florence, whose merchants traded a great variety of goods and whose bankers dominated investments and loans throughout Europe. Florence also generated much wealth itself through its high-quality silk and wool manufacturing.

> City economic life was dominated by trade guilds, run by the businessmen of each craft (such as shoemakers) or trade (such as silk) or manufactured good (such as finished wool cloth) which sought to enhance the profits for all guild masters by controlling quality of materials, hours of operation, and wages. The leaders of the major guilds (such as wool or silk manufacturers) became wealthy and powerful, the oligarchs in charge of the government, and often patrons of the arts.

Objective Knowledge and Subjective Visions

> The Renaissance is defined in large part by the development of a new intellectual movement called humanism, which rejected the scholasticism of medieval universities. Instead, humanists called for a rediscovery of classical antiquity, at first Roman, and then beginning in the fifteenth century, Greek. In classical literature, humanists found models of excellent Latin (Cicero), information on science, medicine and the arts (Galen, Vitruvius, and Plato), justification for republican values and even regicide (Cicero), and guidance for the ideal man who had *virtù* (the ability to shape the world around oneself) and sought excellence in every human endeavor.

> Humanism began in the fourteenth century, first as a literary movement, with the writings of Dante, the poetry of Petrarch, and the work of Florentines Boccaccio, Bruni, and Alberti, who all articulated humanist ideals and expressed their great love of antiquity. Early humanists focused on civic humanism, finding justification for republican forms of government and secular values in Greek and Latin texts. Later humanists became Neo-Platonists and established schools for the education of young men according to the new principles.

> Humanists recovered and translated ancient texts, revived the Latin of Cicero to replace medieval Latin, studied Greek, and wrote their own works based on ancient models. Humanists searched for and treasured manuscripts, which were then published by fifteenth century printers to feed an increasingly literate population.

> Humanists created a new educational system based on classical texts, which became the basis for European education for centuries. The key element in the curriculum was the study of ancient texts and the language skills in Latin and Greek needed to understand and write about them with eloquence. Roman and Greek history and political philosophy were also taught in the newly created schools, which were only for boys.

> Under the patronage of Cosimo de' Medici (1389-1464), the scholar Marsilio Ficino (1433-99) established the Platonic Academy, an informal group of Florence's cultural elite.

> Machiavelli's short book *The Prince* is considered the first modern work in political science. In it, he analyzed the actual practices of rulers in terms of their effectiveness without regard to their moral value.

> **AP® Tip** Renaissance individualism and secularism are easily seen in the newly revived literary genres of biography and autobiography, and the artistic genre of portraiture–a useful point to make in essays.

> Perhaps the most noted achievements of the Renaissance were in the visual arts: painting, sculpture, and architecture. At the beginning of the fourteenth century, Giotto had added monumentality and emotionality to painting. In 1420s Florence, Renaissance artists such as the architect Brunelleschi discovered the potential of mathematical perspective and proportionality to transform building design. Brunelleschi designed the Foundling Hospital, the first contemporary building to use rounded Roman arches instead of pointed Gothic arches, and designed and built the first dome in Europe in 900 years, the Duomo of Florence. Donatello sculpted the first nude since antiquity, the Old Testament figure of David. Sculptors aimed to represent the realities and the glories of the human body as they had in ancient times. Artists increasingly turned to classical antiquity for subjects such as pagan gods, goddesses and heroes, as seen in Botticelli's *The Birth of Venus*.

> In Florence, most of the commissions in the early Renaissance came from the commune (city government), guilds, or wealthy merchants. Later in the Renaissance, princely courts (such as the Duke of Ferrara and the Medicis of Florence), churches, and the Vatican itself became major patrons of the arts. The Vatican commissioned both Raphael's *School of Athens* and Michelangelo's Sistine Chapel frescos. Venice, too, became an important artistic center with such noteworthy artists as Titian.

> Two new art forms developed during the Renaissance: landscape painting, which demonstrated perspective, and portraiture, which reflected the dramatic individualism of the day.

> In northern Europe, great artists like Jan van Eyck and Rogier van der Weyden made technological innovations such as the use of oil-based paint (instead of fresco) to create works of striking detail and realism.

> The social status of artists increased enormously during the Renaissance, from artisans to "men of genius"–wealthy, adored and sought after. Artists trained at the workshops of well-established artists, and artistic academies were established by the mid-sixteenth century. Giorgio Vasari wrote an influential art history praising the genius of artists of his own day like Michelangelo.

> One Renaissance ideal, derived from the ancient Greeks, was the "l'umono universale," meaning a man talented in a wide variety of fields. Several artists were praised as models of this Renaissance ideal. Leonardo da Vinci was an inventor, engineer, as well as an extraordinary artist. The architect Leon Battista Alberti also wrote novels, plays, treatises on the family and on mathematical perspective, and invented codes. Michelangelo was a master sculptor, painter, architect, and designer, as well as a recognized poet. Castiglione's influential behavior guide *The Courtier* called on the aristocrats to achieve excellence in many activities.

> Women were generally excluded from this new artistic world; there were no women architects and only one sculptress. There were a number of successful women painters, like Sofonisba Anguissola, who became a court painter for the Spanish monarchs, but most women involved in artistic activity worked as embroiders or painted on porcelain. Women were excluded from the art academies and usually trained with artists, often their fathers.

States and Other Institutions of Power

> North of Rome, these city-states were organized into self-governing communes: either republics (such as Florence) or one-man dynasties known as *signori* (such as Milan). Most were dominated by oligarchies of merchants and wealthy guildsmen who repressed the political aspirations of the *popolo* (common people) and created courts as centers of culture.

→ **AP® Tip** The city-state system is a key element in understanding how the Renaissance was born in a divided Italy. Passionate loyalty to their city-states infused the work of many Renaissance artists and writers. Humanism developed in part to defend the values of republican Florence. As the Renaissance moved outside of the Italian city-states, royal and aristocratic courts became artistic centers. Because the AP® course begins around 1450, it is more likely that an AP® question will focus on Medicean Florence and court culture rather than on the communal republics.

> The Medici banking family came to dominate Florence and later became hereditary dukes. Other important families were the Sforza in Milan and the Borgias, including Pope Alexander VI and his notorious son Cesare Borgia.

> Southern Italy, the Kingdom of Naples, was ruled by the King of Aragon.

> In France, the Hundred Years' War (1337-1453) ended with the expulsion of the British (except from Calais). Charles VII strengthened the royal treasury with two new taxes, the *gabelle* on salt and the *taille* on land. His son Louis XI (the "Spider King") conquered Burgundy and brought other provinces into the kingdom through marriage, war, and inheritance.

> In England, the Hundred Years' War was followed by infighting among the nobles known as the War of the Roses (1455-1471) and won by the Tudor family, who set about enhancing royal power and prestige by dominating the nobles. Parliament continued to meet but the royal council held the real power. Troublesome aristocrats were tortured and secretly tried in the Star Chamber. The Tudors restored domestic stability, encouraged economic growth, and empowered the monarchy.

→ **AP® Tip** Advances in military technology such as artillery and the longbow enabled common men to wield weapons. First used by the English in the Hundred Years' War, these weapons transformed the armies of the European powers. Armies grew larger and more expensive, pushing governments to seek new sources of revenue, and over time became tools of the development of nationalistic feeling and the enhancement of royal power.

> Both France and Spain developed national churches under the effective authority of the king by the early sixteenth century. François I negotiated the Concordat of Bologna with the Papacy, giving the French monarch virtual control of Church officials in France. Ferdinand and Isabella won from the Papacy the right to appoint bishops in Spain. Later in the century, these concessions made it easier for the monarchs to resist Protestantism.

> In Spain, the royal goal of uniformity in religion led to the 1492 expulsion of those Jews who would not convert (about 150,000 people) and the expulsion of Muslims in 1609. An all-Spain Inquisition was established in 1478 to ferret out false *conversos* or New Christians, and stress was placed on "purity of blood," implying Jewishness was a hereditary condition.

Individual and Society

> While the word 'class' itself was not in use, social gradations based on wealth were widely acknowledged, particularly in towns where wealthy merchants gained much political power. Nevertheless, the basic medieval social order (those who fight, those who pray, those who work) retained influence, with nobles holding onto prestige and power.

> By the end of the fourteenth century, *les quenelles des femmes* (debates about women)–their character, intellectual abilities, and nature, and what type of education they should receive–was avidly discussed, mostly by learned men and some women, particularly writers like Christine de Pizan and women humanists like Cassandra Fedele. Women humanists and artists, by and large excluded by their male counterparts, struggled to assert the legitimacy of their intellectual and artistic activities. Much of this discourse touted the virtuous wife and the domestic ideal although many women worked (at 1/2-2/3 the wages of men). The debate intensified when such powerful rulers as Elizabeth I of England and Isabella of Castile challenged gender stereotypes.

❯ The printing press using movable type was developed in the Germanic states by Gutenberg and other metal-smiths in the mid-fifteenth century. The press and the increasing availability of inexpensive paper vastly reduced the cost of producing books and sparked an exponential growth in the output of printed books (somewhere between 8 and 20 million were printed within a half century of the publication of Gutenberg's Bible in 1456) by a large number of printers. The printing press transformed the lives of ordinary people as well as intellectuals, reducing the gap between the illiterate who relied on oral culture and the literate. Governments and churches feared the new technology and censored books, but also used the printing press for their own purposes. Both the Renaissance and the Reformation (next chapter) spread so wide and deep because the fast-growing printing industry fed an ever-growing market of readers.

❯ A good number of black slaves came to Europe in the fifteenth century; by 1530, the Portuguese sold about 4,000-5,000 each year to the markets of Seville, Barcelona, Marseilles, and Genoa. In some Portuguese cities, the slaves and free blacks comprised about 10 percent of the population. In western Europe, free blacks worked in virtually all occupations and, on the Iberian Peninsula, sometimes intermarried with the Spanish.

❯ During the Renaissance, families began to live as nuclear families, in their own households, rather than sharing the home with the older generation in extended family homes. Renaissance economic and political life was organized in many ways by family. The Medici, for example, were a highly successful banking family who took the reins of political power in fifteenth century Florence.

National and European Identity

❯ The Italian peninsula was divided into numerous city-states, which asserted their sovereignty even though they were technically under the rule of the Holy Roman Empire, the Papacy, or local nobles. Renaissance-era city-states provided a basis for ideas of identification of a unique Italian culture.

❯ Italian city-states were constantly at war with each other, which left them vulnerable to the ambitions of the centralized nation-states of France and Spain. Periodically, they would form an alliance to prevent any one state from domination and to restore a balance of power.

❯ In Italy, the flowering of Renaissance humanism and artistic innovation was encouraged by, and reflected, Italy's division into many small states. In France and England, the adoption of Renaissance literary and artistic values became part of the development of national culture as kings increased their prestige by patronizing the arts.

❯ Spain became a territorially unified state. The *Reconquista,* the 700-year-old struggle to regain Spain as a Christian state from Muslim rule, was completed in 1492 with the conquest of Granada by Ferdinand of Aragon and Isabella of Castile. Ferdinand and Isabella followed a common policy of dominating the aristocrats and enhancing their political authority, but did not unite their states. Their grandson, the Holy Roman Emperor Charles V, was the last great dynastic ruler of large areas of western and central Europe, including Spain, the Netherlands, and Austria.

❯ The terms "race," "people," and "nation" were used interchangeably during this period.

❯ Printed books encouraged communication among readers and served to unite people who read to discuss the ideas espoused in print materials. The printing press allowed for the development and spread of common language among nations.

McKay Chapter 12 Focus Questions

1. How did politics and economics shape the Renaissance?

2. What new ideas were associated with the Renaissance?

3. How did art reflect new Renaissance ideals?

4. What were the key social hierarchies in Renaissance Europe?

5. How did nation-states develop in this period?

CHAPTER 13
Reformations and Religious Wars, 1500–1600

Areas of Focus: Germanic states, England, France, Switzerland, the Netherlands

Main Events: the development of Lutheranism, Calvinism, and other forms of Protestantism; the Catholic Reformation; religious violence

Key Figures:

- Martin Luther: initiated the Protestant Reformation in 1517
- John Calvin: theologian and magistrate in Geneva
- Michael Servetus: dissident; executed in Calvinist Geneva
- Katharina von Bora: wife of Martin Luther
- Henry VIII: king of England; brought Protestantism to England
- Henry II: king of France; issued the Edict of Nantes promising religious toleration to Protestants in France
- Charles V: Holy Roman Emperor; fought for decades against Protestantism in Germanic states
- Philip II: king of Spain and defender of Catholicism; launched the Spanish Armada against England
- Elizabeth I: long-reigning queen of England; systemized the doctrines and practices of the Church of England
- Paul III: reforming pope; supervised the Council of Trent

AP® Themes
Interaction of Europe and the World

> Christianity was already divided before the Reformation began. Most people In Russia and eastern Europe belonged to one of the several national Orthodox churches, sharing theology but divided by language, while most people in central and western Europe were Catholics, all saying the Mass in Latin. There were also Christian sects in the Middle East, some affiliated with the Papacy, others independent.

> One result of the Reformation was an increase in religious fervor among many Christians. Protestants and Catholics alike sent missionaries to Latin America, Asia, and Africa. Most of the native population in the New World was converted to Catholicism.

Poverty and Prosperity

> In the Germanic states, peasants latched onto the new Protestant ideas, while in France, England, and Scotland, the urban middle classes were drawn toward Calvinism. The commercial classes found the Calvinist emphasis on labor and hard work especially appealing. This phenomenon has led to impassioned debate among historians about the intersection of capitalism and Calvinism.

> **AP® Tip** The possible connection between the rise of capitalism in northern Europe and Calvinism was first articulated by Max Weber, a sociologist in late nineteenth century Germany. See McKay pages 748-749 of Chapter 22 for a discussion of his ideas. Weber's claim, that the growth of Calvinism in northern Europe was linked to the rise of capitalism there, led to numerous works challenging this assertion—sometimes on Marxist lines and sometimes on religious lines.

> In early sixteenth century Germany, the economic condition of the peasantry was generally worse than it had been in the previous century and was deteriorating. Crop failures in 1523 and 1524 aggravated religious tensions, and no doubt, were a factor on the Peasants' Revolt of 1525.

Objective Knowledge and Subjective Visions

> There were long-standing criticisms of the church prior to the Reformation, aimed at church practices—simony (the selling of offices); nepotism; pluralism (the holding of more than one office by a church official) and its typical accompaniment, absenteeism; and the luxury and wealth of the papacy. Anticlericalism—the disparaging of priests for drunkenness, cupidity, and sexual immorality—was also widespread.

> Martin Luther, an Augustinian monk and professor at the University of Wittenberg, was consumed by religious doubts. When the church authorized the selling of indulgences (deeds promising forgiveness of sins and reduction of time in purgatory), Luther responded with his famous Ninety-five Theses (1517), which challenged the theological justification for indulgences and other Catholic doctrines about the powers of the Papacy. When Charles V called upon Luther to recant at the Diet of Worms in 1521 or face excommunication, Luther refused and, protected by the elector of Saxony, escaped persecution. Luther married, wrote voluminously (both prose and hymns), translated the Bible into German, and formed a new church. Lutheranism spread in northern Germany and to Scandinavia.

> Luther's key ideas can be summarized with three slogans: [1] "justification by faith alone"– rejecting the Catholic notion of "good works"; [2] *solo scriptura"* Scripture, the Bible, is the only authority– rejecting the religious authority of the Papacy and Church councils; and [3] "the priesthood of all believers"–rejecting the formal, hierarchical institution headed by the pope.

> **AP® Tip** Most of Luther's key ideas were first articulated by John Wyclif in the fourteenth century; see Chapter 11 [p. 340]. What's important to understand is how the intersection of these ideas and political goals of various rulers made them successful in the sixteenth century in the Holy Roman Empire. While Jan Hus, a Czech nationalist and follower of Wyclif was burned at the stake for heresy at the Church Council of Constance in 1415, Luther was protected from such a fate by the elector of Saxony.

> Ulrich Zwingli, who disagreed with Luther about the nature of the Eucharist, believed that the Scriptures were the words of God. He devoted his life to reforming the church in Zurich and established the Swiss Reformation.

> John Calvin stressed predestination, the belief that God had decided at the beginning of time who would be saved and who damned. In Geneva, Calvin established a theocratic state in which city laws were determined by religious values. Gambling, the theater, dancing, prostitution, and the like were all banned. Calvinism's sober, strict vision became the most widespread variety of Protestantism. John Knox brought it to Scotland, and it also spread to the Netherlands, England (the Puritans), and France (the Huguenots).

> There was great variety among radical Protestants. Some sought to establish a new society with communal values and eschewed private property. Some, such as Michael Servetus, who was executed in Geneva for heresy, denied the Scriptural basis of the Trinity. The Anabaptists denied the validity of infant baptism. Most radical Protestants rejected the notion of an established church and were persecuted by other Protestants and Catholics alike.

❭ The Reformation spawned much impassioned intellectual discourse over religion. There were furious intellectual and theological debates in person and in books over the role of the priest in religion, the relationship between church and state, the language to be used for the Mass, what happens during the Eucharist, the rights of the individual, monasticism, the primacy of Scripture, and what determines salvation. Many of these issues were conveyed in printed broadsides and satirical cartoons.

➤ **AP® Tip** Although Protestants read and respected the Old Testament, Jews were vilified for holding onto their faith. Luther wrote several anti-Semitic tracts.

Below is a chart highlighting differences among the different religious groups. Note that for the Calvinists and radicals, only their differences with the Lutherans are listed, as they are all Protestant divisions.

Denomination				
Theological Point	**Catholic**	**Lutheran**	**Calvinist**	**Radicals: Anabaptist**
Afterlife	Heaven, Hell, Purgatory	Heaven, Hell (No purgatory)		
Role of Church	crucial for salvation Hierarchy	justification by faith alone	salvation predestined	
Role of Priests	perform miracle of the Mass; hear confession; offer penance	priesthood of believers; ministers as teachers/leaders	ministers as moral arbiters	ministers as community leaders
Eucharist	transubstantiation	real presence		
Baptism	infant	infant		adult
Church/State Relations	universal church; church above state	state above church	state and church together	religious conscience outweighs state law
Language of Liturgy	Latin	vernacular		
Church Decoration	elaborate, showing the glory of God	simple	austere; no images	

❭ Protestantism encouraged literacy. Initially, the spread of Luther's ideas was made possible by illustrated broadsides, often with anti-papal cartoons. With Luther's translation of the Bible into German and similar translations made into the vernacular by Protestants elsewhere (including the King James Bible in early seventeenth century England), as well as the theological emphasis given to Scripture, ordinary people, including women, were increasingly taught to read.

❭ Calvinists were iconoclasts, that is, destroyers of religious images. Believing that such images broke the Ten Commandments, they frequently destroyed the art in ornate former Catholic churches. Calvinist churches by contrast were austere, with little or no decoration. The Catholic Church responded by embracing the Baroque style with its elaborate, exuberant decorations.

States and Other Institutions of Power

❭ Political developments and wars of this period were intimately connected with religious movements and challenges to the Catholic Church and its supporters. In every country in western and central Europe, religion and politics intersected.

❭ The long political and military effort led by Holy Roman Emperor Charles V to stop Protestantism ultimately failed. The Peace of Augsburg in 1555 granted each prince or ruler within the empire the right to choose Catholicism or Lutheranism, to which all his subjects were to adhere or move. With this division, the possibility of the Germanic states unifying into a centralized state dimmed.

> The establishment of the Church of England by Henry VIII led to substantial opposition from those loyal to the Catholic Church, such as Sir Thomas More (author of *Utopia*), who was executed for that belief, and Henry's daughter Mary Tudor, whose five-year reign (1553–1558) temporarily restored Catholicism in England. Under Elizabeth I (r. 1558–1603) an uneasy compromise was reached in doctrine and practice in England, although fundamental religious differences between the official Church of England and Puritans flared up again with great intensity in the seventeenth century.

> In France, the struggle over religion led to civil war and violent outbursts such as the notorious St. Bartholomew's Day massacre of the Huguenots (Calvinists) on August 24, 1572. Henry of Navarre, leader of the Protestant forces, ultimately won the war but converted back to Catholicism to achieve domestic peace. In 1598, he issued the Edict of Nantes granting religious liberty to the Huguenots in 150 towns. His practical political compromise identifies him as a *politique,* a ruler whose decisions was based on state interest rather than religion.

Individual and Society

> In response to the Protestant threat, the Catholic Church initiated internal reforms, ended abuses like simony, improved the education of priests, and initiated new orders. The Ursulines, founded by Angela Merici, focused on the education of women, while the Jesuits, founded by Ignatius Loyola, saw themselves as soldiers of Christ. They took a special oath to the pope, proselytized in the New World and Asia, and created educational institutions for the Catholic elite. At the same time, at the Council of Trent in the mid-sixteenth century, the church refused to modify its theological doctrines. By and large, the Catholic Reformation proved successful in preventing the further spread of Protestantism after the sixteenth century.

> In the Germanic states, peasants flocked to Lutheranism, seeing the principle of social equality in its doctrine of a "priesthood of all believers." In 1525, the peasants rose up in rebellion. The German Peasants' War was triggered by crop failures, noble seizure of common lands that had been traditionally farmed by peasants, and unjust rents and taxes. The peasants believed that their demands conformed to the Scriptures and sought support from Luther. Although initially sympathetic, Luther soon decried the lawlessness of the peasants and wrote a tract urging the nobles to suppress and if necessary kill the marauding hordes. The peasants were brutally suppressed, with about 75,000 killed.

AP® Tip Some historians have argued that Luther's support of the princes over the peasants encouraged Germans to be obedient to the state.

> Protestantism is often associated with growing individualism, as each individual was to meet his God directly, and with secularism, as nearly all Protestants rejected the monastic ideal, insisting that a good Christian life was to be lived in this world, not away for it. On the whole, though, Protestantism was neither secular nor tolerant of individualism.

> Women's roles were enhanced by Protestant notions of marriage as the bedrock of Christian communities. While women were not allowed to preach in Protestant churches, they were encouraged to read the Bible and take charge of the religious education of their young. Marriage in this period began to be seen as a partnership. As convents were closed in Protestant areas, unmarried women no longer could find a socially acceptable role for themselves in convent life.

> The Council of Trent ended the widespread practice in Catholic areas of informal or private marriages. Marriages were now to be performed by priests in public.

> Protestants in general rejected the Catholic idea that marriage was a sacrament and saw it rather as a mutual contract. Most Protestant churches allowed divorce, although it remained rare.

> Protestants abhorred prostitution and closed brothels that had been licensed by medieval town governments.

> The period 1550–1650 was the height of the witchcraft craze, when hundreds of thousands of people, mostly women, were accused of witchcraft. Those accused of acting on behalf of Satan were interrogated, tried, and often tortured. Some 40,000–60,000 were put to death. Surprisingly, few people were executed for witchcraft in strongly Catholic states like Italy and Spain; the greatest numbers of victims were in the areas of greatest religious conflict. In countries like England, where the legal rights of the accused were protected, relatively few "witches" perished.

National and European Identity

> In 1500 there was one Christian church in western Europe to which all Christians at least nominally belonged. One hundred years later there were many.

> Protestantism in most places enhanced the power of the monarch or prince. Protestant churches were national churches whose liturgy was spoken and written in the vernacular, and typically Protestant churches were under the authority of the ruler in one way or another.

> Around the year 1500 many rulers in the Germanic states, under the titular authority of the Holy Roman emperor, saw Protestantism as a way to break free of the emperor, enhance their own authority, and fill the coffers of the state with confiscated church properties like monasteries. The support of these princes, particularly the elector of Saxony, was crucial for the success of the Protestant reformers.

> In England, the Tudor king Henry VIII, unable to win a marriage annulment from the pope (desired because he lacked a male heir), established a national Church of England (with parliamentary support) with himself as its head.

McKay Chapter 13 Focus Questions

1. What were the main ideas of the reformers, and why were they appealing to different social groups?

2. How did the political situation in Germany shape the course of the Reformation?

3. How did Protestant ideas and institutions spread beyond German-speaking lands?

4. What reforms did the Catholic Church make, and how did it respond to Protestant reform movements?

5. What were the causes and consequences of religious violence, including riots, wars, and witch-hunts?

NOTES:

CHAPTER 14
European Exploration and Conquest, 1450–1650

Areas of Focus: France, Spain, New Spain

Main Events: texploration and colonization of Asia, Africa, and the New World; the Columbian Exchange

Key Figures:

- Prince Henry: "the Navigator," promoted Portuguese navigation and exploration
- Bartholomew Diaz: first to round the Cape of Good Hope in southern Africa.
- Vasco da Gama: rounded the Cape and reached India
- Christopher Columbus: "discovered" the New World in 1492
- Francisco Pizarro: conquistador of the Incas of Peru
- Doña Marina: Natuatl-speaking native American, interpreter for Cortés
- Hernán Cortés: conquistador of the Aztecs of Mexico
- Michel de Montaigne: created the personal essay form, wrote "On Cannibals"
- Ferdinand Magellan: led the first expedition that circumnavigated the globe
- Amerigo Vespucci: Florentine explorer; first to label the lands Columbus discovered as the "New World," his name was the basis for the term "America"
- Jacques Cartier: explored the St. Lawrence river in Canada
- William Shakespeare: playwright and actor; incorporated elements of the global economy and discoveries in his plays
- Bartolomé de las Casas: Dominican monk who praised the native population and criticized Spanish colonization practices
- Juan de Pareja: artist of half-African descent, originally a slave; subject of portrait by Velasquez
- Philip II: King of Spain: oversaw Spanish empire in New World and Philippines

AP® European History Themes
Interaction of Europe and the World

> Before the encounters of the fifteenth century, there were already well-established trade routes among Europe, Asia, the Middle East, and Africa, but Europeans did not yet dominate them. Much of this trade, centered in the Indian Ocean and the South China Sea, especially in the ports of Malacca, and Calicut, was in spices, Chinese porcelain, sugar, textiles, and similar goods. China's population and trade grew enormously after the fall of the Mongol empire to the Mings in the fourteenth century. The explorations of the Chinese Admiral Zheng He were extraordinary in size and distance but the Ming rulers did not build on their success. African trade, mostly in gold and slaves, was centered in the Mamluk Egyptian Empire, directed from the prosperous and highly cultured city of Cairo, and in the wealthy kingdom of Mali, whose king Mansa Musa made a famous pilgrimage to Mecca displaying enormous wealth.

> In the Middle East, the wealthy Ottoman Empire, which had conquered Constantinople in 1453, was continually expanding both territorially and commercially from the fifteenth century on. This worried the European powers and encouraged their interest in finding new trade routes to Asia.

> Until the voyages initiated by the Portuguese and Spanish rulers, Venice and Genoa dominated trade in spices and other luxury goods imported from Asia in exchange for European manufactured goods, including firearms and precious metals acquired in Egypt and North Africa. Genoese merchants provided much of the capital, personnel, and skill to the Iberian monarchs. Slavery, largely of young girls, was a large part of this Italian trade.

> The encounter between the Old World and the New affected every aspect of life: economic, political, intellectual, and social—on both continents. It marked the beginning of European ascendancy of the rest of world and established patterns of economic exploitation, racialist thinking, and the blending of populations and cultures that mark the long-legacy of colonialism.

> European conquest of powerful kingdoms like those of the Aztecs and the Incas was made easier by local resentments held by subjected peoples and other internal weaknesses.

> The impact of the encounter with Europeans on the peoples of the New World was devastating, with estimates of 95 percent of the native population dying off from disease and exploitation. The entire culture of the natives was transformed by their encounter with the Europeans.

> A new global economy emerged in this period, with Europeans bringing goods from the New World to Europe and Asia and buying Asian goods with New World silver to take back to Europe, Africa, and the New World for sale. As the Chinese insisted on payment in silver, a triangular international trade developed, with silver from Peru sent to Manila to exchange for Chinese silks then sold in Europe or back in the colonies. China absorbed about half of the world's production of silver.

> This trade included the import and sale of African slaves in the New World, where they were put to work producing sugar and other commodities of high value in the world market.

Poverty and Prosperity

> The global economy brought new goods such as sugar, Chinese silk, and porcelain into the homes of increasing numbers of Europeans, along with new sources of wealth and prestige.

> Spain had a huge surge in national wealth as a result of the gold and silver mined in its colonies in the New World, especially after the 1545 discovery of silver mines in Potosí (modern Bolivia), leading to its *siglo d'oro,* or Golden Age. As China demanded payment for its goods in silver, silver was a key element in global trade.

> Europeans experienced a price revolution exacerbated by the infusion of gold and silver from the New World into Spain. Inflation spread throughout the continent, with prices doubling or even quadrupling in much of Europe. Inflation put a squeeze on government budgets and on those with fixed incomes, such as aristocrats whose income was limited by customary rents on their lands.

> New crops from the New World—particularly corn and the potato, and later the tomato— transformed the European economy and diet. In turn, the economy and diet of the New World was transformed by the introduction of European crops and livestock, especially sugar and wheat, sheep, horses, pigs, and chickens. This system is commonly known as the Columbian Exchange. Its darker side was the exchange of disease, with European diseases like smallpox causing unprecedented death tolls among the natives of the Americas.

> The slave trade was lucrative for European capitalists. Slaves remained relatively rare on the continent, but the importation of black slaves from Africa to European colonies in the New World, probably some 10 million in all, made the slave trade a greatly valued component in the expanding commercial economy.

> The history of sugar is intricately tied in to the history of slavery. Increasing demand in Europe led to the establishment of the plantation system, manned by slaves, in the Caribbean. Some 10 million

slaves were brought to the New World over the course of four centuries, with the largest number going to Brazil.

> Spain introduced the *encomienda* system to its New World colonies to manage its many plantations and the treatment of the Native Americans. Conquerors were given the right to demand forced labor from the Indians, though officially enslaving them was banned.

Objective Knowledge and Subjective Visions

> Exploration was made possible by numerous technological innovations, many from Asia, such as the magnetic compass, the lateen sail, and gunpowder. The Portuguese development of the caravel, replacing the galley ship, enabled larger cargos to be carried. Great advances in mapmaking were also made in this period. Ptolemy's *Geography*, brought to Europe by Arab scholars in 1410, vastly improved geographical knowledge. Invented by the ancient Greeks and perfected in the Islamic world, the astrolabe allowed mariners to plot their latitude.

> The idea of a new world was first articulated by Vespucci. Columbus believed until his dying day that he had reached Asia.

➡️ **AP® Tip** Thomas More's *Utopia*, discussed in Chapter 12 (pp. 369), was set in the New World.

> Encounters with the "primitive" natives of the New World stirred the imagination of European intellectuals, most notably the French writer, Michel de Montaigne. In the sixteenth century he created a new form of writing, the personal essay. One of these essays, "On Cannibals," challenged the labeling of New World natives as savages or barbarians. He argued that such terms reflected discomfort with new ideas and experiences rather than a rational understanding of them. William Shakespeare's work reveals the impact of the new discoveries and contacts of his day. In his play *The Tempest*, Shakespeare explored race relations with an encounter of Europeans and natives on an unnamed island, and in *Othello* the title character is a Moor, a Muslim of North African origin.

> Cosmography, natural history, and geography aroused enormous interest among educated people in the fifteenth and sixteenth centuries. One of the most popular books of the time was the fourteenth century *The Travels of Sir John Mandeville,* which purported to be a firsthand account of the author's travels.

> European artists were fascinated with images of "the other"—the natives of Asia, Africa, and particularly the Americas. In the Spanish-controlled areas of the New World a popular genre of paintings known as *castas* depicted couples composed of individuals of different ethnic origin and their children.

> As Europeans' involvement in the slave trade grew, they drew on and developed ideas about Africans' primitiveness and barbarity to defend slavery and even argue that enslavement benefited Africans by bringing Christianity to pagan peoples. Slavery became identified with blackness. Europeans found Biblical justifications for their racist ideas.

States and Other Institutions of Power

> European exploration was made possible by the growth of government power. The reassertion of monarchical authority and state centralization in the fifteenth century enabled rulers to provide the massive funds needed for exploration.

> Portugal led the way in empire expansion, starting in 1415 with the conquest of Ceuta in northern Africa, and then the exploration of the entire African coast. After a route to India via the Cape of Good Hope was discovered in 1497, Lisbon became the entrance port for Asian goods into Europe. In 1500, a Portuguese fleet claimed Brazil for the Crown.

> The two most famous Spanish conquistadors were soldier-explorers Hernando Cortés and Francisco Pizarro, who defeated the Aztecs and Incas respectively. Spain grew wealthy from the hordes of silver from the mines in Potosí in modern-day Bolivia, but experienced rapid inflation.

> Among the most famous explorers were Columbus (Genoese); Vasco da Gama (Portuguese), the first explorer to round the coast of Africa (1498); and Ferdinand Magellan (Portuguese), who first circumnavigated the globe (1522). The Florentine Amerigo Vespucci's name was given to the New World. While many explorers were Italian, the Italian city-states did not participate in colonization.

> Spain and Portugal signed the Treaty of Tordesillas in 1494 dividing the New World between them. Portugal took Brazil; most of the rest went to Spain.

> Spain and France introduced European political concepts into its colonies in the New World. Intendants were royal officials possessing broad political, military, and financial powers. Portugal used similar officials called *corregidores*. Spain ruled its American colonies, divided into New Spain in North America and Peru in South America, through viceroyalties.

> The colonization of the New World accelerated the economic and political ascendancy of the Atlantic states over the Mediterranean and central European states.

Individual and Society

> Religious motivations for exploration were galvanized by Spain's successful *Reconquista*, by legends like that of Prester John, widely believed to have established a Christian kingdom somewhere in Africa, and by the expansion of Islam into Europe following the Ottoman conquest of Constantinople in 1453.

> Religious motives were important in European colonization. In the New World, missionaries—mostly Franciscans, Dominicans, and Jesuits—spread not only Christianity but also European methods of agriculture and the idea of loyalty to the Crown. Huge numbers of Indians were converted, although their new faith was often based on cultural misunderstandings and imbued with elements of their original faiths. In the English colonies on the Atlantic coast of North America, various groups of religious dissidents founded colonies, including Puritans in Massachusetts, Catholics in Maryland, and Quakers in Pennsylvania.

AP® Tip Many historians see the exploration and conquest as outgrowths of Renaissance culture, which fostered curiosity and the search for individual glory.

> The consequences of the European conquest and colonization were devastating for the native peoples of the New World. Disease to which indigenous people had no immunity claimed the lives of millions. Overwork, malnutrition, and hunger from forced labor killed many more. Estimated death tolls vary, but they go as high as 95 percent of the pre-conquest population.

> Exploration and colonization offered opportunities of adventure and wealth for ambitious young European men and havens for religions dissidents.

> Europeans interbred with the native populations and imported slaves, creating new populations and ethnicities. In Spanish America the complex feelings of self-identity gave rise to a new vocabulary, such as *mulatto* and *mestizo,* that sought to define racial mixing. In the Portuguese, Spanish, and French colonies, substantial populations of free blacks descended from the freed children of these unions. In English colonies, masters were less likely to free children they fathered with female slaves.

> Where English and Spanish women accompanied the men as colonial settlers, European languages and culture took root; where women did not, as in European colonies in West Africa and Asia, indigenous peoples retained their own languages and religion. The English maintained an attitude of cultural superiority toward the natives of the New World and segregated them both physically and socially, while in the French colonies, settlers were encouraged to develop relationships with local people.

National and European Identity

> Spain, newly unified as a territorial state after defeating the last Moorish kingdom in 1492 (also the year of Columbus's first journey), became a hugely powerful state in the next century and competed with the Dutch, the English, and the French both abroad and within Europe.

> The Dutch, although still officially under Spanish rule until 1609, became an international power, with valuable colonies in Indonesia (the Spice Islands), western South Africa, and the Americas (parts of Brazil and New Amsterdam, taken by the British and renamed New York in 1664). The Dutch aggressively competed with other European powers, taking Ceylon from Portugal and capturing the Spanish silver fleet. The Dutch West India Company and the Dutch East India Company played a big role in the slave trade and brought great wealth to the Dutch Republic, making possible the extraordinary effusion of art and science of its Golden Age.

> Widespread slavery created new ideas of European racial superiority and African inferiority.

McKay Chapter 14 Focus Questions

1. What was the Afroeurasian trading world prior to the era of European exploration?

2. How and why did Europeans undertake ambitious voyages of exploration?

3. How did European powers acquire colonies in the Americas, and how were they governed?

4. How was the era of global contact shaped by new forms of exploitation, commercial exchange, and forced migration?

5. How did the encounters shape cultural attitudes and beliefs in Europe and the rest of the world?

NOTES:

CHAPTER 15
Absolutism and Constitutionalism, ca. 1589–1725

Areas of Focus: France, Spain, Austria, Prussia, Russia, the Ottoman Empire, England, and the Netherlands

Main Events: absolutism, the Thirty Years' War, the English Civil War and constitutionalism

Key Figures:

- Louis XIV: the "Sun King" and founder of French absolutism
- Jean-Baptiste Colbert: finance minister to Louis XIV; mercantilist
- Charles I: Stuart king of England who lost the civil war and was executed by Parliamentary forces in England
- Oliver Cromwell: military ruler of England under the Protectorate
- William and Mary: king and queen of England after the Glorious Revolution
- Peter the Great: tsar; westernizer of Russia
- Ferdinand III: Habsburg emperor; expanded and centralized Austrian power
- Frederick William the Great: elector; founder of Prussian absolutism
- Suleiman the Magnificent: Ottoman sultan at the height of its power
- John Locke: English political philosopher promoting constitutionalism
- Thomas Hobbes: political theorist in favor of strong centralized government; offered secular defense of absolutism
- Peter Paul Rubens: Baroque artist who glorified monarchs

AP® European History Themes
Interaction of Europe and the World

> As England, France, the Netherlands, Russia, Austria, Prussia, Spain, and the Ottoman Empire organized centralized states—either as absolute monarchies or as constitutional regimes—trade was a key element in providing financial underpinnings to these regimes. Mercantilism in France, England, and the Netherlands led to an intensification of international trade and competition between states. Colonies were key elements of mercantilism, encouraging European colonial expansion abroad.

> The Russian and Ottoman Empire were huge landmasses containing overlapping areas in Europe, the Middle East, and Asia.

Poverty and Prosperity

> ❯ Mercantilism was the dominant economic policy in this period. It was characterized by the active intervention of the state in the economy to increase its supply of gold and silver by promoting exports and reducing imports. In France, Jean-Baptiste Colbert, Louis XIV's finance minister (1665–1683), subsidized local manufacturing, imposed protectionist tariffs, abolished domestic tariffs, created new textile industries, invited foreign craftsmen to France, and promoted colonial growth. In England, Oliver Cromwell also enacted mercantilist legislation, such as the Navigation Act of 1651, which required goods coming into England or English possessions to be transported on English ships.

> ❯ The population and economy of central Europe was devastated by the Thirty Years' War; it would take two centuries to rebound.

> ❯ Spain's economy declined partially because of the competition of the Dutch and the English, who built up their shipbuilding industries and established hugely successful trading companies in the East and West Indies. Spain also suffered from declining manufacturing, a small middle class, the continuing effects of inflation, and the exhaustion of its mines in the New World.

> ❯ The Dutch merchant marine was the largest in Europe, and trade and commerce brought the Dutch the highest standard of living in Europe and perhaps in the world.

Objective Knowledge and Subjective Visions

> ❯ Both constitutionalism and absolutism had major theorists in England. Thomas Hobbes argued in his 1651 treatise *Leviathan* that in the state of nature, man's life was "nasty, brutish and short." Men should join in a social contract and install themselves under an absolute government to prevent the war of "all against all."

> ❯ John Locke argued in his *Second Treatise of Civil Government* (1690) that men have natural rights to life, liberty, and property, and that governments are instituted to protect those rights. If the government does not do so and becomes a tyranny, men have the right to revolt. Locke advocated constitutional governments in which the people (men with property) have a say in their governments.

> ❯ Baroque art, with its dramatic and elaborate decorations and sensuous colors, was defined in Italy after 1600 and used in the Counter-Reformation to inspire religiosity among Catholics and by absolute monarchs to inspire awe. The Baroque style in the arts flourished especially in Catholic regions: Spain and its Latin American colonies, Austria, southern Germany, and Poland. The greatest Baroque painter was Peter Paul Rubens (1577–1640).

> ❯ Baroque music reached its apogee with Johann Sebastian Bach (1685–1750), a Lutheran from Saxony in Germany, who was an extraordinarily talented composer of religious and secular music.

> ❯ French classicism, the imitation by artists and writers of classical antiquity, dominated the court at Versailles.

States and Other Institutions of Power

➡️ **AP® Tip** Absolutism and constitutionalism shaped Europe's political destiny and are often subjects of comparative questions on how politics intersected with class, economy, and religion.

> ❯ Both constitutional governments and absolutist states experienced important changes in the military. Armies (and, in England's case, the navy) became more professional, larger, more expensive and (except in England) permanent.

> ❯ The two most developed capitalistic states in Europe in the seventeenth century—England and the United Provinces (the Netherlands)—established constitutional governments where sovereignty lay with the people, and the powers of the monarchs were limited by a constitution, either written or unwritten.

❯ England became Europe's first constitutional monarchy with a strong Parliament, with power of the purse and citizen rights granted in the Magna Carta of 1215; but this occurred only after war, revolution, and the execution of the king during the mid-seventeenth century. The changes began to occur during the change of the ruling dynasty in England when, in 1603, the last Tudor and Protestant queen Elizabeth I was succeeded by the Stuarts—Scots, absolutists, and Anglicans with sympathies for Catholicism. Religious conflicts compounded the power struggle between the Stuart monarchs and Parliament dominated by Puritans.

❯ Charles I (r. 1625–1649) came into conflict with Parliament first politically and then militarily. Backing the Catholic supporters of his throne during a period of Puritan unrest, he was forced to summon Parliament to create an army to counter invading Presbyterian Scots. The unforeseen consequence in the resulting English Civil War (1642–1649) was the king's defeat by the New Model Army under Oliver Cromwell and Charles's execution.

❯ After Charles I was executed in 1649, England became a commonwealth or republic in name but a military dictatorship in practice. Oliver Cromwell's Protectorate (1653–1658) repressed Catholicism in Ireland but allowed the Jews to return to England.

❯ The monarchy was temporarily restored in 1660, but when James II (r. 1685–1688) actively promoted the Catholic cause, Parliament offered the crown to James's Protestant daughter, Mary, and her husband, William, the Stadholder of Holland. This peaceful Glorious Revolution of 1688 permanently established constitutionalism, and the Bill of Rights in 1689 guaranteed civil liberties.

⟶ **AP® Tip** The English Cabinet system developed in the eighteenth century when the Stuarts died out and the new royal dynasty had little interest in governing. Parliament's power was enhanced as its members (MPs) began to formulate policy and execute programs. Robert Walpole was the first prime minister.

❯ The Netherlands became a republic. Each of its seven provinces had their own Estate (assembly) but all shared a common executive officer, the Stadholder, and a federal assembly for foreign affairs. The Dutch were highly prosperous and by far the most religiously tolerant state in Europe at the time, particularly for Jews.

⟶ **AP® Tip** Some historians have used the English Revolution to create a model of revolutions. The first stage leads to reform as most people see the need for political change. In the next stage, radicalization and fierce conflicts among the revolutionaries over values and class interests lead to violence, repression, and civil war. One-man rule restores order, and, ultimately, there's restoration of key elements of pre-revolutionary political system. This pattern fits the French and Russian Revolutions as well as many revolutions around the world. Such a model is useful to distill the narrative of extremely complex revolutions.

❯ In France, Austria, Prussia, and Russia, traditional limitations on the power of the monarch disappeared as the monarchs established themselves as absolute rulers. In absolutism, sovereignty was held by the king who ruled with divine right and without limitation from church, tradition, or nobles. The aristocracy, the dominant social class, had to be forced or enticed to give up their traditional political rights.

⟶ **AP® Tip** Students sometimes see "absolutism" as synonymous with "dictatorship." No seventeenth- or eighteenth-century monarch, however absolute, could be called a dictator by today's standard. Hereditary monarchs ruled without institutional constraints and their heirs later inherited their power; twentieth- and twenty-first-century dictatorships rarely outlived their founders. They are fundamentally different forms of power and control. Modern dictatorships extended the impact of their rule into social, economic, and cultural realms and private lives to a far greater extent than absolute monarchs.

❭ The absolute monarchs shared a number of traits and policies: long reigns; standing armies composed primarily of infantry employed, trained, and outfitted by the state; higher state costs; the maneuvering of religious and cultural life for political purposes; and the transformation of royal relationships with the nobles.

❭ One key difference between the development of absolutism in France and that in central and eastern Europe was the treatment of the nobles. In France, their status was manipulated and their political power was reduced as the rich bourgeoisie became allies of the kings against the nobles, while in central and eastern Europe, monarchs were able to dominate the nobles who, in general, were willing to give up their political power in exchange for greater control of the serfs, whose burdens intensified.

❭ The French monarchs used royal officials, known as *intendants*, often of bourgeois origin to execute royal policies in the provinces and spy on local nobles. Louis XIV, the longest ruling French king, built an impressive palace with huge gardens outside of Paris in Versailles and required the nobles to reside there for at least part of the year, where they participated in elaborate court rituals under royal control. Louis XIV, calling himself the "Sun King" and implying that he was the center of the universe, ruled without relying on advisors such as Cardinal Richelieu. He never called the Estates-General, France's parliament, into session even once.

❭ The Habsburgs tamed the Bohemian nobility but struggled to subjugate the Hungarian nobles. The Thirty Years' War began in 1618 when Bohemian nobles attempted to assert their independence from the Holy Roman emperor and win the right to practice Protestantism. It grew into a war involving many states. The belligerents were divided into the Catholic League (the Habsburgs) against the Protestant Union (Denmark, Prussia, and Sweden). France, though Catholic, supported the Protestant side in order to weaken the Habsburgs. The Peace of Westphalia of 1648 permanently crippled the Holy Roman Empire by recognizing the independent authority of hundreds of German princes and added valuable territories to Prussia.

❭ In Prussia, the Hohenzollern's Frederick William, the "Great Elector," and his successors built up a powerful court centered in Berlin and a highly centralized state. Over time Prussia was able to expand its territories with its highly trained army. Frederick William convinced the nobles, known as *Junkers,* to relinquish political power in exchange for enhanced control over their serfs. Frederick William I transformed Prussia into a militaristic state emphasizing soldiers' virtues of obedience, hard work, and discipline and thus created the best army in Europe. His bureaucracy was highly efficient and generally honest.

❭ Russia's Romanovs based in Moscow, established order after the instability of several centuries of rule by the Mongols and then Ivan the Terrible. They expanded their lands to include Siberia and Ukraine and some Muslim states in the south, and crushed a rebellion of the warrior bands known as Cossacks. They built up the army and bureaucracy, expanded serfdom, and enhanced the power of the Orthodox Church. Peter the Great created a new ranking system for nobles [known as boyars] based on service to the state. He enhanced royal power by defeating the Swedes in war, building a new capital, instituting widespread cultural and social changes, and introducing Western attitudes and technology.

❭ After its Golden Age, Spain declined in the seventeenth century for economic, religious, and political reasons. These included the expulsion of the Moriscos (Muslim converts to Christianity) and a series of weak and overspending kings who left the administration of the state in the hands of ministers. English and Dutch competition in the New World, combined with the running dry of its silver mines, reduced Spain's trade in the Americas while manufacturing and commerce were declining at home. Military defeats meant the loss of territories and the independence of Portugal.

❭ French attempts at dynastic expansion led to the War of the Spanish Succession (1701–1714), which Louis XIV countered by a Grand Alliance of other European powers. The Peace of Utrecht, which ended it, marked the end of French expansion. France ceded important territories in the New World to England, which also took control of the African slave trade from Spain.

> The Ottoman Empire was also an absolutist state in that the sultan had sole political power and owned all agricultural lands. There was no hereditary nobility. Its highly effective army, the Janissary corps, was made up of former Christian boys taken from the Balkans; some became high administrators. Religious and ethnic communities called millets were given autonomous self-government, the right to practice their religion, and the right to use their own languages. Under Suleiman the Magnificent, Istanbul became a great center of culture and commerce.

	France	**Austria**	**Prussia**	**Russia**
Dynasy	Bourbon	Habsburg	Hohenzollern	Romanov
Most Important King/Years Ruled	Louis XIV 1643/1661–1715 (54 years)	Leopold I 1658–1705 (47 years)	Fredrick William, the "Great Elector" 1640–1689 (48 years)	Peter the Great 1682–1725 (36 years)
Conquests/Wars	Franche–Comté; Alsace–Lorraine; lost War of the Spanish Succession 1714; largest army in Europe	Hungary; Transylvania; defeated Ottoman siege of Vienna 1683	Built militaristic state with small but well-trained army; best army in Europe	Defeated Sweden in the Great Northern War; acquired Baltic states
Use of the Arts/Culture	The splendor and function of the Versailles palace as a center for government set the standard for other absolutist monarchs	Vienna was center for arts and music; Baroque art and music flourished; German language dominant over the many ethnicities		St. Petersburg as new capital city; westernized nobles' education, attire, social life
Allied Class	Wealthy bourgeoisie	Nobility	Nobility (Junkers)	Nobility (boyars)
Religious Issues	Revoked Edict of Nantes 1685; 200,000 Huguenots leave	Catholicism used to create national identity and forge loyalty to the Crown	Religiously tolerant; welcomed Huguenots from France	Holy Synod run by government official appointed by the tsar

Individual and Society

> As the feudal lords of seventeenth century central and eastern Europe gained authority, and the cultural gap between lords and peasants grew, the lives of peasants worsened considerably.

> While few feudal obligations remained for the peasants of western Europe, most lived at subsistence level, with bread as the primary element in their diet. Some small peasant landowners lived better, but the majority were vulnerable to famine, and there were numerous riots over the high prices of bread in bad times. French nobles opposed to financing the monarchy's wars and government policies rioted in a series of uprisings known as the Fronde (1648–1653), but the rebellions died out and reinforced the desire for a strong monarchy.

> In Russia, Ivan the Terrible (r. 1533–1584) attempted to make commoners servants of the tsar, binding them to their towns and jobs so he could tax them. Many fled the country and joined Cossack armies.

> Aristocratic women played important roles in absolutist courts not only as wives and mistresses, but also as power brokers. In the Ottoman Empire, the sultan's concubines lived in the harem in the palace and vied to produce the next sultan.

> The Thirty Years' War (1618–1648) was the last of the great religious wars in Europe; the concluding Peace of Westphalia guaranteed more than 300 princes within the Holy Roman Empire the right to

choose Catholicism, Lutheranism, or Calvinism as their state religion. Subjects in these states were obligated to observe the religion of the prince, or leave.

> In the Ottoman Empire, the millet system granted religious freedom to non-Muslims in exchange for the payment of taxes; thus there was almost no compulsion for conversion, unlike in most other absolutist states. The Ottoman Empire was a highly diverse society.

> After the revocation of the Edict of Nantes that had given religious toleration to the Huguenots, some 200,000, including many high-skilled artisans, left France for welcoming Protestant lands.

National and European Identity

> Peter the Great, who had traveled widely in western Europe, instigated westernization of Russian dress, cultural habits, and educational systems. He demanded the Russian nobles shave their beards, and encouraged men and women to socialize together. After defeating Sweden in a war, he built the city of St. Petersburg with forced labor on the Baltic as a model of urban planning. He also instituted unigeniture, the inheritance of family estates by one son alone, a very unpopular policy.

> In France, Louis XIV revoked the Edict of Nantes that had given the French Protestants, the Huguenots, religious toleration in order to establish a unified state religion and support unified legal system in France.

> Under the system of mercantilism, the establishment of colonies became tied to expressions of national identity and power in England, France, and the Netherlands.

McKay Chapter 15 Focus Questions

1. What were the common crises and achievements of seventeenth-century European states?

2. What factors led to the rise of the French absolutist state under Louis XIV, and why did absolutist Spain experience decline in the same period?

3. What were the social conditions of eastern Europe, and how did the rulers of Austria and Prussia transform their nations into powerful absolutist monarchies?

4. What were the distinctive features of Russian and Ottoman absolutism?

5. Why and how did the constitutional state triumph in the Dutch Republic and England?

CHAPTER 16
Toward a New Worldview, 1540–1789

Areas of Focus: England, France, Italy, Austria, Prussia, Russia

Main Events: the Scientific Revolution, the Enlightenment, enlightened absolutism

Key Figures:

- Nicolaus Copernicus: Polish astronomer; argued for the heliocentric theory of the universe
- Johannes Kepler: Danish astronomer; discovered three laws of planetary motion
- Galileo Galilei: physicist, first to use the telescope; proved Copernican theory
- Isaac Newton: physicist and mathematician; discovered law of gravity
- William Harvey: physician; rediscovered the circulation of the blood
- Francis Bacon: articulated value of empiricism and the scientific method
- René Descartes: mathematician, geometrician, philosopher
- John Locke: philosopher; defended constitutional governments and civic rights
- Voltaire: philosopher; author of *Candide,* satirist; opposed organized religion
- Jean-Jacques Rousseau: philosopher; promoted radical democracy
- Denis Diderot: philosopher; editor of the *Encyclopedia*
- Baron de Montesquieu: political scientist; articulated the separation of powers
- Adam Smith: argued for laissez-faire capitalism; opponent of mercantilism
- Cesare Beccaria: advocate of reform of criminal law and the prison system
- Moses Mendelssohn: Jewish philosopher; promoted Jewish Enlightenment
- Joseph II: Habsburg emperor; implemented Enlightenment ideas
- Frederick the Great: Prussian king, friend of Voltaire, reformer
- Catherine the Great: Russian tsar, enlightened monarch

AP® European History Themes
Interaction of Europe and the World

⟶ **AP® Tip** This chapter describes the scientific and intellectual movements that became the foundation of modern Western civilization, The rationalistic, scientific, secularist orientation of Europeans established during this time is considered the key element in how the West came to dominate the world in the next century. Mastery of these key ideas is crucial for understanding Europe's history and its impact on the globe.

> Awareness of cultural differences between Europe and the rest of the world led to comparisons. Philosophers wrote on China and Islam, in particular, but had divided opinions, some praising these societies as more advanced than Europe, others critical of them for their backwardness, despotic governments, and religiosity.

> Rousseau in particular articulated the idea that the "natural man" found in less developed parts of the world was superior to the civilized man in Europe.

Poverty and Prosperity

> Initially, there were few practical improvements in technology as a result of the Scientific Revolution, but by the eighteenth century, the empirical approach led to technological innovation and improved machinery.

→ **AP® Tip**   The practical results of these intellectual movements can be seen in the application of scientific principles to agriculture that prompted the Agricultural Revolution and the rapid growth of European population discussed in the next chapter (Chapter 17).

> Adam Smith wrote *The Wealth of Nations* in 1776, in which he attacked mercantilism for its restraint on market forces, and argued instead for laissez-faire or free enterprise capitalism in which the state stays out of the economy. He believed that an unfettered economy would provide the greatest overall social benefit. This doctrine became a key part of the success of the British and American economies in the nineteenth century.

Objective Knowledge and Subjective Visions

> The Scientific Revolution, a transformation over the seventeenth century that drew on long-term developments in European culture rather than a sudden change in attitudes, was a profound revision in the methods of ascertaining truth and knowledge of the physical world. Before the seventeenth century, disciples of "natural philosophy" found answers to scientific questions in classical authorities like Aristotle, Ptolemy, or Galen, but afterward they used the experimental method, observation, and mathematical analysis.

> The use of reason to ascertain of the workings of the physical world ("rationalism") inspired a new generation of philosophers, commonly known by the French term "philosophes," who used reason to understand the human world, or the social sciences. The Age of Reason held the optimistic premise that society could be improved by the use of reason and observation freed from religious and classical authorities.

→ **AP® Tip**   The twentieth century saw the rise of political and intellectual movements that challenged the basic premise of the Enlightenment–its exaltation of human powers of reason. Fascism rejected this idea calling instead for "thinking with the blood" and for intense nationalism rather than the tolerance and internationalism of the Enlightenment. Many other writers saw reason as a chain rather than a source of liberation.

> John Locke (English, 1632–1704), in addition to asserting the legitimacy of republicanism and the right of revolution, articulated the concept of *tabula rasa*, that man is born a blank slate with no innate ideas or original sin; thus creating modern psychology and the powerful political notion that humanity can be remade (*Essay Concerning Human Understanding,* 1690).

> Baron de Montesquieu (1689–1755) and Voltaire (1694–1778) both used satire to criticize their native France. Montesquieu's *The Spirit of Laws* developed the idea of separation of powers and a system of checks and balances to protect liberty. Voltaire relentlessly criticized the hypocrisy and intolerance of organized religion. His best-selling novel, *Candide,* lampooned virtually every aspect of society and the philosophy known as optimism.

> The Enlightenment saw a publishing explosion and a "reading revolution," with an expanded community of readers who read more on the arts and sciences than on religion.

> Philosophers wrote dictionaries and encyclopedias to enlighten the common man. Pierre Bayle's popular *Historical and Critical Dictionary* (1697) fostered skepticism. Denis Diderot and Jean le Rond d'Alembert filled their hugely influential seventeen volume *Encyclopedia* (1765) with technical and scientific knowledge and denunciations of intolerance, repression, immorality, and legal injustice.

> The most influential of the later philosophers was Jean-Jacques Rousseau (1712–1778). He denied the primacy of reason (thereby fostering early-nineteenth century Romanticism) and articulated a radical republican vision: the people have sole sovereignty but are to be led by those few who know the "general will," or the common interests of all the people, a doctrine that would underlie twentieth-century totalitarianism.

> Before the Enlightenment, the accepted theories of natural philosophy—such as Ptolemy's and Aristotle's geocentric models of the universe—reinforced religious thought. This approach to the natural world was later supplanted by the Enlightenment concept of secular "rationalism."

> During the eighteenth century, Enlightenment philosophers—most notably Voltaire—attacked organized religion as oppressive, superstitious, and inimical to free thought. Many philosophers were deists, believing in God as creator but not redeemer, who gave man reason to understand his universe. Deists supported separation of church and state.

> Pierre Bayle (French, 1647–1706) was a famous skeptic who demonstrated that human beliefs were historically varied and often mistaken, and that nothing, not even God's existence, could be known beyond all doubt.

> Led by Prussian philosopher Moses Mendelssohn (1729–1786), a Jewish Enlightenment movement (called the Haskalah) fostered greater contact with the Christian community and urged states to give Jews civil rights. Only Austria's Joseph II did so. Catherine the Great established the Pale of Settlement (1791) where Russian Jews were required to live.

> Within the "public sphere," intellectuals came together to discuss important issues relating to the intersection of society, the economy, and politics.

> Artists participated in the Scientific Revolution and the Enlightenment by painting experiments, scientific illustrations, medical school classes, and salon scenes.

> Women artists were important illustrators, noted for botanical paintings. Illustrated texts popularized the new science.

> Rococo, with its soft pastels, ornate interiors, and sentimental portraits and lush paintings with cupids, was popular throughout Europe.

Scientific Field	Major Figures	Theories and Discoveries
Astronomy	Nicolaus Copernicus (Polish), 1473–1543	Copernican hypothesis; heliocentric theory, spherical planetary orbits
	Tycho Brahe (Dutch), 1546–1601	Improved planetary observational charts
	Johannes Kepler (German), 1571–1630	Three laws of planetary motion; elliptical orbits proved mathematically
	Galileo Galilei (Florentine), 1564–1642	Used telescope to observe the moons of Jupiter, sunspots, the moon's craters
	Isaac Newton (English), 1642–1727	Unified theory of the universe, same laws operate on earth and in the heavens; law of universal gravitation
Chemistry	Robert Boyle (Irish), 1493–1541	First to create vacuum tube; Boyle's law
Physics	Galileo Galilei (see Astronomy)	Conducted experiments on motion; proved the law of acceleration of falling objects
Medicine	Andrea Vesalius (Flemish), 1514–1564	Dissected human bodies; wrote important book on anatomy
	William Harvey (English), 1578–1657	Discovered circulation of the blood, function of the heart
	Paracelsus (Swiss), 1627–1691	Pioneered the use of medicinal drugs
Scientific Method and Philosophy of Science	Francis Bacon (English), 1561–1626	Promoted science as socially useful and advocated empiricism and inductive reasoning, asserting that knowledge comes from the senses and experiments
	René Descartes (French), 1596–1650	Creator of analytical geometry; argued that sensory knowledge was unreliable. Scientific truth needed deductive reasoning and mathematics. All substances could be divided into "matter" or "mind," the physical or spiritual, and one had little to do with the other.
	Isaac Newton (see Astronomy	Combined mathematics and empiricism

States and Other Institutions of Power

❯ Most royal or ducal families founded scientific societies and promoted research.

❯ In the eighteenth century, absolute monarchs in Austria, Prussia, and Russia adopted some Enlightenment ideas, reforming legal and educational systems and improving agriculture.

❯ The most radical enlightened monarch was Joseph II of Austria (r. 1780–1790), famous as Mozart's patron, who abolished serfdom and instituted religious toleration—reforms nullified by his successors.

❯ Frederick II of Prussia ("Frederick the Great," r. 1740–1786) called himself the "first servant of the state" and made significant administrative and legal reforms, improved education, and abolished torture. At the same time, he maintained serfdom and extended the privileges of the nobility, on whom he depended to serve as officers in his army.

❯ Catherine the Great of Russia (r. 1762–1796), a financial supporter of Diderot's Encyclopedia after the French government banned it, restricted the use of torture and improved education and government. But after relying on nobles to suppress a peasant uprising, she gave them more control than ever over their serfs.

❯ Most enlightened monarchs took some steps toward religious toleration.

Individual and Society

> Scientific societies excluded women, but women were very much involved in informal scientific communities, such as salons. Women interested in science were illustrators, model makers, and astronomers, and a few did experiments or wrote on science. The important translation of Newton's major (Latin) work, the *Principia Mathematica*, into French was done by a woman, Madame du Châtelet.

> The philosophers met at salons—uncensored evenings of discussion on literature, science, and philosophy held in the private homes of sophisticated and wealthy women.

National and European Identity

> There was growing awareness of how culturally different peoples in Asia and Africa were from Europeans.

> The Enlightenment, while forged in France, was an international movement.

> Neoclassicism, an art style based on a selection (canon) of work from classical antiquity and the Renaissance, was the dominant style. This style was used to create national symbols and support loyalty and nationalism among citizens.

> In the War of the Austrian Succession (1740–1748), Frederick the Great expanded Prussia by taking Silesia and its valuable mineral resources from Maria Theresa of Austria.

> In the late eighteenth century, the Russian, Austrian, and Prussian rulers dismembered Poland, where the monarchy was weak. Each took a share of its former territories; independent Poland ceased to exist.

> During the Enlightenment, European notions of racial and ethnic superiority began to morph into racism. Hume and Kant wrote classifications of humans by race following botanical and biological models, although Diderot and the Scottish philosopher James Beattie argued that no culture was intrinsically more worthy than any other.

> An international community of scholars developed, linked by journals and the scientific societies or academies founded in most major cities. Lending libraries and coffeehouses offered commoners public spaces for debate.

McKay Chapter 16 Focus Questions

1. What revolutionary discoveries were made in the sixteenth and seventeenth centuries, and why did they occur in Europe?

2. What intellectual and social changes occurred as a result of the Scientific Revolution?

3. How did the Enlightenment emerge, and what were major currents of Enlightenment thought?

4. How did Enlightenment thinkers address issues of racial and social difference, and how did new institutions and social practices diffuse Enlightenment thought?

5. What impact did new ways of thinking have on political development and monarchical absolutism?

NOTES:

CHAPTER 17
The Expansion of Europe, 1650–1800

Areas of Focus: western Europe, Atlantic states and their colonies

Main Events: the enclosure movement, Agricultural Revolution, rural industry, population growth, mercantilism and colonial wars, the Atlantic slave trade, economic liberalism

Key Figures:

- Adam Smith: Scottish economist; leading proponent of laissez-faire capitalism
- Arthur Young: English proponent of scientific agriculture; reported on rural conditions in France and England
- Olaudah Equiano: African slave; wrote influential autobiography, opposed slavery
- Benjamin Franklin: American diplomat, scientist, printer; advocate of the Enlightenment
- Captain James Cook: discovered eastern shore of Australia and the Hawaiian islands
- Jethro Tull: agricultural innovator; inventor of the seed drill

AP® European History Themes
Interaction of Europe and the World

> The war known as the French and Indian War in North America was the overseas extension of French-English conflict on the continent of Europe known as the Seven Years' War. In both cases, England emerged the victor winning valuable territories as well as the dominant position in the lucrative slave trade. France continued to rely on its colonies in Haiti and other islands in the Caribbean as sources of great wealth.

> Spain's colonial empire grew in size when it acquired Louisiana and was able to move west to California. Indigenous peoples were held on the colonial estates through debt peonage.

> European exploration of hitherto unknown areas continued. James Cook discovered the east coast of Australia and Hawaii.

> International trade grew more complicated, with intricate connections between the Atlantic trade and that in the Pacific and Indian Oceans.

> Europeans fought less among themselves as they focused more and more on commerce. In Africa, they used the shore method of trading, meaning they traded with African dealers to bring the slaves to their ship. This rising demand for slaves made some African merchants wealthy. They bought more and more European and colonial goods, including firearms, which was a factor in a rise in warfare among African states.

> The population of Africa stagnated and possibly even declined during this period.

> As more details about the slave trade and slavery became public, a movement to abolish slavery grew by the late 1680s, becoming Britain's first mass movement. In 1807, the British Parliament abolished the slave trade and slavery itself in 1833.

Poverty and Prosperity

> The domestic system of manufacturing and the Agricultural Revolution (1650–1850) developed to the greatest degree in England and to a lesser degree in the Low Countries.

> The domestic or "putting-out" system, also known as the cottage industry, involved merchant capitalists who would bring materials to peasants, such as raw wool to be spun into thread, or thread for weavers to weave into cloth. The merchant controlled the entire process, avoided guild regulations, paid low wages, and thus was able to produce textile and household goods inexpensively. In this way rural families could earn cash and supplement their incomes, but relations between the merchant capitalists and the rural laborers were often contentious.

> The Agricultural Revolution led to a huge increase in the amount and variety of foodstuffs. The goal of its proponents was to increase agricultural yield by using new methods to revitalize the soil, which had been planted in the open-field system for centuries. Instead of failed harvests every eight or nine years, continuous "crop rotation" and planting novel crops were used to restore fertility and provided new foods for humans and animals as well: potatoes, turnips, peas, beans, clovers and grasses. The growth of productivity led to an increase in the number of cattle and sheep, which in turn meant more high-protein food for consumers and more fertilizer [manure] for the soil.

> To implement improvements and allow for greater experimentation, some landowners joined together to enclose the common fields that had been used by the tenant farmers for grazing, firewood, foraging, and gleaning as part of the open-field system. Such enclosures created larger fields for the landowners but forced the displacement of many small farmers. Elsewhere, peasants held onto their traditional rights and prevented enclosure.

> England led in enclosing land; half was already enclosed by 1700. Most of the rest of the land was enclosed by parliamentary legislation in the eighteenth century. The enclosure movement was a huge transformation of village life. In effect, most of the land in England was held by a few landowners as the majority of small landowners became rural wage earners in a process called proletarization.

> The landowners of large estates used new equipment like the seed drill promoted by English innovator Jethro Tull (1674–1741). They learned drainage and water control from the Dutch and cultivated marginal lands. Agriculture became a capitalistic, market-oriented business.

> Great Britain, formed in 1707 by the union of England and Scotland, strengthened its shipbuilding industry and gained a virtual monopoly on trade with its American colonies through its Navigation Acts (1651–1663), which disallowed importing goods on the ships of its foreign competition.

> Population growth increased the market for manufactured goods and dampened the wages of workers.

Objective Knowledge and Subjective Visions

> The discipline of economics was founded during this period. Adam Smith, a Scot, discovered the law of supply and demand as the basis of economic life. His seminal work—*Inquiry into the Nature and Causes of the Wealth of Nations* (1776)—criticized mercantilism and argued for capitalism, with a limited government role to allow for the free operation of the economy, which would benefit consumers and nations alike. His theories formed a classic argument for economic liberalism. This book catapulted his ideas regarding capitalism into the public sphere.

> There was much discussion about the proper role of guilds, which had grown dramatically in the seventeenth century. Smith opposed them for their interference with the natural operation of the law of supply and demand, and he spurred support for their abolition.

> Eighteenth-century painters portrayed the newly grown, bustling, cosmopolitan cities, scenes of rural life, the exotic peoples of the colonies, and the hard work of slaves. *Casta* painting was a new artistic genre depicting mixed race couples in the New World.

> Skilled artisans across Europe espoused the values of hand craftsmanship and limited competition as opposed to the mechanized production system, which devalued the worker.

States and Other Institutions of Power

> In the age of the Atlantic economy (1650–1790), governments inextricably intertwined politics and economics in their mercantilist policies.

> Economic (and maritime) advantage was the main issue in the eighteenth century English-French mercantilist wars (1701–1763).

> The Atlantic states—France, England, and Holland—eclipsed Portugal and Spain and fiercely competed with each other for trade in Asia and Africa. The Dutch East India Company (established 1602) took over the spice trade from Portugal in Indonesia and Ceylon, only to face competition from the British East India Company (established 1600).

> The British took over French concessions in India as a result of the War of the Spanish Succession (1701–1714) and in 1764 defeated the Mughal emperor. By the early 1800s the British had gained economic and political dominance over much of India.

> In the New World, where the Dutch had already lost most of their colonies, France and England competed with each other and with Spain. England's mercantilist policies were highly successful. France and England fought several wars for colonial domination. After the last—the Seven Years' War—the 1763 Treaty of Paris ratified British victory on all colonial fronts; they won former French holdings in the Mississippi and Ohio River Valleys, Canada, and most of India.

> France derived great wealth from its remaining colony of Haiti, a slave-based plantation economy producing sugar and coffee.

> Spain acquired Louisiana and expanded its empire in western North America. Spanish landowners used debt peonage to keep indigenous workers bound to them.

> In 1807, the slave trade in the British Empire was banned by Parliament, largely due to a political mass movement, the first ever in Britain, in which women played an important role.

Individual and Society

➤ **AP® Tip** This chapter focuses mostly on social history, that is, changes in the lives of ordinary people. AP History curricula and exams have increasingly focused on social history. It is now seen as important as the deeds and thoughts of great men and women, wars, and governments.

> Women entered the paid labor force in hitherto unknown numbers, which gave them greater authority in the household.

> Leisure time was reduced in this "industrious revolution" as people worked harder.

> As the traditional rights of peasants and rural laborers were lost, many former small landowners moved to cities, which grew in size.

> With expanding armies, many men were conscripted or joined the military.

> Population growth had been slow until 1700, when it began to skyrocket, reaching a growth rate of 1 percent per year. The cause was more a reduction of the death rate, likely due to the increasing supply of food, than an increase in the birthrate. In England, inoculations against smallpox began to reduce deaths there. In the 1720s, the periodic recurrences of plague ended. Better public health, better methods of safeguarding food supplies, more building of canals and roads, and less destructive wars all helped reduce death rates.

> Wealthy Creoles (American-born people of Spanish ancestry) and their counterparts throughout the Atlantic colonies—the colonial elite—took pride in assimilating fine European ways of life.

> Atlantic cultural identities and race relations throughout the colonies were complex. Some mixed-race populations (such as those in the Spanish and French Caribbean) were embraced, while others were kept in slavery.

❯ The conversion of native peoples of the New World remained a key goal for Europeans. The Spanish sent many missionaries who built missions and acted as agents of cultural exchange, so that Catholicism in its colonies in Central and South America was syncretic, filled with elements of native religious practice. Conversion of the natives in North America was less successful. Jews, as white Europeans, were ineligible for enslavement, but they were discriminated against in European colonies.

National and European Identity

❯ While the European economy was transformed by the agricultural revolution and the domestic or cottage system of manufacturing, the competition among the European powers intensified. Colonial exports and imports became more and more important, particularly to England's economy.

❯ After 1700 Britain became the undisputed leader in the Atlantic slave trade. London was the wealthiest and largest city in Europe. Relying on African merchants and rulers to provide slaves, this trade was a major source of wealth until the slave trade was banned in the British Empire in 1807.

❯ In 1707, the United Kingdom came into being with the union of England and Scotland. After this, the term Great Britain came into common use.

❯ Great Britain was formed by the union of England and Scotland in 1707 beginning a process of unification that was both supported and challenged by various national groups.

McKay Chapter 17 Focus Questions

1. What important developments led to increased agricultural production, and how did these changes affect peasants?

2. Why did the European population rise dramatically in the eighteenth century?

3. How and why did rural industry intensify in the eighteenth century?

4. What were guilds, and why did they become controversial in the eighteenth century?

5. How did colonial markets boost Europe's economic and social development, and what conflict and adversity did world trade entail?

CHAPTER 18
Life in the Era of Expansion, 1650–1800

Areas of Focus: western Europe

Main Events: illegitimacy explosion, more widespread education, consumer revolution, Methodism

Key Figures:

- Jean-Baptiste de la Salle: founder of a series of Christian schools
- John Wesley: founder of Methodism
- Jean-Jacques Rousseau: Enlightenment philosophe who advocated progressive child care
- Thomas Paine: author of *Common Sense*
- Edward Jenner: discovered the principles of inoculation, performed first smallpox inoculation in England
- Madame du Coudray: midwife; author of *Manual on the Art of Childbirth*
- Rose Bertin: fashion designer, successful entrepreneur
- James Gillray: English satirist

AP® European History Themes
Interaction of Europe and the World

> The European consumer revolution could only happen because of the availability of cheap imports from colonies in the New World. Cotton, particularly, was key in making nice clothes important to the lower social classes, as it was relatively inexpensive and could be easily both dyed and washed.

> The idea of vaccination against smallpox was brought to England by Lady Mary Wortley Montagu who took it from Ottoman inoculation practices. Edward Jenner discovered the efficacy of using cowpox (1796) and made a smallpox vaccine less dangerous.

> Europeans drank large quantities of coffee from the New World and tea from Asia. Sugar, cigars or other forms of tobacco, and chocolate also were commonly available. Drinking good quantities of tea or coffee helped people stay awake during the Industrial Revolution (discussed in Chapter 17) where ordinary people were working longer hours and harder.

Poverty and Prosperity

> A burgeoning consumer culture emerged in the elite and among people of modest means who could buy cheap reproductions of luxury goods and affordable clothes made out of new fabrics like cotton.

> The consumer revolution was aided by marketing campaigns as fashion merchants took over from courtiers. Homes also changed as privacy and individual household goods became seen as necessary.

> Peasants, landless laborers, and urban workers believed in the idea of a fair "just price" that could be imposed by government decree if necessary. When prices rose above acceptable levels, they often rioted.

Objective Knowledge and Subjective Visions

> The expansion of the size of the reading public allowed for the proliferation of published materials such as cheap broadsheets, and set the stage for the popularity of the novel in the nineteenth century.

> Artists portrayed the lives of ordinary people both in cities and villages, with images such as market scenes, weddings, and family scenes, often showing the interactions among people of different social classes.

States and Other Institutions of Power

> Several monarchs expanded the educational opportunities of their subjects. Prussian King Frederick I made elementary education mandatory in 1717 for both boys and girls.

> The Jesuits, seen as politically dangerous, were expelled from France by Louis XV in 1763. The order was dissolved by the pope ten years later (and restored in 1814).

> The Jansenists, dissident Catholics in France, were strong in their opposition to Bourbon absolutism and were persecuted by the French monarchs.

Individual and Society

> Religious fervor increased over the eighteenth century in various parts of Europe. The parish church remained central to the community, but it was subject to greater state control.

> Pietism also stressed emotional religiosity and inspired a strong Protestant revival spreading outward from Germany.

> In Catholic communities, the church retained its vibrancy due to the exuberance of Baroque art and the close connections between parish priests and the laity.

> Jansenists in the Spanish Netherlands and France called for a return to austere Christianity. Much of France's urban elite became Jansenists.

AP® Tip Numerous AP European History Exam document-based questions have focused on the social history of the early modern period; for example, the 2000 DBQ addressed peasant rituals and the 2007 DBQ was about attitudes toward children. They are available on the College Board Web site. The documents in these DBQs are worthwhile reading, and they make great practice exercises.

> Nuclear families were the norm in Europe at this time, which was unusual in world history where most people elsewhere lived in extended families. Most people married in their twenties, waiting until they had the means to establish independent households. This combination of late marriage and nuclear-family households, rare around the globe, is considered to be a key element in European economic advantage over other parts of the world, as it typically meant the marriage of two adults who may already have acquired some capital before marriage. It also fostered gender equality unlike the inequality fostered by the typical wide gap in the ages of the husband and wife at marriage in earlier times in European history and generally around the world.

> Young people often worked away from home, boys as apprentices or day laborers and girls as domestic servants or employees hired by guilds. Such work was unregulated and many youths were abused at work.

> Prostitution was less and less tolerated. More repressive laws were passed, but the practice continued to flourish because of the irregular employment of young women.

> Homosexuality was thoroughly condemned, but homosexual and even lesbian subcultures began to emerge in Paris, Amsterdam, and London.

> In villages in the first half of the eighteenth century, social control was maintained through community pressure and rituals like *charivari*, a shaming ritual for people who broke social norms. Premarital intercourse was common but generally led to marriage in cases of pregnancy.

> As these controls weakened in the second half of the eighteenth century, illegitimate births became much more common; about one-third of all births were illegitimate in the late eighteenth century. Condoms made from sheep intestines became available, but they were expensive. Commoners, who relied on coitus interruptus, rarely used them. The illegitimacy explosion was concentrated in northern and central Europe.

> As abortion was illegal, women with unwanted babies had few choices. Some committed infanticide while others left their babies in urban foundling hospitals, favorite charities of the rich but with horrific mortality rates.

> Poor women nursed their babies and often served as wet nurses to the children of the well to do. Rural wet-nursing was a widespread business, particularly in northern France, linked with high infant mortality rates. Many upper-class women were encouraged to breast feed their children by works such as Rousseau's *Emile*. Wet-nursing raised the infant mortality rate.

> Historians long thought that high childhood mortalities (typically two or three out of every five babies died) might have led parents to limit their emotional attachments to children. Ample documentary evidence, however, shows great emotional attachments to infants, even those who died at very young ages. With Enlightenment philosophes rethinking the use of strict and severe discipline, as in Rousseau's popular work *Emile* (1762), the educated elite began to give their children freedom of movement in their dress, to nurse them themselves, and to educate both sons and daughters.

> In Catholic areas, the education of the children of the elite was managed by the Jesuits, and for the poor, by parish schools. Education in Prussia was at mandatory state schools; in Scotland education was under the Presbyterians, and in England in religious-based "charity schools." The result was a surge in literacy and a growth in the reading public.

> Under the influence of the Enlightenment, children began to be considered innocent and natural, and were given greater tenderness and care.

> People spent their leisure time enjoying blood sports like cockfighting and boxing, going to urban pleasure gardens, theater, or commercial spectator sports. Both urban and rural Catholics delighted in the often-ribald carnival festivities before Lent. Games originating from peasants' sports—such as boxing—became professionalized and commercialized. Elite private schools fostered the growth of organized, rule-laden sports and attitudes about masculinity that went with them.

> The consumer revolution transformed the ways people asserted their self-identity. As the colonies produced inexpensive cotton cloth colored with various vegetables dyes, fashionable clothes and luxury goods became ways to express individuality, leading to a huge growth in the size of wardrobes even among lower-class people.

> The diet of Europeans noticeably improved in the eighteenth century, with a greater variety of vegetables and the consumption of sugar and tea. Upper-class people enjoyed formal teas, while ordinary people drank tea to provide energy for work.

> New attitudes about privacy and intimacy led to the designation of specific rooms for sleeping and other functions, replacing the former households where many functions took place in the same room.

> Hygiene improved when doctors began to urge their patients to bathe, overriding previous ideas that bathing could be dangerous.

> Medical care was typically given by apothecaries, faith healers using herbal medicines, midwives (all women), and physicians and surgeons (all men). Army surgeons made some improvements in field amputations. When forceps were invented, physician-surgeons attacked the qualifications of midwives. An important text written by Madame du Coudray in 1757 did much to improve midwifery practice.

> Vaccination against smallpox began when Lady Mary Wortley Montagu brought back Ottoman inoculation practices to England, and it improved when Edward Jenner discovered the efficacy of using cowpox (1796).

National and European Identity

> Books, printed on cheap paper, were mostly religious texts, stories, practical guides, almanacs, or pamphlets simplifying Enlightenment ideas.

> Caricaturists like James Gillray and satirical artists like William Hogarth were popular in eighteenth century England.

> In both Spain and France, monarchs were able to create a type of national Catholic churches as they took greater control over religious practice and appointments.

> Methodism was a widely popular movement in eighteenth century England, created by the energetic preacher John Wesley (1703–1791). He wanted to restore emotionality to individual religious faith and offer the assurance of salvation to all by rejecting predestination.

> Popular beliefs were increasingly under attack by the critical rationalism of the enlightened elite as well as by secular authorities.

McKay Chapter 18 Focus Questions

1. How did the expansion of agricultural and trade (Chapter 17) contribute to changes in daily life in the eighteenth century?

2. What were the main areas of improvement in the lives of the common people in the eighteenth century, and what aspects of life remained unchanged or even determined?

3. How did Enlightenment thought (Chapter 16) affect education, childcare, medicine, and religion in the eighteenth century?

NOTES:

CHAPTER 19
Revolutions in Politics, 1775–1815

Areas of Focus: France, North America, Saint-Domingue (Haiti)

Main Events: the American Revolution, the French Revolution, the Reign of Terror, Napoleonic reign and wars, the Haitian War of Independence

Key Figures:

- Thomas Jefferson: American influenced by the Enlightenment; author of *The (American) Declaration of Independence*
- George Washington: general in charge of the Continental Army, first American President
- King Louis XV: unsuccessful in his attempts to refashion the tax system; had a series of scandalizing mistresses
- King Louis XVI: last absolute monarch in France; executed January 1793
- Marie Antoinette: Austrian-born queen of France; executed later in 1793
- Marquis de Lafayette: aristocrat, general who fought on the side of the revolutionaries in America, head of the French National Guard created by the National Assembly
- Abbé Sieyès: author of *What is the Third Estate*, influential pamphleteer; key figure in Napoleon's rise to power
- Maximilien Robespierre: leader of the Jacobins, dominant member of the Committee of Public Safely who ruled during the Reign of Terror, advocate of terror as an instrument of virtue
- Georges Jacques Danton: leader of the Girondists, on the Committee of Public Safety; executed on order of Robespierre
- Mary Wollstonecraft: author of *A Vindication of the Rights of Women* (1792)
- Olympe de Gouges: author of *The Declaration of Rights of the Woman Citizen*; purged during the Reign of Terror
- Napoleon Bonaparte: general for the Republic, emperor of France 1803–1815; took power in a coup
- Francisco Goya: Spanish painter of war including anti-Napoleonic scenes
- Toussaint L'Ouverture: freed slave, key military leader of the Haitian revolt against the French government
- Jacques-Louis David: dramatic painter of the Revolution and Napoleon
- Alexander I of Russia: czar; opposed Continental system, defeated Napoleon's invasion of 1812
- Louis XVIII: Bourbon restored to the French throne in 1814
- Edmund Burke: founder of British conservatism; argued in his *Reflections on the Revolution in France* (1790) that it would lead only to violence, disorder, and tyranny

AP® European History Themes

Interaction of Europe and the World

> Three important revolutions happened within the span of 20 years—the American, the French, and the Haitian. The destinies of both the Haitian and the American revolutions were closely tied to what happened in France.

> The American Revolution against British rule in the colonies and the resulting 1789 United States Constitution inspired reformers in France. The French government supported the rebels, which weakened its finances substantially, one of the long-term causes of the 1789 Revolution. The Haitians broke out in rebellion when the National Assembly refused to give the newly won rights of Frenchmen to the colonies. After a series of on-again, off-again rebellions and relations with France and some shifting loyalties, Haiti won its independence in 1804; however, its great leader, Toussaint L'Ouverture, was arrested by French troops and died in a French prison the next year.

> Napoleon had re-established slavery in the colonies in 1799 after it had been abolished by the Convention. When Haiti became independent in 1804, it marked the first successful revolution in Latin America and the only successful slave rebellion in history. In the wake of his failure to secure Haiti, Napoleon sold Louisiana to the United States in 1803.

> The ideals of the French and American Revolutions spread around the world inspiring republican and radical movements for the next two centuries.

Poverty and Prosperity

> Among the major causes of the French Revolution was the huge debt held by the monarchy because of its costly wars and its aid to the American colonies in their war against the British. France lacked a central bank and paper currency.

> The harvests in 1788 were poor, which led to soaring bread prices and high urban unemployment as demand for manufactured goods dried up.

> The National Assembly, following laissez-faire ideas, banned monopolies, guilds, and workers' associations, which served bourgeois interests but not those of the urban poor.

> In 1790, new paper currency, *assignats,* was issued. It was backed by confiscated church lands.

> The Committee of Public Safety created a type of socialistic economy, with nationalized workshops and maximum prices and rationing for key goods.

> **AP® Tip** These economic programs that would later become important elements of the many socialist parties—minimum wage, price controls on key commodities, forced requisitioning of food crops from farmers during wartime, and the idea of the "right to work" (i.e. that should the private sector not be able to provide employment for all those who seek it, the state would seek ways to provide them with an job and income). The first three ideas will also appear during the civil war after the Russian Revolution (see Chapter 25).

> Napoleon established the Bank of France in 1800. France was way behind its chief competitors: the Bank of England was established in 1694, the Bank of Amsterdam in 1609.

> **AP® Tip** Students of U.S. history will recognize the battle over the idea of a national bank from Alexander Hamilton to President Andrew Jackson.

Objective Knowledge and Subjective Visions

> The widely popular pamphlet by Abbé de Sieyès—*What Is the Third Estate?*—defended the legitimacy of the demands of the bourgeoisie in 1789.

> The National Assembly deprived the church of its right to tithe and confiscated its lands. In 1790, the Civil Constitution of the Clergy made priests employees of the state and put the church under the authority of the government, to which clergymen had to swear allegiance. Only about half the clergy swore the loyalty oath.

> The Convention attempted to de-Christianize France with a new calendar eliminating all religious elements, and by encouraging the Cult of Reason and creating civic holidays.

> The Catholic Church and the government of France were reconciled through Napoleon's 1801 Concordat with the pope, in which Catholics were granted freedom of religion and Napoleon gained political power and influence over the church.

> Songs and political art were key ways people unified around the Revolution. Liberty was often personified as a woman.

> Napoleon spread Enlightenment ideas throughout Europe, but he repressed dissent, censored and banned newspapers, and persecuted intellectuals resisting him. He used plebiscite to mask the end of democratic government in his reign.

> Napoleon favored Neoclassicism and had himself portrayed as a Roman emperor.

> The revolution provoked strong denunciations by those believing in the "divine right of kings" and by conservative philosophers like Edmund Burke who eloquently argued in *Reflections on the Revolution in France* (1790) that rapid reform would lead only to tyranny and chaos. Burke was opposed to "divine right of kings" and defended constitutional government but saw the revolution as leading not to more freedom but to chaos and tyranny. Instead he argued for slow change under the management of well-educated and trained elites.

> Napoleon was seen by some as a romantic hero and painted as such by artists like Jacques-Louis David.

> Spanish artist Francisco Goya made powerful antiwar paintings and drawings during the French suppression of a Spanish revolt against their rule.

→ **AP® Tip** There was relatively limited public opposition to Napoleon. Madame de Staël, daughter of Jacques Necker (Louis XIV's finance minister and a reformer], novelist, was a fierce opponent of Napoleon's policies (see Chapter 21).

States and Other Institutions of Power

→ **AP® Tip** The French Revolution and the reign of Napoleon Bonaparte marked the transition from the feudal to the modern state. Many college courses in Modern European History begin there. While some historians find the origins of modern Europe in the Enlightenment or the Industrial Revolution, there is no doubt that the forces of nationalism, the ideologies, and the mass politics that define modern history found their origins in the French Revolution. In addition, it set the model both for later revolutions and for a new type of popular, progressive, but authoritarian ruler.

> The last two French kings, Louis XV (r. 1715–1774) and Louis XVI (r. 1774–1792), were inadequate leaders, and their libertine behavior led to a desacralization of the monarchy. (Background to the Revolution follows; more information on what happened in each stage is to be found in the chart below.)

> In 1787, facing financial crisis, Louis XVI called an Assembly of Notables to approve a general tax on landed property, but the Assembly insisted that the Estates General—the traditional legislative body—be called to approve such a significant change. When the king tried to impose the tax by decree, it was invalidated by the Parlement of Paris, which had the right to approve royal decrees before they could become law. In 1788, his hand forced, Louis XVI called the Estates General into session for the first time in 175 years. An outburst of discussion everywhere in France accompanied the election of delegates, leading to a general agreement on the desirability of creating a constitutional monarchy and guarantees of individual liberty.

> When the Estates General had last met in 1614, each estate met separately and had one vote. In May 1789, the third estate called for the three estates to meet together and vote by delegate, which led to crisis and began the Revolution.

> **AP® Tip** The revolutionaries had a tripartite slogan—*Liberté, Egalité, Fraternité*—that was shared by all classes in the beginning. But liberty, equality, and fraternity (brotherhood or nationalism) are often contradictory, and the different classes stressed different goals, which destroyed their early unity. A chart to help you remember the various stages of the revolution follows, using the revolutionary slogan: the first stage of the revolution focused on liberty, the "second revolution" on equality, and the third stage, Napoleon's rule, with fraternity.

The following table traces the development and resolution of the French Revolution through the various governmental bodies ruling France through 1815.

Political Aspects of the Governments of France, 1789–1815	
The First Stage: "Liberté"	
National Assembly (1789–1791)	> The delegates of the third estate declared themselves the National Assembly in June 1789 and swore the Tennis Court Oath not to disband until they had written a constitution for France. This was a radical assertion of sovereignty. > When the king responded by calling out the troops, angry Parisians (sans-culottes, artisans, and small traders) gathered arms and stormed the Bastille on July 14. The king relented; the National Assembly replaced the Estates General. Bastille Day is now France's national holiday. > In the summer of 1789, peasants rose up in a spontaneous rebellion against their feudal lords, which perpetuated widespread fear of landlord retaliation (the Great Fear). This fear intensified the rebellions, and on August 4, 1789, the nobles of France voluntarily relinquished their individual feudal privileges. Feudalism was abolished. > The National Assembly issued the Declaration of the Rights of Man and of the Citizen (August 27, 1789), which guaranteed legal equality before the law, representative government, and individual freedoms. > Seven thousand armed Parisian women marched on Versailles in October to protest high bread prices and brought the royal family back to Paris from Versailles. > France was reorganized into eighty-three departments, a structure retained to this day.
Constitutional Monarchy and Legislative Assembly (1791–1792)	> Louis XVI reluctantly accepted a new constitution that made him a limited monarch. > The kings of Austria and Prussia announced their readiness to go to war to protect the French monarchs. The French Legislative Assembly responded, in April 1792, by declaring war on Austria. > The king and queen attempted to flee Paris but were captured; the attempt to escape the country convinced many that they were traitors. A Parisian crowd stormed the royal palace at the Tuileries in August 1792. When the king sought refuge at the nearby Legislative Assembly, they instead arrested and imprisoned him. > Radical clubs such as the Jacobins formed to advocate for the urban masses.

The Second Stage: "Egalité"	
The Republic and the National Convention (1792–1795)	❭ The National Convention, dominated by Jacobins, declared France a republic in September 1792 and wrote a very liberal constitution that was never put into effect. Because of war abroad and disorder at home, a twelve-man Committee of Public Safety, led by Robespierre, was installed as the government in April 1793.
	❭ The Convention convicted the king of treason and executed him in January 1793.
	❭ Rebellions against the Paris government arose in 1793 in the Vendée region of western France and in Lyons in central France, mostly for royalist, Christian, and localist reasons.
	❭ The Committee of Public Safety established special courts to prosecute dissidents, rebels, and traitors; some 40,000 French citizens were executed or died in prison, and hundreds of thousands more were arrested. This was known as the Reign of Terror (1793–1794).
	❭ The French army managed to hold off the Prussians and Austrians, and the Convention declared war on Britain, Holland, and Spain. An all-out military mobilization, including a draft, led to success on the battlefield and made the efficacy of ideologically committed and nationalistic troops evident. The French army held on to Haiti against the Spanish and English and repressed rebellions at home.
	❭ As the political conflicts within France intensified, Robespierre ordered the execution of his critics, including long-standing collaborators like Georges Jacques Danton. Moderates in the Convention then arrested Robespierre, who was guillotined in July 1794. This so-called Thermidorian Reaction (named for Thermidor, the month of the revolutionary calendar in which it occurred) ended the radical stage of the Revolution.
The Directory (1795–1799)	❭ A five-man committee and an indirectly elected legislative assembly ran France but faced opposition from conservatives and had little popular support. It ruled dictatorially.
	❭ Napoleon Bonaparte—a Corsican noble and dedicated revolutionary who had risen rapidly as an artillery officer and as a general with glorious victories in Italy—was seen by opponents of the Directory as strong and charismatic. In November 1799, Napoleon and two others staged a coup d'état. Napoleon became first consul, a move approved by the majority of French voters in a subsequent plebiscite. Napoleon offered internal order and national glory.
The Third Stage: "Fraternité"	
The Consulate and the Empire (1799–1814)	❭ The codification of the civil and criminal laws was one of Napoleon's most important accomplishments. The Napoleonic Code established equality under the law for all French men and the sanctity of private property, but it also limited the rights of many and stripped away some of the gains in rights given women in earlier stages of the Revolution.
	❭ Napoleon streamlined the bureaucracy, created equality of opportunity, and granted amnesty to 100,000 nobles who had emigrated during the Revolution.
	❭ Napoleon's regime was repressive. Newspapers were censored or shut down, and a secret police was established to ferret out and detain political opponents.
	❭ Napoleon crowned himself emperor in 1804, which was also approved by plebiscite.
	❭ A planned invasion of England was thwarted by British victory at Trafalgar in 1805. Napoleon tried to restrict British trade with the rest of Europe. This "continental system" led to smuggling and a counter-blockade against France.
	❭ In the New World, Napoleon had less success. The Haitians had revolted in 1791, and their revolutionary leader Toussaint L'Ouverture was increasingly independent of France. Napoleon, who had re-established slavery in the colonies in 1799, had L'Ouverture arrested and brought to France, where he died. His followers routed the French forces, and Haiti became independent in 1804, marking the first successful revolution in Latin America and the only successful slave rebellion in history. In the wake of his failure to secure Haiti, Napoleon sold Louisiana to the United States in 1803.

	❯ Napoleon's Grand Empire reached its zenith in 1810. Only England stayed outside his orbit. Napoleon abolished feudalism in conquered states, but his imposition of French ideas and high taxes sparked nationalistic reaction, such as in Spain in 1808. Napoleon was ultimately undone by his invasion of Russia in 1812. The Grand Army of more than half a million men was forced to retreat from Moscow in one of the greatest disasters in military history. Britain, Austria, Prussia, and Russia formed a coalition in the Treaty of Chaumont and defeated Napoleon in 1814.
The Restored Bourbon Monarchy (1814–1815)	❯ Napoleon abdicated in 1814 and went into exile on Elba, and the Bourbons were restored but as constitutional monarchs. Napoleon returned to power the following year for 100 days, but he was defeated on the battlefield of Waterloo by the combined European powers and sent into exile on a distant island, where he died in 1821.

Individual and Society

❯ Among the causes of the 1789 Revolution was the long-standing legal division of 25 million French people into one of three estates: the clergy, or first estate, which numbered about 100,000; the nobility, or second estate, which numbered about 400,000; and the third estate, made up of everyone else from the wealthy middle class to peasants, about 98 percent of the population. Both the first and second estates enjoyed tax exemptions and legal privileges. Many of the bourgeoisie and nobles were linked by marriage and business ties, and they shared Enlightenment ideas.

❯ Women were excluded from the 1789 *Declaration of the Rights of Man and of the Citizen,* and later the Convention banned women's political clubs. Olympe de Gouges published her own version of the Declaration in protest, and in 1792 Mary Wollstonecraft published *A Vindication of the Rights of Woman.* Napoleon restricted the rights of women and enhanced the authority of husbands over wives and children. Women couldn't do business or have bank accounts on their own. Men were no longer forced to recognize or support their illegitimate children, a key demand of lower-class women.

❯ The Committee of Public Safety abolished slavery in Haiti and all other French territories. Slavery was reinstated in the colonies by Napoleon.

❯ Napoleon set up elite schools for able young men of all classes to provide greater equality of opportunity. These still serve to create France's professional elite.

❯ Under Napoleon's Napoleonic Code, women, children, and employees all lost rights. Employees were made more vulnerable to their bosses as their rights to collectively bargain were eliminated. Freedom of the press and speech were also limited.

AP® Tip The revolution attempted to change many aspects of French culture. A new calendar ended the seven-day week and replaced Christian holiday with revolutionary holidays. People greeted each other as "citizen" rather than with the class-bound titles used before the revolution. Fashion also changed. The social class known as the *sans-culottes*—the poor and the lower middle class, too poor to buy stockings, who wore long pants and inspired the new style of men's clothing that came to dominate later in the nineteenth century and still holds today. Citizens, both men and women, were expected to wear the tricolor cockade on their hats to show their support for the revolution. The revolutionary government introduced the metric system, used in France to this day. Much of the revolution and the opposition to it was based as much on cultural and social issues as it was on political and economic acts of the government.

National and European Identity

> The French Revolution of 1789 overthrew the Old (Ancien) Regime, the feudal structure and government of the absolute monarchs and challenged notions of European identity throughout the continent.

> Napoleon's armies won Austria's Italian and German holdings in 1801, defeated Austria and Russia at the Battle of Austerlitz in 1805, and defeated Prussia at Jena in 1806. He then abolished the Holy Roman Empire and replaced it with the Confederation of the Rhine, establishing a foundation for the unification of modern Germany

McKay Chapter 19 Focus Questions

1. What were the factors leading to the revolutions of the late eighteenth century?

2. Why and how did American colonists forge a new, independent nation?

3. How did the events of 1789 result in a constitutional monarchy in France, and what were the consequences?

4. Why and how did the French Revolution take a radical turn, which included terror at home and war with European powers?

5. How did Napoleon Bonaparte assume control of France and much of Europe, and what factors led to his downfall?

6. How did slave revolt on colonial Sanit-Domingue lead to the creation of the independent state of Haiti in 1804?

NOTES:

CHAPTER 20
The Revolution in Energy and Industry, ca. 1780–1850

Areas of Focus: Great Britain, continental Europe

Main Events: invention of the steam engine, the Industrial Revolution, the factory system, urbanization, reactions to industrialization

Key Figures:

- James Hargreaves: inventor of the spinning jenny; increased the amount of thread that could be spun
- John Kay: inventor of the flying shuttle; increased speed of handloom weaving
- Richard Arkwright: invented the water frame for spinning thread
- Samuel Crompton: invented the mule, a hybrid spinning machine, by combining features of the water frame and the spinning jenny
- Thomas Newcomen and Thomas Slavery: invented the first steam engines
- James Watt: reconfigured early steam engines to make them work without danger of explosion
- George Stevenson: built the first successful steam locomotive
- Thomas Malthus: English classical liberal; explained poverty as a result of overpopulation in relation to limited food supply
- David Ricardo: English classical liberal, economist; came up with the "iron law of wages," which argued that labor is a commodity that responds to the law of supply and demand
- J.M.W. Turner: English artist; dramatically painted railroads and other industrial scenes
- William Cockerill: English carpenter who established a large textile factory in Belgium and helped begin industrialization there
- Sir Robert Peel: English factory owner; proposed legislation restricting working hours of children
- Frederick Engels: author of *the Condition of the Working Class in England* and later collaborator with Karl Marx; harsh attacker of the capitalist class
- Robert Owen: progressive factory owner: ended child labor in his factories and educated children instead, created worker-friendly communities, involved in creating forerunner of Trade Union Congress

AP® European History Themes
Interaction of Europe and the World

> The Industrial Revolution transformed Europe and had an equal or even greater impact on the entire world. Economic, social, political, and intellectual elements were intertwined in this process.

> The Industrial Revolution established European superiority over the rest of the world. The differences in life styles, material conditions, and civil society established by the middle of the nineteenth century, remain sources of regional inequality in our contemporary world, except for those non-European nations that successfully industrialized, particularly Japan and the U.S., in the nineteenth century.

→ **AP® Tip** The invention of the cotton gin by the American, Eli Whitney, made the production of raw cotton faster and cheaper, and spurred the transformation of the British textile industry from wool to cotton. Cotton has many advantages: it can be washed and dyed easily, and can be manufactured more easily and cheaply to meet growing demand.

> Many countries on the periphery of and outside of Europe had only tentative steps towards industrialization throughout most of the nineteenth century. Russia only industrialized seriously starting in the 1880s. Egypt adopted British technology but couldn't compete with England. Both Russia and Egypt relied on their agricultural exports. In India, the large native textile industry was harshly damaged because it couldn't compete with the less expensive British imports, partially because they were unburdened by tariffs, Britain brought raw Indian cotton to the UK for manufacturing and then sold finished cloth back to the Indians. China was too disrupted by civil disorder in the nineteenth century to be able to industrialize in any organized way; ironically it is now the U.S.'s chief economic rivalry. Japan industrialized quickly after the U.S. forced it open to trade in 1853.

Poverty and Prosperity

> The Industrial Revolution began in the textile industry—the most important sphere of manufacturing for centuries—when the cottage industry could not meet increasing consumer demand. Inventions increased production: The spinning jenny produced multiple threads from one spinning wheel, and the water frame—using waterpower to operate spinning machines, thread making machines, and power looms—moved workers from the cottages to factories by the late eighteenth century.

> Early industrialists, coming from varied backgrounds, were often in precarious financial straits and cut production costs, including jobs and wages.

> Working conditions in early factories were terrible—regimented, unsafe, and brutal.

> Factories increased the demand for power provided by coal. The steam engine was invented in the 1760s to pump water out of coal mines, and it soon became the linch-pin of the industrial economy.

> By 1850, Britain was covered with railroad tracks, which radically reduced the cost of shipping and opened previously inaccessible markets. As a result, Britain became the "workshop of the world," increasing Britain's share of the world's industrial output tenfold.

> Continental states lacked British sources of capital for investment but had to compete with Britain. Capitalists imported British technology and workers, and numerous clever Englishmen went abroad to set up industrial enterprises.

> By the mid-nineteenth century, Britain was moving toward free trade, with no import or export duties, and had repealed tariff protection laws; elsewhere economic nationalism dominated.

> Around this same time, workers began to see an improvement in their wages and disposable income. Real wages, meaning what they could purchase with their earnings, went up during the 1840s.

Objective Knowledge and Subjective Visions

> The Industrial Revolution was made possible by a series of inventions, first in the textile industry and then in the coal industry. Artisans or entrepreneurs typically made the inventions.

> Laissez-faire capitalism, as articulated by Adam Smith and others, grew to dominate in Britain by the middle of the nineteenth century when Britain adopted free trade. Its proponents articulated the importance of self-improvement and argued that those who remained poor did so because of their own failures.

> Population growth was of much concern to observers at the time. Thomas Malthus argued in his famous work, *Essay on the Principle of Population* (1798), that population always grows faster than

the food supply, meaning that poverty is inevitable unless there are "positive checks" to population growth (such as war or epidemics) or "prudential restraint" of young people (marrying late and limiting reproduction).

> Stockbroker and economist David Ricardo articulated the "iron law of wages," arguing that wages would always sink to subsistence level because of overpopulation.

> Numerous reformers described the terrible living and working conditions of the working classes. The Tory [Conservative] party set up various committees to investigate conditions in the mines and factories under the idea that the traditional role of the elite is to protect the lower classes. Legislation was subsequently passed to reduce the hours of children and women and to prohibit their employment in industries considered unsafe for their health. The liberals as a whole were opposed to state intervention in the economy.

AP® Tip Thomas Malthus, David Ricardo, and Adam Smith are considered "classical liberals." The terms *liberal* and *conservative* had quite different meanings in the nineteenth century than they did in the twentieth. Liberals encouraged the passing of the Combination (anti–trade union) Acts (1799) and legislation freeing up the craft guilds on the basis that unions and guilds restricted the free operation of the market. Conservatives pushed for various factory and mine acts to protect workers and reduce the freedom of industrialists to operate without any regulation. They tended to argue for tariff protection to prevent inexpensive imports from hurting native businesses.

> Romantic writers, such as the poets William Blake and William Wordsworth, lamented the loss of the rural lifestyle and protested the conditions of the urban poor.

> After visiting Manchester, Friedrich Engels (1820–1895), later a colleague of Karl Marx, wrote passionately about the horrific factory conditions in his *Conditions of the Working Class in England*. He bluntly blamed the middle classes for their exploitation and mistreatment of the workers. Engels and Marx argued that the poverty of urban workers was worse than rural poverty, because of relentless competition for jobs and demands on workers.

> Some contemporaries of Marx and Engels believed that conditions were improving for the workers. Andrew Ure described good conditions in cotton factories in 1835. Edwin Chadwick, a reformer and government official, asserted that the poor had more disposable income than they had had before.

> A number of important artists—including J.M.W. Turner and Claude Monet—were fascinated by the steam power of trains and the majesty of train stations and railway bridges.

> Many artists portrayed factory life. Illustrations of young girls working in coal mines were instrumental in getting the Mines Act of 1842 passed.

States and Other Institutions of Power

> Industrial workers emerged as a political force when they began to organize and advocate for political change. The Combination Acts from 1799 to 1824 banned unions in Britain. Anti-capitalist sentiments were expressed in newspapers, strikes, and protests. Over time they turned into political movements. In the 1830s, an attempt to create a national union failed. A few unions, like the machinists, won benefits.

> In the 1840s, many British workers joined the Chartists, a reformist movement for political democracy whose greatest demand was universal manhood suffrage. Their hope was to reform the economic system by first reforming the political system. This was the largest mass movement anywhere in Europe at the time. Others became involved in political organizations to limit the workday and to lower bread prices by abolishing protectionist tariffs against foreign wheat (the Corn Laws; see Chapter 21).

> Parliament established commissions to investigate conditions in the mines and factories. It passed legislation to restrict abuses, such the Factory Act of 1833, which limited the hours of children, and the Mines Act of 1842, which banned women from working as miners.

> On the continent, industrialization developed with significant involvement of government, quite a different pattern than in Britain, where the government was little involved. Belgium and soon Prussia was industrializing by the 1830s, and made important advances in business-friendly banking. By the outbreak of World War I in 1914, industrialization had progressed to a significant degree in Germany, Belgium, and France, but much less so in Italy, Russia, and Austria-Hungary. Governments used tariff protection to protect industries, to build roads and canals, and to fund the construction of railroads.

Individual and Society

> Men and women working together, often unsupervised and in physically uncomfortable or dirty conditions, led to an easy intimacy, reducing adherence to strict religious rules about sexual behavior. This partially explains the explosion of illegitimate births in the late eighteenth century

> Urbanization, population growth, and significant changes in the social structure and family life accompanied industrialization.

> In the early years of industrialization, workers in factories and coal mines were often abandoned orphans—boys and girls as young as five or six—or women, who were paid very little for working long hours. They labored under strict and often brutal discipline.

> Many cottage workers were not willing to work in the new cotton mills because of the monotony of machine labor and the loss of the freedom to choose when to work. Those who made the switch continued their tradition of working as family units, with parents disciplining and working alongside their children. Parliament's Factory Act (1833) ended this pattern of the family working together.

> Overall, the living and working conditions of laborers were terrible until around 1850. Workers' purchasing power did not improve in the early years of industrialization. Statistical analysis shows that living conditions and wages declined until 1820. Many early factory workers lived in poorhouses, a type of industrial prison where they had to work to keep their lodging and food.

> By around 1840, real wages went up and the standard of living improved; poor people could afford cotton outer clothing and underwear, and they ate more varied food.

> Industrial workers typically worked some fifty days more a year in 1830 than farm laborers had worked in 1760. They worked about eleven hours per day.

> Population increased dramatically, more than doubling in eighty years, providing both more laborers and more consumers.

> Women had played an important role in many early enterprises but later were excluded and prohibited from certain industrial employment. Factory work became gendered, and the notion of "separate spheres" with a new ideal of domesticity emerged. Women were paid substantially less than men for the same work and given the poorer jobs. Over time, working-class women became less likely to work full-time, as that made it difficult to take care of babies and the household.

> Some workers resisted industrialization. Luddites, mostly artisans, protested vehemently against machine manufacturing by destroying machines.

> Even with industrialization under full sway, farming was still the primary occupation for the majority of British workers in 1850, and domestic service was the second largest occupation.

> Robert Owen (1771–1858), a successful manufacturer who believed that workers would be more productive if treated well, formed cooperative, socialistic communities of workers.

National and European Identity

> Britain had a unique combination of factors that fostered industrialization as the solution to the economic needs of its rising population: a huge colonial empire that provided guaranteed markets as well as tax revenues and raw materials; wealth from trade in slaves and other goods; a well-developed shipbuilding industry; canals and plentiful rivers; highly productive agriculture; a national bank to provide credit; a mobile labor force; and substantial natural resources of coal and iron.

> Belgium was the first European nation to industrialize. It took the leadership in banking innovations to foster business. France, Belgium, and Germany implemented industrialization at the governmental level, particularly in their investment in building extensive railroad networks.

> In 1834 the *Zollverein,* a customs union of Germanic states, formed to remove trade barriers and forge common economic policies. This would later be an important step towards German unification.

> The Great Exhibition of 1851 at the Crystal Palace—so called because it was made of glass and iron—demonstrated Britain's industrial exuberance.

> The Industrial Revolution began in Britain, already a powerful nation with a stable political life, and made Britain the dominant world power for the next 100 years.

> Class-consciousness in both middle and working classes rose as the industrial system created clearer demarcations in occupation and lifestyle.

McKay Chapter 20 Focus Questions

1. Why did the Industrial Revolution begin in Britain, and how did it develop between 1780 and 1850?

2. How did countries in Europe and around the world respond to the challenge of industrialization?

3. How did work evolve during the Industrial Revolution, and how did daily life change for working people?

4. How did the changes brought about by the Industrial Revolution lead to new social classes, and how did people respond to the new structure?

NOTES:

CHAPTER 21
Ideologies and Upheavals, 1815–1850

Areas of Focus: Great Britain, France, Prussia, Austria, Greece

Main Events: new ideologies and movements, Romanticism, the Metternich system, Great Reform Bill of 1832, the 1848 revolutions, Irish potato famine, The *Communist Manifesto*

Key Figures:

- Klemens von Metternich: Austrian foreign minister and leading conservative politician in the post-Napoleonic period; issued Karlsbad Decrees to limit opposition
- Charles X: king of France; repudiated the limited monarchy established in 1815 leading to the revolution of 1830
- Louis Philippe: "the bourgeois monarch," succeeded Charles X; overthrown in the Revolution of 1848
- Louis Napoleon: nephew of the late Emperor; elected President of France in 1848
- Louis Kossuth: leader of Hungarian rebels in 1848 against the Austrian Empire
- Franz-Joseph: Austrian emperor from 1848 to 1916
- Friedrich Wilhelm IV: king of Prussia during the 1848 Revolution; refused to accept the crown offered by the Frankfurt Assembly
- Henri de Saint-Simon: French Utopian socialist; enthusiastic about the potential of industrialization, called for society to be led by engineers, scientists and industrialists
- Charles Fourier: French Utopian socialist; called for small communities to be formed based on cooperation not coercion, free love, equality between men and women, and communal ownership of property
- Robert Owen: British industrialist, advocate of trade unions; created utopian communities of workers without child labor, educating children in common, and treating workers well
- Louis Blanc: author of *the Organization of Work,* leading advocate on the national workshops in the French 1848 revolution
- Pierre-Joseph Proudhon: author of *What is property?*—an important early anarchist text (his answer: "theft")
- Karl Marx and Friedrich Engels: authors of *The Communist Manifesto,* which articulated a trenchant, class-based analysis and criticism of capitalism, and argued that scientific socialism made revolution inevitable
- Percy Bysshe Shelley, William Wordsworth and John Keats: British Romantic poets
- Walter Scott, Victor Hugo, George Sand: Romantic novelists
- Jacob and Wilhelm Grimm: collectors of Germanic fairy tales for both nationalistic and Romantic motivations
- J.M.W. Turner, John Constable, Eugène Delacroix: Romantic painters
- Ludwig van Beethoven, Frederick Chopin, Franz Liszt: Romantic composers
- Germaine de Staël: female author and advocate of women's rights, opponent of Napoleon Bonaparte

AP® European History Themes

Interaction of Europe and the World

> This chapter deals very little with the world outside Europe, although to be sure the ideas and ideologies developed in the period between the end of the Napoleonic period and 1848– conservatism, nationalism, liberalism, and socialism in particular–had a huge influence on every country on the globe, and were particularly important in the twentieth century.

> France conquered Algeria in 1830, marking the rebirth of French imperial ambitions. It will hold Algeria until the 1960s.

> The notion of the balance of power that held sway at the Congress of Vienna will dominate European politics and affect imperial competition in the nineteenth century.

> In Latin America, revolutionaries and nationalists took advantage of European political turmoil to forge independent nations. Creole elites and effective generals like Simon de Bolívar and José de San Martín threw off Spanish rule. Most Latin American states became independent and Spain lost its U.S. empire.

AP® Tip This was when the U.S. issued the Monroe Doctrine, asserting its leadership role in Latin America and warning Europeans to stay out of the Americas.

Poverty and Prosperity

AP® Tip The mutual relationship between economic and political changes that fused and reinforced each other after 1815 has been called a "dual revolution." Although they appear in two separate categories here, the economic and political developments of this time are intricately related. Review the political changes in conjunction with the economic.

> Shortly after the end of the Napoleonic wars, Britain imposed high tariffs on the import of foreign wheat. This led to increased unemployment, higher cost of living for workers, and protests. The Tory government suspended the rights of peaceful protests and habeas corpus, and passed the Six Acts to prevent the formation of unions. An orderly protest in Peterloo, Manchester was broken up brutally with government troops.

> Political change from the Great Reform Bill of 1832 and the Chartist movement created a new coalition of workers and liberals. The repeal of the Corn Laws in 1846 meant the victory of free trade in England. This allowed the import of cheaper wheat from eastern Europe, and reduced the cost of living for workers.

> The House of Commons passed legislation to address the worst abuses of the factory system, limited the employment of children and women, and gave them a ten hour workday in 1847.

Objective Knowledge and Subjective Visions

> Conservatism insisted that traditional ruling elites and values would conserve stability, while liberalism, socialism, and nationalism would lead to revolution, violence, and less freedom.

> Liberalism, which stressed freedom, had two strands. *Political liberals* fought for constitutional government, equality before the law, the expansion of suffrage, and civil liberties. *Economic or classical liberals* opposed all hindrances to the free operation of the market. Businessmen enthusiastically joined in, frequently working with political liberals to secure their economic interests, but they often wanted to limit suffrage.

> Socialism generally sought a just society to benefit the common people with a planned economy. Socialists wanted either the abolition or restriction of private property in favor of ownership by communes or by the state in the name of the people. Count Henri de Saint-Simon called for industrial development directed by a technocratic elite; fellow Frenchman Charles Fourier established small model communities with free choice in work and love. Louis Blanc, who played a key role in the 1848 revolution in France, demanded the government provide full employment. Pierre Proudhon was an anarchist who articulated a profoundly socialist idea in his 1840 pamphlet *What Is Property?* His answer, "Property is theft," denied the legitimacy of private property.

> Karl Marx and Friedrich Engels, in the *Communist Manifesto* (1848), called upon the workers to revolt. Marxism is both a theoretical analysis of history and society as well as an impassioned call for political action. It asserts that all profit is exploitative, that history is about class struggle between two classes in any society—the owners of the means of production (farms, factories, and so on) and those who work for them. Marx argued for a materialistic, deterministic view of history.

> Romanticism was less an ideology than a movement with many threads: some romantics being conservative or even reactionary, others liberal or nationalistic. It appealed to many young artists, writers, and composers. Rejecting Enlightenment rationalism and classicism, romantics lamented the changes brought by the Industrial Revolution and sought to live free of social conventions and materialism amid the power of nature.

> In music and art, romanticism lasted for most of the nineteenth century. Painters (John Constable, Eugène Delacroix, Joseph M. W. Turner) used dramatic scenes, exotic subjects, and intense colors. Romantic composers expanded the size of the symphony orchestra and the range of musical forms, and they wrote with emotionality and sometimes with nationalistic intent. Great composer-pianists like Franz Liszt performed before huge, adoring crowds at new concert halls. Ludwig van Beethoven was the archetypal romantic artist, a genius with a tortured life whose music was deeply affective.

States and Other Institutions of Power

> The profoundly conservative Congress of Vienna restored the legitimate monarchs displaced by Napoleon's rule, and (with a few exceptions) undid the changes he had made. The four victorious powers (the Quadruple Alliance of Russia, Prussia, Austria, and Great Britain) gained some lands, not entirely at the expense of France, which lost relatively little territory.

> After the Napoleonic wars, the major European powers (including France) formed a series of alliances and met periodically to enforce the peace settlement through military action, repressing liberal revolts in Spain and Sicily in the early 1820s. This system, enacted by Austrian foreign minister Klemens von Metternich, was generally successful until 1848; although Greece, Belgium, and the American colonies held by Spain gained independence in the intervening years.

> Metternich imposed political repression in the German Confederation (Austria, Prussia, and 37 other states) through the infamous Carlsbad Decrees (1819), which restricted freedom of assembly and the press and academic freedom in German universities.

> **AP® Tip** A good cross-period comparative topic might contrast the decisions and long-term consequences of the Congress of Vienna (1814–1815) with the Treaty of Versailles after World War I (1919; see A *History of Western Society,* Chapter 25, pp. 852–859).

> Great Britain underwent significant political change in 1832 when the Great Reform Bill redistributed the seats in Parliament, expanded suffrage, and made the House of Commons more important than the House of Lords. The number of voters increased by about 50 percent to 12 percent of the adult male population.

> Liberals in Parliament in the 1820s pushed through legislation providing civil rights for Catholics and Jews. In alliance with workers in the Anti–Corn Law League, they won repeal of these laws in 1846. Workers pushed for greater democracy in the Chartist movement, with 6 million people signing petitions that were soon rejected by the House of Commons.

> France became a constitutional monarchy when the Bourbons were restored in 1814. Charles X became king in 1824 and tried to restore unlimited monarchy. He repudiated the Constitutional Charter of 1814, censored the press, and reduced voting rights. In 1830, Parisian artisans, with many other groups, brought down the government. The new king, Louis Philippe (r. 1830–1848), restored the Constitutional Charter and called himself the "king of the French people." But many saw the "bourgeois monarchy" as corrupt, indifferent to the needs of the people, and resistant to electoral reform. These frustrations burst forth in Paris in the spring of 1848, sparking revolutions in most European states except England and Russia.

> **AP® Tip** The revolutions of 1848 are complex, multifaceted, and often confusing to students. Use the table below to clarify the chief events and issues in France, Austria, and Prussia. Get a clear sense of the conflicting ideologies involved so you can understand the shifting alliances of the revolutions.

> The year 1848 was an extraordinary and unprecedented one in which governments were toppled; kings and ministers fled; various promises were made to the people; and nationalism, liberalism, socialism, romanticism, and economic crises played various roles. Overall, the revolutions of 1848 achieved relatively little, as autocratic rulers successfully repressed nationalistic and socialistic forces. There were some permanent changes, however: the abolition of serfdom and slavery and the establishment of universal manhood suffrage in France, and some acknowledgement of the legitimacy of constitutionalism in most other states.

Individual and Society

> In Ireland in the 1840s, the potato crop failed because of blight. The Great Famine (1845–1851) and terrible diseases killed about one and a half million people and forced another one million Irish to flee the country. Ireland was the only area in Europe to lose population in the nineteenth century.

> Religious conflicts played little role in the post-Napoleonic period, except in Ireland. Catholics and Jews won some civil rights in Britain and in Prussia.

National and European Identity

> Greece was able to win independence from the Ottoman Empire after a difficult war; Russia took a greater role as protectorate of the Eastern European Christians still under Ottoman rule.

> Powerful ideologies—conservatism, liberalism, nationalism, and socialism—developed in the early nineteenth century but were not mutually exclusive. Many nationalists were liberals; others were conservatives. Socialists were more isolated. Marxian socialism rejected nationalism, arguing that class, not nationality, determined identity.

> Nationalism had several strands. *Cultural nationalism* asserted that each nation (or people) has a distinct identity based on common language, food, music, and often, but not always, religion. Nationalists used emotionally-laden symbols, folk legends, music, and (after 1850) mass education to create their "imagined communities." *Political nationalism* in already formed states meant love of country and efforts to enhance its prestige and power. In the multinational Austrian, Ottoman, and Russian empires, cultural nationalism grew into political demands for independence for subject nationalities.

Causes and Results of the 1848 Revolution			
Country/Chief Movements	Initial Successes	Problems	End of the Revolution
France: Liberalism and Socialism	Artisans and laborers barricaded the streets of Paris; Louis Philippe abdicated. The Provisional Government abolished slavery in the colonies and the death penalty. Parisian workers got a ten-hour workday. National workshops provided public works projects for the unemployed.	Divisions grew between workers wanting social and economic change and the middle classes wanting only political change. In May, moderates won in the first election with universal manhood suffrage. The new government canceled the national workshops.	A spontaneous uprising in Paris, the "June Days," ensued. Some 10,000 people died in its repression. In December, Louis Napoleon, the nephew of the late emperor, was elected with a huge majority and created an authoritarian regime
The Austrian Empire: Nationalism and Liberalism	Subject nationalities such as the Hungarians sought both independence from Austrian rule and liberal constitutions. In Vienna, students and workers rebelled and Metternich fled. The Habsburg emperor Ferdinand I promised a constitution and abolished serfdom	The peasants were content with their gains, but the middle classes feared the socialism demanded by workers. The Hungarian nationalists alienated the Slavic minorities in their part of the empire, and Czech nationalists fought German ones	The emperor abdicated in favor of the eighteen-year-old Francis Joseph. The loyal army crushed radicals in Prague and Vienna. Russian troops ended the Hungarian republic. Nationalism re-surged throughout the empire in the second half of the nineteenth century
Prussia: Liberalism and Nationalism	Prussian liberals were supported in March 1848 by artisans and factory workers; together they forced King Frederick William IV to make concessions	Liberals wrote a constitution for a unified Germany at the Frankfurt assembly. They elected the king of Prussia as emperor	Frederick William refused to take a "crown from the gutter." He took back control of Berlin, and he restored autocracy

> ❯ *Marxian Socialism* argued that the victory of the urban industrial class—the proletariat, over the industrial ruling class—the bourgeoisie—was inevitable because of the laws of scientific socialism and would create a just society. This view of European identity challenged the growing trend towards cultural and political nationalism.

> ❯ Romanticism flowered in English and French literature (William Wordsworth, Sir Walter Scott, Victor Hugo, George Sand).

> ❯ After the Congress of Vienna, the Austrians feared liberalism and nationalism from two strong subject peoples, the Hungarians (Magyars) and the Czechs (Bohemians), and dozens of other peoples in the empire.

> ❯ The British laissez-faire policies resulted in a slow, inadequate response to the Irish potato famine of the 1840s, which would later prompt Irish patriots to recall the tragedies of the famine when campaigning for home rule, land reforms, and independence from Great Britain.

McKay Chapter 21 Focus Questions

1. How was peace restored and maintained after 1815?

2. What new ideologies emerged to challenge conservatism?

3. What were the characteristics of the Romantic Movement?

4. How and where was conservatism challenged after 1815?

5. What were the main causes and results of the revolutions of 1848?

NOTES:

CHAPTER 22
Life in the Emerging Urban Society, 1840–1914

Areas of Focus: England, France, Germanic states

Main Events: Darwinian evolution, rebuilding of Paris, public health reform, Poor Law of 1834, Social Darwinism, foundation of new sciences and social sciences, Realism is literature and the arts

Key Figures:

- Edwin Chatwick: English health reformer
- Louis Pasteur: French discoverer of germ theory
- Joseph Lister: developed antiseptic principles reducing infections and disease
- Charles Darwin: founder of evolutionary biology
- Jeremy Bentham: English philosopher, founder of utilitarianism; influenced Poor Law of 1834
- Napoleon III: French emperor until 1870; rebuilt Paris
- Baron Georges Haussmann: urban planner who transformed Paris from a medieval to a modern city
- Gustav Droz: author of *Papa, Mama and Baby*, bestselling advice book on parenting
- Jean-Baptiste Lamarck: French naturalist; argued that animals develop characteristics that are transmitted to the next generation
- Herbert Spencer: English philosopher, founder of Social Darwinism
- Max Weber: German sociologist; studied bureaucracy, connections between religions and economic life
- Émile Durkheim: French sociologist; studied religions and suicide
- Ferdinand Tönnies: German sociologist; contrasted "community" and "society"
- Gustav Le Bon: French sociologist; examined the pull of emotional crowds for the alienated masses
- Franziska Tiburtius: German feminist leader; medical doctor
- Dimitri Mendeleev: Russian chemist; codified the periodic table
- Gustav Courbet, Honoré Daumier: French realist painters
- Émile Zola, Honoré de Balzac, Gustave Flaubert: French realist novelists
- George Eliot, Thomas Hardy: English Realist novelists
- Leo Tolstoy: author of *War and Peace*; Realist and moralizer

AP® European History Themes
Interaction of Europe and the World

> The public health spread quickly in industrial Europe and from there to the United States. New waste treatment and sewage plants were built in Europe and North America to reduce disease and water pollution.

> Similarly, medical care improved with the use of disinfectants and sterilization and many diseases began to disappear.

> The first transatlantic telegraph cable was completed 1858.

> Europeans adopted technology from the U.S., such as the horse-drawn streetcar and later the electric streetcar.

> Utilitarianism had great influence in the United States.

Poverty and Prosperity

> Real wages, the purchasing power of earned income, were increasing for the working classes of Europe in the second half of the nineteenth century, especially in Britain, where they doubled between 1850 and 1906.

> Public transportation systems were built by private companies in London and by city governments on the continent to help industries and cities expand and reduce congestion. Europeans adopted two American innovations—the horse-drawn streetcar in the 1870s and the electric streetcar in the 1890s. Public transport use grew phenomenally after 1886.

> Domestic servants—mostly women—were the largest single group of unskilled workers, and their numbers grew during this era. Women frequently married and transitioned to working-class families, but those who did not often joined the sweated industries, which paid low wages by the piece for goods made in the home.

Objective Knowledge and Subjective Visions

→ **AP® Tip** It might seem that the various threads of this chapter—philosophical and scientific ideas, urban planning, and social history—have little to do with each other. In fact, intellectuals were responding to visible changes in urban life around them and proposing solutions to problems. Philosophy and social science was largely rooted in reality.

> There were major advances in scientific knowledge with the discovery of the fundamental laws of thermodynamics, the periodic table, and electromagnetism. The practical application of science, as in the new chemistry industry, increased its prestige. The Enlightenment's faith in progress seemed verified by improvements visible everywhere.

> Charles Darwin's (1809–1882) theory of evolution fundamentally altered conceptions about human origins and development. It was enormously influential. Darwinism was applied by thinkers such as Herbert Spencer (who came up with the phrase "survival of the fittest") to human society in a doctrine known as Social Darwinism, popular with the middle classes. It proposed that humans engage in a fierce struggle for survival, and that the poor are so because they are unfit.

> One of the most influential ideas of the nineteenth century was Utilitarianism, developed by Jeremy Bentham. It argued that social problems had to be examined scientifically, even mathematically, with the goal of producing "the greatest happiness for the greatest number."

> Late nineteenth century literary authors turned to realism, using prose more often than poetry, to report on contemporary social conditions and the daily life of the middle and working classes. They wrote about previously taboo topics including adultery, slums, strikes, violence, and alcoholism. Social determinists, they believed that heredity in conjunction with environment determined human behavior. The three great realistic authors in France were Honoré de Balzac, Gustave Flaubert, and Émile Zola. George Eliot and Thomas Hardy were two important British realists.

> In Russia, the masterful Leo Tolstoy wrote *War and Peace* about the French invasion of Russia in 1812.

> Artists too turned to realism, portraying urban life in its exciting variety, from elegant dinner parties to dance halls. French painters Gustave Courbet, Jean-François Millet, and Honoré Daumier painted scenes of laboring workers and peasants, using somber colors and simple composition. Illustrations in magazines and newspapers highlighted the plight of the urban poor.

Feild of Study	Main Figures and Works	Key Ideas
Medicine	Edwin Chadwick, 1840s	Disease is spread by filth.
	Louis Pasteur, 1850s	Disease is spread by germs.
	Joseph Lister, 1860s	Antiseptic principle: surgical procedures must be clean.
	Robert Koch, 1870s	Specific bacteria cause specific diseases.
Biology	Charles Darwin *On the Origin of Species,* 1859; *The Descent of Man,* 1871	Species change through evolution, caused not as Lamarck suggested by inheritance of acquired characteristics, but by accidental mutations. These give certain members of a species advantages in their environment so that they survive, while others without these traits die out; the survivors reproduce, spreading their characteristics through populations; all life forms have evolved through the "struggle for survival
Political Economy	Jeremy Bentham	Utilitarianism, the rational calculation of social problems to achieve "the greatest good for the greatest number
Sociology	Max Weber	Argued in the Protestant Ethic and the Spirit of Capitalism that ideas and beliefs are the dynamo of historical change; studied modern bureaucracies and leadership.
	Emile Durkheim	Quantitative sociologist, studied suicide and religion, developed concept of anomie (rootlessness).
	Ferdinand Tönnies	Compared community to society, analyzed alienation of modern society.
	Gustav Le Bon	Argued that alienated masses will be attracted by crowds and emotionality.

> There was a general decline in church attendance and donations throughout Europe in the late nineteenth century, more in working-class urban neighborhoods than in middle-class or rural ones. Most people continued to have their children baptized, but religion played a reduced role in their lives, except in areas where religion thrived as the core of ethnic identity, as with Irish Catholics in Protestant Britain and Jews in Russia.

> Protestant and Catholic churches were conservative and were seen as such by the working class, who generally were dissatisfied with the social order and customs that conservatism upheld.

> Religious people were greatly offended by the Darwinian theory of natural selection, but it was relatively quickly accepted by the mass of the population and tolerated by most religious establishments.

> The first modern consumer industry, fashionable clothes for middle-class women, developed by the late nineteenth century. Ready-to-wear clothes were sold in newly created department stores. This development was centered in Paris.

States and Other Institutions of Power

> Urban planning was instituted all over Europe. Governments built or subsidized public transportation systems, theaters, office buildings, museums, and middle-class housing. They razed slums and improved sanitation and sewage systems.

> In Britain, reformer Edwin Chadwick applied Jeremy Bentham's utilitarian ideas to report on the new Poor Law enacted in 1834. His findings, published in 1842, ignited a nationwide public health movement and resulted in Britain's first public health law in 1846.

> In France, Napoleon III (r. 1848–1870) undertook a massive rebuilding of Paris. Under the direction of Baron Georges Haussmann, the old Paris disappeared. Broad boulevards, parks and squares, new sewage and water systems, and apartment buildings in new residential areas replaced the medieval city.

Individual and Society

> By 1851, more than half of the British population lived in cities. Urban life was awful in the early nineteenth century, with overcrowded housing, rampant diseases like cholera, widespread poverty, inadequate sewage systems and toilets, and no public transportation.

> As urbanization intensified, reformers sought to make cities safe and livable. Cheap iron pipes were installed underground to carry sewage away and to provide clean water. Overall, the public health movement saved millions of lives; death rates dramatically declined after about 1880 in what has been called a "great silent revolution."

> Everywhere in Europe, but particularly in Britain, the gap between rich and poor grew more noticeable. The aristocrats, still wealthy and influential, divided their time between grand country estates and splendid townhouses. Many intermarried with the wealthy middle classes and engaged in capitalistic exploitation of their own resources. There was substantial inequality of wealth and income.

> The two ever-more important social classes—the middle classes (about 20 percent of the urban population) and the working classes (about 80 percent)—were each subdivided into several subclasses.

> The middle classes: The upper-middle class, highly successful in commerce, banking, and industry, mimicked the aristocracy. The middle-middle class of small industrialists and professionals like lawyers and physicians was less wealthy but solidly comfortable. The lower-middle class—the small shopkeepers, tiny manufacturers, and low-level shop or office workers—often had incomes no higher than those of skilled workers. Still, they were firmly committed to their middle-class status, forever seeking to move up in society and to distinguish themselves from proletarians. Teachers, nurses, and dentists achieved respectable middle-class status in this period.

> The working classes: The working classes were divided by the level of skill required for their work. Highly skilled workers such as cabinetmakers, masters of technology like railroad engineers and machinists, and managers like factory foremen became the labor aristocracy. They adopted middle-class values. The middle working class, semi-skilled workers, felt superior to the huge numbers of unskilled workers, street vendors, and day laborers who performed, in desperate competition, menial tasks. Working-class women often worked at home on sewing machines producing garments in a new version of the domestic system.

> The middle classes lived puritanically but well, followed fashion, read novels, and went to concerts and the opera. For the working class, drinking, going to music halls, and participating in (and betting on) spectator sports were the most popular leisure activities. The need to read racing forms encouraged literacy.

> Romantic love began to replace arranged marriage in the middle classes as the best way to achieve human happiness, although in middle-class families in France, economic concerns still took precedence. There were many strict rules for courtship, engagement, and marriage. Inequality of rights in marriage was part of a pattern of patriarchal relationships.

> Sexual standards for the working classes were much looser, with more acceptance of premarital sex.

> By the mid-nineteenth century, illegitimacy rates among the working classes declined as contraceptives like condoms and the diaphragm became more available and affordable. Unplanned pregnancies led increasingly to marriage and the establishment of two-parent households, which reflected the increase in working-class respectability and economic standing. In most working-class families, kinship ties remained strong, as middle-class ideas of respectability and romantic love strengthened working-class relationships.

> Prostitution was widespread, although it usually provided only temporary employment for poor women. Men of all classes patronized prostitutes, though the upper and middle classes supplied the majority of their earnings. Prostitution was an important social issue. In Britain laws were passed to supervise and medically treat prostitutes, in an attempt to control venereal disease.

> Gender roles changed dramatically. Men and women were seen as inhabiting "separate spheres": husbands the breadwinners, wives the household managers. Only poor women worked outside the home. Managing a household was a complicated, time-absorbing task. The ideal home for the middle-class was a single-family home, with designated areas for separate functions and decorated ostentatiously.

> Middle-class women began to agitate for equal legal rights and access to education and employment, as married women had few legal rights or work options. Feminists achieved some victories, but women were still barred from universities and most professions. Socialists argued that women's issues were a diversion from the goal of liberation for the entire working class.

> Child-rearing practices changed with the decline in the infant mortality rate. Middle-class women made greater emotional commitments to their children and increasingly breast-fed them rather than employing wet nurses. They invested a great deal in each child. More parents limited the number of children they had, leading to a decline in the birthrate and the shrinking of family size to about six by the 1890s and to about four by the 1920s.

> As young children became less and less of an economic asset when various labor laws prevented them from working, working class parents had fewer children and devoted more attention to their future success, aided by a growing supply of parenting guides and experts. Rigid gender roles for parents emphasized the need to control the child's sexuality.

> Middle-class children had fewer means to escape parental control that their working-class compatriots who would start to become financially independent much earlier.

> Fashion too distinguished the social classes. Women's costumes reflected their changing roles in society. The binding corset was replaced first by the bustle and later by the brassiere. The English created the tailored women's suit.

National and European Identity

> The Industrial Revolution transformed Europe from a rural society based on agriculture and ruled by the aristocracy to an urban, industrial society dominated by the bourgeoisie.

McKay Chapter 22 Focus Questions

1. How did urban life change in the nineteenth century?

2. What did the emergence of urban industrial society mean for rich and poor and those in between?

3. How did urbanization affect family life and gender roles?

4. How and why did intellectual life change in this period?

NOTES:

CHAPTER 23
The Age of Nationalism, 1850–1914

Areas of Focus: Germany, Italy, England, France, United States, Austria, Russia, the Ottoman Empire

Main Events: unification of Italy and Germany, 1905 revolution in Russia, Revisionism, revolution in France and the founding of the Third Republic, Victorian England

Key Figures:

- Napoleon III: emperor of France until 1871
- Alfred Dreyfus: first Jewish officer in the French army falsely accused of treason; divided France
- Otto von Bismarck: German Chancellor, forger of German unification; established welfare state in Germany
- Kaiser Wilhelm I: first ruler of unified Germany
- Giuseppe Mazzini: called for Italy to unify as a democratic republic based on the will of the people
- Giuseppe Garibaldi: popular Italian nationalist leader of the Red Shirts; liberated Sicily
- Count Camilio Cavour: prime minister of Piedmont, architect of Italian unification
- Pope Pius IX: issued the *Syllabus of Errors* attacking liberal ideals
- Victor Emmanuel II: first king of unified Italy
- Franz Joseph: Austrian emperor and king of Hungary
- Alexander II: tsar, reformer; abolished serfdom in Russia
- Sergei Witte: finance minister of Russia; promoted industrialization
- Nicholas II: tsar; established a duma during the 1905 Revolution, resisted reform
- Abdulhamid II: Ottoman sultan; halted reform movement and turned away from Westernization
- Eduard Bernstein: advocate of "revisionism" rather than radical Marxism
- William Gladstone: Liberal prime minister of Britain; fought for home rule for Ireland
- Benjamin Disraeli: Conservative prime minister of Britain, imperialist; expanded the suffrage
- Count Arthur de Gobineau and Houston Stewart Chamberlain: racialist theorists; champions of the white "Aryan" race
- Theodore Herzl: Austrian journalist, founder of Zionism

AP® European History Themes
Interaction of Europe and the World

> In the United States, deep divisions arose between the industrialized, urban North and the agricultural South. Northern whites felt their labor system was economically and morally superior to the slave-based agriculture system of the South. The U.S. victory over Mexico in the 1848 war added vast territory to the U.S. and spurred conflict over the expansion of slavery there. Divisions led to the Civil War, which lasted from 1861 to 1865. The North won the war, preventing secession of the South and ending slavery. The Homestead Act spurred western settlement and the various amendments to the Constitution in the wake of Northern victory ended slavery and gave political rights to the former slaves.

> Europeans were involved with the U.S. Civil War. France took advantage of the U.S. government's involvement in the civil war to set up a puppet state in Mexico for several years. Britain had grown dependent on cotton imports from the U.S. South, which in turn had entrenched slavery further earlier in the century. The U.S. civil war led Britain to import more cotton from Egypt.

Poverty and Prosperity

> In most European countries, as industrialization deepened, national wealth increased and the industrial classes became more prominent. Unions became legal in most of western Europe, and as their membership skyrocketed, they began to play important political roles, using less radical rhetoric and focusing on collective bargaining for better wages and benefits.

> When the tsar emancipated the serfs, it freed up the labor force and capital in Russia, and industrialization fostered by the government produced rather quick and marked change.

> **AP® Tip** There is a useful parallel between Russia and the United States here. Both countries developed large plantation agriculture, both used forms of unpaid labor (serfdom in Russia, chattel slavery in the U.S.), and both liberated that population in the 1860s, which freed up their economies and contributed to their rise as major world powers in the twentieth century.

Objective Knowledge and Subjective Visions

> In response to rising anti-Semitism, an Austrian Jewish journalist in Paris, Theodor Herzl, delineated a new idea, Zionism. He sought the creation of a Jewish homeland to provide Jews with the benefits and protection of the nation-state. Assimilation, Herzl argued, would ultimately not work. The First Zionist Congress met in 1897.

> As socialist parties became less radical and workers more moderate, some socialist intellectuals— such as Eduard Bernstein in Germany—turned away from radical revolution and espoused Revisionism, arguing that socialism would be achieved through electoral politics and unions.

> Pope Pius IX (pontificate 1846-1878) issued the *Syllabus of Errors* (1864), which denounced rationalism, liberalism, and socialism. In 1870, the papacy articulated the doctrine of papal infallibility.

States and Other Institutions of Power

> **AP® Tip** This chapter offers a wealth of information for analysis of successful modernization (Germany, Italy, England, France) and incomplete efforts (the Russian, Ottoman, and Austrian Empires). These three empires collapsed at the end of World War I, and understanding their weaknesses at the end of the nineteenth century is crucial for understanding why that happened.

> In France, Louis Napoleon Bonaparte was overwhelmingly elected president in December 1848. He staged a coup d'état in December 1851, and he declared himself Emperor Napoleon III the following year. He established an authoritarian government but won widespread approval by modernizing the economy, building railroads and housing, transforming Paris, and giving workers the right to form unions and to strike.

> The end of Louis III's regime, after its defeat by Germany in the Franco-Prussian War in 1871, led to the last major Parisian revolution, the Commune. The Communards wanted a radical state with separation of church and state, equal rights for women, and workplace reform. The Commune was brutally repressed after two months. France became a republic permanently in 1871 and over time won the allegiance of the next generation with a strong state public school system, legalization of unions, and imperial expansion. About twenty-five years later, political divisions over the Dreyfus affair, when the first Jewish officer in the French army was falsely accused of treason, tore the Third Republic apart.

❯ Socialist parties grew in size and importance, and over time became less radical. They formed the Socialist International in 1864.

❯ Russia was a vast multinational state under absolutist rule. Russia's defeat in the Crimean War (1853–1856) and its rapid population growth revealed the need for industrialization. Tsar Alexander II liberated the serfs in 1861, with peasants collectively given land for which they had to pay. He also established new local elected assemblies (zemstvos) and equality before the law, liberalized education, reduced restrictions on Jews, and encouraged industrialization. Radical anarchists, using terrorism to try to bring down the government, assassinated him. His successors, Alexander III (1881–1894) and Nicholas II (1894–1917), rejected reform and repressed political dissent.

❯ Russia's regression became all too apparent in its humiliating defeat by Japan in 1905, which led to a revolution. Liberals sought to turn Russia into a constitutional monarchy, radical Marxists led a (still illegal) labor movement, non-Russian nationalities wanted autonomy, and peasants resented their continuing poverty. Nicholas II made concessions on civil rights and allowed a parliament (the Duma), but autocracy remained, with the apparatus but not the reality of limited monarchy.

❯ The Ottoman Empire continued to lose power and territory into the nineteenth century. Realizing that modernization of industry, technology, and military forces was needed; statesmen launched an era of reforms (the Tanzimat) in 1839. Reforms established equality before the law for Muslims, Christians, and Jews; liberalized commercial laws, and encouraged Western education and secularism. In 1908 the Young Turks, a group of patriotic officers and intellectuals, seized power, and forced political reforms.

❯ Britain's two great parties had towering leaders in the nineteenth century: Benjamin Disraeli for the Conservatives and William Gladstone for the Liberals. Extensive social legislation (national health insurance, unemployment benefits, old-age pensions) was passed, and suffrage was extended, though not to women. Militant suffragettes such as Emmeline Pankhurst publicly protested. Gladstone hoped to pacify Catholic Irish nationalists with home rule or self-government, but the minority Irish Protestants—living mostly in Ulster—resisted any change, and the issue remained unresolved.

❯ In the early twentieth century, the power of the House of Lords was limited after they had vetoed the People's Budget passed by the Commons. Substantial social welfare legislation was passed before the outbreak of World War I under the leadership of David Lloyd George, Liberal Party Prime Minister.

Individual and Society

➔ **AP® Tip** As the political, ideological, and economic landscapes of European nations diverged, so did the social and cultural particularities of their people. While this chapter focuses more on the political upheaval and modernization under way (as do most questions about this period of history), nationality became an increasingly important part of identity.

❯ The demand for representation (suffrage) followed in the wake of industrialization, as did improvements to education and standard of living.

❯ European Jews had long been under severe restrictions, but liberalism and revolutionary sentiment—asserting the equality of all men—argued against such discrimination. Jews were granted civil rights in France in 1791, and legal equality in newly unified Germany in 1871. Many Jews responded gladly to the opportunities to succeed in professionals previously denied to them, such as medicine, journalism, academics, and law.

❯ Membership in trade unions skyrocketed at the end of the nineteenth century. A strong labor movement developed, and socialist parties grew continually in importance, albeit differently in their separate states. By 1912, the German Social Democratic Party held the most seats in the Reichstag. The Second International unified the various socialist parties in a common analysis of Marxism and goals. Socialism became not only a political movement but also an important identity for most working class Europeans.

National and European Identity

> Racism, of which political anti-Semitism is one form, flourished in Europe at the turn of the twentieth century, sometimes combined with Social Darwinism.

> Nationalism brought forth impressive buildings sponsored by governments—from memorials to statues to government centers to cultural institutions. Art promoted nationalism with portrayals of historic events, landscapes, and portraits.

> Although unsuccessful during the 1848 revolutions, nationalism became the dominant force in Europe in the second half of the nineteenth century and directly led to World War I. Appealing to people across class lines and political philosophies, the nation-state became the focus of strong nationalist sentiments that grew even deeper as suffrage increased.

> Most western European states developed into one form or another of parliamentary democracy, whereby the party that wins the majority of seats in the parliament forms the cabinet and the head of the party becomes prime minister. Mass politics led to a proliferation of parties except in England, where two main parties alternated in power.

> Conservatives were often able to manipulate the liberal- or socialist-leaning masses by using aggressive foreign policies to appeal to nationalism.

> Most newly emancipated Jews in western and central Europe joined the middle classes and became fervent patriotic nationalists. But at the same time, anti-Semitism grew more virulent. Partially a reaction against liberalism and modernization—which had propelled the Jews forward, partially a response to economic competition, and partially drawing on long-standing anti-Judaism. Modern anti-Semitism was distinguished from former versions in that the vilified group was the Jewish race, not the Jewish religion. Anti-Semitism was most virulent in Russia and eastern Europe. In Russia, Jews were the occasional victims of mass attacks called pogroms, which were encouraged by the tsarist government. Political anti-Semitism was used by Karl Lueger to win election as mayor of Vienna.

> The Austro-Hungarian Empire, created in 1867, contended with the nationalistic demands of its many subject nationalities. The dual monarchy—one king wore both crowns—gave Hungary virtual independence and rule over some of the minorities in the empire. In the Austrian half, ethnic Germans felt threatened by the Slavs, especially the Poles and the Czechs. In their part of the empire, the Hungarians insisted that their language be used in government and schools, creating huge resentment among ethnic minorities of the region.

> By 1914, nationalism had evolved into an almost universal faith in Europe and the United States, and it appealed to the broad masses of society. Nationalism generally reduced social tensions and the responsive nation-state improved city life.

> The unifications of Italy and Germany fulfilled nationalist dreams and changed not only the face of Europe but also its balance of power. The weakest of the Great Powers in 1862, Germany would became the most powerful state in Europe less than a decade later.

The Unifications of Italy and Germany		
	Italy (1859–1870)	Germany (1866–1871)
Dominant State and Leading Figures	Kingdom of Sardinia-Piedmont Count Cavour (prime minister) Victor Emmanuel (king) Giuseppe Garibaldi (militia leader)	Kingdom of Prussia Otto von Bismarck (chancellor) William I (king)
Problems Facing Unifiers	Resistance of Catholic Church; Sicily under Bourbon control; Lombardy and Venetia under Austrian control	"Small" Germany (without Austria) vs. "big" Germany (with it); reluctance of Catholic states to join largely Lutheran nation
Wars and Stages of Unification	1859—War with Austria: Lombardy awarded to Piedmont 1860—Other states vote to join; Turin, then Florence as capital 1866—Venice added 1870—Rome added	1864—War with Denmark over Schleswig-Holstein 1866—Victory in Austro-Prussian War eliminates Austria from the new state 1867—North German Confederation, with twenty-two states as members 1870–1871—Prussian victory in Franco-Prussian war; Germany gains Alsace-Lorraine
Outcomes	Constitutional monarchy Rome capital of unified Italy Papacy loses the Papal States, withdraws into the Vatican, and has hostile relationship to Italy Some lands still held by Austria Limited suffrage Conflicts between industrial north and the mostly agricultural and feudal south Socialist Party formed Christian Democrats dominate	Strongest European state Federal empire headed by a kaiser (emperor) Individual provinces under traditional rulers A parliament elected by universal male suffrage but its approval not required for military or foreign policy decisions Relationship with France contentious Bismarck goes after perceived domestic enemies: first Catholics (a process called Kulturkampf), then the socialists, instituting Europe's first social welfare legislation (social security, etc.) to co-opt them Social Democrats become the largest party

McKay Chapter 23 Focus Questions

1. How did Napoleon III seek to reconcile popular and conservative forces in an authoritarian nation-state?

2. How did conflict and war lead to the construction of strong nation-states in Italy, Germany, and the United States?

3. What steps did Russia and the Ottoman Empire take toward modernization, and how successful were they?

4. What general domestic political trends emerged after 1871?

5. How did popular nationalism evolve in the last decades of the nineteenth century?

6. Why did the social movement grow and how revolutionary was it?

NOTES:

CHAPTER 24
The West and the World, 1815–1914

Areas of Focus: Britain, France, Belgium, Germany, Italy, Asia, and Africa

Main Events: Berlin Conference, European takeovers of African and Asian states, South African (Boer) War, the opium trade, the Great Rebellion in India, Meiji restoration in Japan, the Boxer Rebellion in China, the great migration

Key Figures:

- Otto von Bismarck: chancellor of Germany; organized the Berlin Conference of 1885
- Cecil Rhodes: prime minister of Britain's Cape Colony; conquered eastern South Africa, Rhodesia and Botswana
- Leopold: king of Belgium; ruled the Congo harshly
- Sir Herbert Kitchener: general; conquered Sudan for Britain
- Commodore Matthew Perry: U.S. naval officer; used gunboat diplomacy to open Japan to Western interests
- Tzu His: dowager empress of China, its last imperial ruler
- Mohammad Ali: Ottoman-appointed ruler of Egypt; modernizer
- Rudyard Kipling: wrote "The White Man's Burden"
- Henry Labouchère: wrote "The Brown Man's Burden"
- Eduard Said: literary scholar; analyzed "Orientalism"
- J.A. Hobson: leading critic of imperialism in Britain
- Joseph Conrad: author of *The Heart of Darkness*

AP® European History Themes
Interaction of Europe and the World

> The three decades before World War I (1914–1918) were the high point of European expansionism. European states—particularly France and Britain, and Belgium, Italy, and Germany to a lesser extent—competed to take, either peacefully or forcefully, valuable colonies in Asia and Africa. These decades intensified Europe's relationship with the rest of the world, and deeply transformed both.

> The scramble for Africa was the single most remarkable development in the new imperialism. In 1850, only a small part of Africa was colonized: Mozambique and Angola (by Portugal), Algeria (by France), and South Africa (by the Dutch). In the 1880s and 1890s, virtually the entire continent of Africa was carved up, mostly between the British (who aimed for a "Cape to Cairo" empire) and the French, with Italy, Belgium, and Germany also taking important colonies. The British took South Africa from the Dutch in the brutal South African Boer War of 1899-1902 and gave it nominal independence in 1910. They took control of the Suez Canal and ruled Egypt indirectly.

> No colony was as notorious for its brutality as the Congo, the personal colony of the King of Belgium, Leopold. Perhaps some 10 million Congolese were killed or maimed by the colonists who punished them severely (cutting off hands and feet) if they didn't meet their quotas for rubber. As outrage grew, Leopold was forced by an international conference in 1908 to give up his personal control and hand the Congo over to the Belgian government.

> Parts of Asia were also taken over by Europeans: Indochina by the French, Indonesia by the Dutch, and Central Asia by Russia. China was forcibly opened up to western trade by the British in the Opium Wars of the 1840s, as was Japan by the "gunboat diplomacy" of the United States a decade later. India was Britain's "Jewel in the Crown," under direct rule of Parliament after the 1857 Great Rebellion. Direct rule by Britain would last there until 1947, when India and Pakistan gained independence.

> Responses to imperialism varied. Within Europe, socialists generally opposed imperialism while nationalists were enthusiastic. In the colonies, traditionalists sought to preserve native culture and sometimes organized violent resistance, while Westernizers espoused what they considered to be superior Western models and values. In India, a Western-educated native elite did most of the administrative and military work of imperial control and established the Indian National Congress in 1885. In Japan, the feudal state was abolished, the emperor restored by Meiji reformers, and Western-style political, economic, and educational institutions were adopted. In China, native resentment over European spheres of influences broke out in the violent Boxer Rebellion in 1900. The Qing Dynasty lost prestige when it was unable to prevent Western penetration and was overthrown in a revolution in 1912 that established a republic.

> Sixty million Europeans emigrated between 1815 and 1932, mostly going (although not necessarily permanently) to areas of previous European settlement; this is one reason European expansion had such impact around the globe. Twenty million of the migrants came from the British Isles, and more than half of those emigrated in the decade before World War I. National groups left Europe at different times: the British and Irish from the 1840s on, the Germans in the 1850s and 1880s, and the Italians and the Russian Jews around 1900.

> The United States accepted the largest number of immigrants, but less than half of the total. Most of the migrants were young unmarried farmers and artisans, not usually the impoverished. White settlers in sparsely populated areas (such as the Argentine or American plains) benefited easily at the expense of natives. When it was possible, between a third and a half of migrants returned home.

> Although not in numbers as large as Europeans, a significant number of Asians (mostly Chinese, Japanese, Indians, and Filipinos) left their homelands to work as indentured laborers in mines and on plantations in the United States, Africa, and Latin America. European migrants disliked the influx of Asian migrants and by the 1880s were constructing "great white walls"—discriminatory laws designed to prevent Asians from settling permanently.

> Christian missionary work was highly successful in Africa but much less so in India, China, and the Muslim world.

Poverty and Prosperity

> Industrialization widened the gap between the industrialized states and the rest of the world. Areas that did not industrialize during the nineteenth century (namely Africa, Asia, and Latin America) came to be subject to political or economic imperialism.

> World trade expanded enormously before World War I, growing in value to about twenty times what it had been in 1800, sped up by new technologies like the steamship and transoceanic telegraphic cables.

> Britain's already far-flung empire gave it the basis for expansion when industrialization produced too many cheap goods for absorption by the domestic market. Once free trade became its law,

Britain turned quickly into the world's emporium, selling goods produced at home around the globe and stimulating the exploitation of colonial resources for export to Europe, such as jute, hemp, and rubber and popular foodstuffs like tea, coffee, and sugar.

> The Germans, the French and the British, flush with capital from their own industries, made enormous investments overseas, mostly to other industrial nations.

Objective Knowledge and Subjective Visions

> Technological innovations in the second half of the nineteenth century were crucial to Europe's success. Steamships easily traveled around the world and could go upriver, allowing Europeans to penetrate to the interior as never before. New ports and the newly constructed Suez Canal (between the Mediterranean and the Red Seas) and Panama Canal (connecting the Pacific and the Atlantic in Central America) made trade faster, more efficient, and more profitable. European superiority in weapons and medicine made the "new imperialism" possible.

> Social Darwinism combined with racism postulated competition among the white peoples for survival and their (rightful, it argued) exploitation of "inferior" races like blacks and Asians.

> Tabloid journalism (called the "yellow press" in the U.S.) promoted nationalism and imperialism.

> Imperialism was a divisive issue. Critics saw European wealth as stolen from exploited colonized peoples, but others argued that Europe's expansion was a rightful product of scientific and technological advances, capitalistic business organization, and a distinct worldview.

> Influential British writer Rudyard Kipling's poem "The White Man's Burden" eloquently conveyed the humanistic mandate of imperialism, while a satire of it by British member of Parliament Henry Labouchère called "The Brown Man's Burden" indicted imperialism as racist, exploitative, and brutal. Joseph Conrad's *The Heart of Darkness* showed the corrupting influence of imperialism. These European critics provided an ideological basis for independence and liberation movements.

> European imperialism had a great impact on the arts at home, as artists were fascinated by, and thus absorbed and incorporated, the artistic styles of Africa and the East, vastly different from traditional European styles. Artists often portrayed exotic elements of colonized peoples and conveyed the excitement of travel in posters and advertisements.

> Songs of conquering armies became part of the popular musical lexicon and travel guides became popular reference tools for Europeans traveling to the colonies. Orientalist images and products were ubiquitous in Europe.

States and Other Institutions of Power

> Prior to the 1880s, conservatives like Otto von Bismarck opposed imperialism as unnecessary, burdensome, and dangerous. But by 1900, most leaders, including Bismarck himself, favored imperialism.

> "Effective occupation" was the rule for takeover set by the 1884–1885 Berlin Conference, called by Jules Ferry and Bismarck to avoid conflicting claims among the Europeans that might lead to war, and to prevent any one power from dominating Africa.

> Tabloid journalism promoted nationalism and imperialism, as did special-interest groups like shippers and shipbuilders, settlers, missionaries, humanitarians, military men, and colonial officials.

> **AP® Tip** The two major periods of European expansion had many similarities but important differences. The following comparative chart highlights the chief differences. In studying the new imperialism of this period, be sure to consider its social impact at home as well as in the colonies and the political controversies.

European Expansion, ca. 1400–1900		
	European Colonization 15th–18th Centuries	European Imperialism 19th Century
Dominant European States Competing with Each Other	Britain, France, Spain, Holland, Portugal	Britain and France (later Germany, Belgium, and Italy)
Areas Colonized	Coastal ports in Africa, Indian subcontinent, Indonesia; entire territories in the Americas	Coastal and interior regions in Africa and Asia
Chief Motivations	"Gold, God, Glory"	Strategic outposts for navies, exclusive control over resources, guaranteed markets for goods, national prestige
Goods Sought in Colonies	Gold, slaves, spices, rum, molasses, sugar	Rubber, minerals, diamonds, tea, coffee
Political Control	Native governments of colonies in Asia and Africa left intact; direct rule in New World	Direct European rule or indirect rule in spheres of influence or through protectorates
Relationship of Europeans and Natives	Respect for native rulers; disdain for cultural practices; Christianizing missions	Disdain for native rulers and "racially inferior" Asians and Africans; "White Man's Burden" to civilize the "half-savage and half-child" natives

Individual and Society

> European population doubled in the nineteenth century and by 1914 accounted for 38 percent of the world's population. After 1900 it began to decline.

> Women worked as missionaries, nurses, educators, as well as housewives in the colonies.

> For many, emigration was not only about economic opportunities but also about civic rights and human dignity.

National and European Identity

> Most Europeans and Americans believed that they had a mission to civilize the "barbarian" peoples of the world, to bring the benefits of modern medicine, education, political democracy, and Christianity—the glories of Western civilization—to the primitive peoples of the world, and to end barbaric practices.

> As imperialism grew, so did criticisms of it. The British economist J. A. Hobson in his 1902 work *Imperialism* delineated the classic Marxist analysis that imperialism existed because the rich needed to invest their excess capital, and in fact damaged the home country whose taxpayers bore the brunt of the costs. Workers were manipulated by nationalism and diverted from the class struggle, which delayed domestic reform.

> Competition between the European states fostered imperialism. No nation, it was said by the German nationalist historian Heinrich von Treitschke, could be great without colonies. Political control of colonies served economic and nationalist interests. Aggressive imperialistic policies increased tensions among the Europeans, however, and led to wars or near-wars with non-Europeans.

> Domestic problems seemed less important because of successful imperialistic ventures and nationalistic pride. Propagandists for imperialism argued that imperialism benefited not only capitalists but also ordinary workers in that it provided jobs and cheap raw materials that kept down the cost of manufactured goods for them to enjoy.

> Economic motives were prominent for states in the new imperialism. Great Britain was losing its industrial lead to Germany and the United States, which made old colonies like India all the more valuable to Great Britain and caused it to work to secure new colonies. There were also strategic goals of securing safe havens and refueling stations for ships in case of war.

> "Race-mixing"—the mating of European settlers with native women—was widely considered a danger.

McKay Chapter 24 Focus Questions

1. What were some of the global consequences of European industrialization between 1815 and 1914?

2. How was massive migration an integral part of Western expansion?

3. How did Western imperialism change after 1880?

4. What was the general pattern of non-Western responses to Western expansion?

NOTES:

NOTES:

CHAPTER 25
War and Revolution, 1914–1919

Areas of Focus: Britain, Germany, Austria-Hungary, Ottoman Empire, Russia

Main Events: the outbreak of World War I, trench warfare, the Russian Revolution, armistice, the Versailles/Paris Peace Conference

Key Figures:

- Kaiser Wilhelm II: pursued an aggressive foreign policy
- Archduke Franz Ferdinand: heir to the Austrian throne whose assassination sparked the war
- Nicholas II: tsar overthrown in the Russian Revolution
- Rasputin: monk close to the tsar and tsarina
- Vladimir Lenin: Bolshevik revolutionary and ruler of Russia; developed Marxist-Leninism
- Leon Trotsky: Marxist theoretician; organized the Red Army
- Henri-Philippe Pétain: French general; hero of Verdun
- Lord Arthur Balfour: British foreign secretary; issued declaration supporting the idea of the Jewish homeland in Palestine
- Wilfred Owen: author of "Dulce et Decorum Est"
- Woodrow Wilson: U.S. president who negotiated the Versailles Treaties
- Hussein ibn-Ali: Arab magistrate and leader of the Arab revolt against the Ottoman Empire

AP® European History Themes
Interaction of Europe and the World

❯ Although Wilson had articulated a war aim of self-determination of subject nationalities, a mandate system for the former German and Ottoman colonies was established. While in theory the mandates were meant to be temporary, they were seen as continuation of imperialistic control. Many people around the globe were disappointed. Arabs had been promised independence if they joined the war against the Ottoman Empire but were instead put under the indirect rule of Britain and France; Vietnamese hopes for independence from the French were dashed as well.

❯ The League of Nations was created—with a weak executive and no army—to negotiate disputes, act collectively against aggression, and supervise the mandates of the Treaty of Versailles.

❯ The U.S. Senate refused to ratify the terms of the treaty, and the United States effectively turned its back on Europe, beginning a new age of American isolationism. Great Britain followed suit, leaving France effectively without allies.

❯ The broken promises of self-determination after the war led to resentment and caused violence and disorder in the region, still to this day. The roots of the contemporary Arab-Israeli conflict lie in this post-war settlement.

> The Turks rebounded from the near death blow of the war with a strong leader, Mustafa Kemal, who organized a Turkish military force and defeated British and French forces. He created an authoritarian, westernized Turkish republic, separated church and state, established a secular educational system, and granted more rights to women.

> Many soldiers from its colonies, especially India, and from the Commonwealth served in the British forces. New Zealanders and Australians forged national identities with their participation in the Gallipoli campaign of 1915.

Poverty and Prosperity

> To manage the long war, governments abandoned laissez-faire capitalism in favor of the planned economy (where governments decide what is to be produced, who produces it, and how), instituted rationing, set wage and price controls, and limited workers' rights. This was total war, with every aspect of life engaged.

> Germany encouraged the making of synthetic goods like rubber to aid in war material production. With inflation, black markets, food shortages due to the British blockade, and deficit spending, times were difficult in Germany toward the end of the war, with many near starvation.

> Britain was economically better off than Germany because of its empire and imports from the United States.

Objective Knowledge and Subjective Visions

> Vladimir Lenin (1870–1924) modified Marxian ideology by insisting that socialism could be achieved only through revolution, and that it could occur in countries only partially industrialized and partially feudal like Russia—if led by a small, tightly disciplined revolutionary vanguard. Marxist-Leninists took the name Bolsheviks to distinguish themselves from the more democratic Marxists in Russia, the Mensheviks, and later called themselves Communists.

> **AP® Tip** Perhaps in no other war has there been such an outpouring of wonderful literature. Poets stationed on the western front wrote stirring, sometimes grim, poems of their experiences, and after the war, that experience informed virtually every art form. The war became a cultural watershed.

> The war and the Russian Revolution sparked the use of striking propaganda posters.

> The war stimulated technological innovation. In weaponry, tanks on the land and submarines on the sea had significant impact by the end of the war. Chemical warfare, such as the use of mustard gas, was introduced early in the war in the trenches. Wilfred Owen's iconic poem *Dulce et Decorum Est* describes one such gas attack. Airplanes were also used for the first time in war.

States and Other Institutions of Power

> After nearly one hundred years of general peace, rising prosperity, and international power, Europeans began a four-year war that destroyed millions of lives and brought down four European empires—the Russian, Ottoman, Austro-Hungarian, and German.

> **AP® Tip** World War I, the Versailles treaties, and the Russian Revolution were world historical events and are absolutely crucial for an understanding of modern history.

> What might have been a localized conflict between Serbia and Austria became a world war due to a complicated alliance system (the Triple Alliance of Austria, Germany, and Italy versus the Triple Entente of Britain, Russia, and France) that drew states into war. Xenophobia, nationalism, imperialistic competition, and militarism pitted peoples against each other, encouraged an arms race, and weakened internationalism. In this hostile atmosphere, the assassination of the heir to the

Austro-Hungarian throne—Archduke Francis Ferdinand—by a Serb in Bosnia, easily provided the spark for war.

> German-British relations deteriorated when Germany announced plans to expand its fleet and to build dreadnoughts—big-gun battleships. Such tensions made it harder to prevent war.

> The decade before the outbreak of the war saw several international crises and two Balkan wars against the Ottoman Empire.

> When war broke out in August 1914, crowds enthusiastically rallied and young men lined up to volunteer thinking the war would be brief and decisive. Instead, it lasted over four years and had no simple resolution, as victory eluded each of the two sides—the Central Powers (Germany, Austria-Hungary, the Ottoman Empire, and Bulgaria) and the Allies (France, Britain, Russia, and some thirty other states including the United States after 1917).

> The thousand-mile-long western front became a series of trenches with high death tolls due largely to the introduction of the machine gun. Attempts to end the stalemate by force of new weapons and heavy machinery (the tank, airplane bombing, the submarine, mustard gas, and other forms of chemical warfare) and by widening the fighting to other arenas outside of Europe (the Middle East) were largely ineffective. Major battles—such as the Marne (near Paris), Gallipoli (on the Dardanelles), Tannenberg (in East Prussia), Verdun, and the Somme (both on the western front)—each had death tolls of hundreds of thousands on each side for little real result.

> On the eastern front, death tolls were even higher, with huge losses for both Germany and Russia. Fighting was more mobile there, but definitive victories were just as elusive as in the west.

> In order to maintain such a long and damaging war effort, governments permanently increased the scope of their authority to ensure continued popular support and sufficient men and materials for war. Governments on both sides manipulated public opinion through censorship of the press and propaganda, and severely limited civil liberties.

> Initially, virtually everyone supported the war, but by 1916, antiwar sentiment grew. Britain faced, but quickly crushed, a rebellion by Irish nationalists on Easter Sunday in 1916. At the front, too, disillusionment was evident. In May 1917, there was a mutiny in the French forces. Russian soldiers frequently deserted in droves, and the Italian army also collapsed.

> In Russia, the war intensified the discontent long felt about the tsarist regime. Russia's early defeats by the German army, the tsar's direct leadership of a poorly managed war effort, and the lack of democracy led to a spontaneous uprising of the people in March 1917—also known as the February Revolution. Tsar Nicholas II abdicated, and a provisional government was formed. In spring 1917, many Russian soldiers walked away from the front, inspired by the promises of "Peace, Land, and Bread" made by Vladimir Lenin, head of the Bolshevik wing of the Social Democratic Party.

> In November 1917, the Bolsheviks took power in a coup d'état and founded the first Communist regime in the world. Lenin was the head of a new government in which councils (or "soviets") of workers, peasants, and soldiers were to have all the power. Lenin immediately sued for peace, giving in to tough demands from the Germans for territory in the Treaty of Brest-Litovsk of March 1918. Russia was quickly embroiled in a bloody, two-year civil war between the Whites, who opposed communism and the terms of the peace treaty, and the Communist Reds. The Reds won because of the effective leadership of Leon Trotsky, an energetic secret police, and "War Communism," or control of the economy and food supplies. They established the Union of Soviet Socialist Republics, ruled by the Communist Party as the "dictatorship of the proletariat," that lasted more than seventy years.

AP® Tip The Russian Revolution is the last of the three great successful European revolutions, along with the English in the seventeenth century and the French in the eighteenth. While the issues in each varied widely, a certain pattern of revolution can be discerned—reform, radicalization, civil war, dictatorship, and reaction or restoration of some elements of the prerevolutionary state.

> World War I ended on November 11, 1918, after the Germans failed in their last offensive and a revolution forced Emperor William II to abdicate. It ended with an armistice, not a surrender.

> ❯ Germany experienced a revolution, which forced the kaiser to abdicate just before the Armistice, and established the Weimar Republic, dominated by liberals and moderate socialists. Both extreme left and extreme right attacked the new government.

> ❯ The peace settlement of 1919, commonly known as the Treaty of Versailles, was a compromise between French and British desires for revenge on a weak Germany and U.S. president Woodrow Wilson's negotiations for an international organization to prevent further war. Although not defeated on the battlefield, Germany was not invited to the peace conference. The treaty it was forced to accept was punitive. Although it lost relatively little territory (its African colonies to France, Japan, and Britain; Alsace-Lorraine to France; and East Prussia to newly reconstituted Poland), Germany was forced to pay huge reparations, to accept blame for the war, and to limit its army to 100,000 men. Austria lost most of its pre-war territory as Poland, Hungary, Czechoslovakia, and Yugoslavia came into being.

> ❯ Almost everyone was disappointed in the treaties, and those frustrations directly led to the rise of fascism and World War II.

Individual and Society

> ❯ Total war affected every aspect of life on the home front, from gender roles to civil liberties, from government involvement in the economy to fashion. That some 55 million men were mobilized for war meant that just about every family had someone serving in the military. The number of soldiers who lost their lives [more than 8 million] or who were wounded or disabled by the war [more than 20 million] deeply affected social and political life in the years after the war. Many soldiers long suffered from "shellshock," a form of PTSD.

> ❯ Class distinctions lessened both at the front and at home. Labor unions and workers grew in importance and prestige because of their loyalty and cooperation with the war effort.

> ❯ Women took jobs in industry, transportation, and public service at home, and at the front as nurses and ambulance drivers, becoming visible in the public sphere as never before. Postwar disillusionment led to looser sexual morality, which led some women to bob their hair, shorten their skirts, and smoke cigarettes in public. Women were given the vote immediately after the war in Britain, Germany, Poland, and the United States.

> ❯ Religious issues played no role in causing the war, but the experience of the war both at the front and at home encouraged secularism and made religion irrelevant to some.

> ❯ In Russia, the close affiliation of the Russian Orthodox Church with the tsarist regime meant that the new Communist government was extremely hostile to it.

> ❯ Both the provisional government formed in Russia after the February Revolution and the Turkish government under Mustafa Kemal established freedom of religion, which had previously been absent in these areas.

National and European Identity

> ❯ Arab nations were generally unable to attain the freedom vaguely promised to them by the Treaty of Versailles terms. Arab nationalists came together in Damascus in 1919 to call for political independence, but French and British forces took control. Zionist Jews were frustrated as well that the Balfour Declaration was ignored and they were not given their promised homeland.

> ❯ Successful state management of the wartime economy gave credibility to socialism.

> ❯ The war in the Ottoman Empire saw a terrible mass killing on the basis of ethnicity, the Armenian genocide of 1915. The Turkish massacred perhaps a million Armenians, caught between Russian promises of support for their independence and Turkish strategic needs to control the eastern part of their country.

❭ Radical Communists like Karl Liebknecht and Rosa Luxembourg led an uprising against the new government and were murdered by nationalist militias called the Free Corps, who also put down a Bolshevik-style republic in Bavaria. The Nazi Party was founded in 1919. The Social Democratic Party in Germany dominated the early years of the Weimar Republic.

❭ The Ottoman Empire was dismembered by the Treaties. But under the leadership of the able general, Mustafa Kemal, who had defeated the British at Gallipoli in 1915, Turkey was able to renegotiate the peace settlement and retain its territorial integrity. The new peace treaty called for a population exchange—ethnic Greeks in Turkey moved to Greece, ethnic Turks in Greece moved to Turkey—that was a humanitarian disaster. Kemal established and ruled a secular, authoritarian republic.

McKay Chapter 25 Focus Questions

1. What caused the outbreak of the First World War?

2. How did the First World War differ from previous wars?

3. In what ways did the war transform life on the home front?

4. Why did world war lead to revolution in Russia, and what was its outcome?

5. In what ways was the Allied peace settlement flawed?

NOTES:

CHAPTER 26
The Age of Anxiety, 1880–1940

Areas of Focus: Germany, England, France, the United States

Main Events: the Great Depression; the New Deal; consumer society; Modernism in art, architecture, and music; existentialism, surrealism, and Dadaism; post-Newtonian physics; Popular Front government in France; Weimar Germany; radio and mass culture

Key Figures:

- Sigmund Freud: Austrian neurologist, founder of psychoanalysis; "discovered the unconscious"
- Friedrich Nietzsche: German philosopher; challenged traditional values, proclaimed the "death of God"
- John Maynard Keynes: influential British economist; criticized the Versailles Treaty, advocated deficit spending
- Ernest Rutherford: British physicist; split the atom
- T.S. Eliot: American poet; author of The *Wasteland*
- James Joyce: Irish stream-of-consciousness novelist; author of *Ulysses*
- Virginia Wolff: Innovative British novelist
- Ludwig Wittgenstein: German philosopher; developed logical positivism
- Alban Berg: Austrian avant-garde composer of the opera *Wozzeck*
- Igor Stravinsky: Russian composer of the ballet *The Rite of Spring*
- Arnold Schönberg: German composer; developed the 12-tone scale
- Walter Gropius: German architect, co-founder of Bauhaus, architecture based on functionalism
- Marie Curie: Polish-French physicist; discovered radium
- Albert Einstein: German physicist; postulated the special theory of relativity
- Werner Heisenberg: German physicist; developed the uncertainty principle
- Franz Kafka: Czech writer of stories and novels about alienation
- Søren Kierkegaard: Danish theologian, Christian existentialist
- Jean-Paul Sartre: French philosopher, leading existentialist
- Georg Grosz: German Dadaist; satirical artist
- Claude Monet, Edgar Degas, Mary Cassatt: Impressionist artists
- Vincent van Gogh: Dutch artist working in France, post-Impressionist
- Pablo Picasso: Spanish artist working in France, Cubist
- Filippo Tomasso Marinetti: Italian Futurist
- Salvador Dali: Spanish Dadaist artist
- Gustav Stresemann: German Chancellor; stabilized the currency
- Ramsey MacDonald: Labour prime minister of Britain
- George Orwell: British novelist and journalist, author of *1984*
- Franklin Delano Roosevelt, Jr.: president of the United States; initiated the New Deal

- Adolf Hitler: Austrian-born German nationalist and fascist, leader of the Nazi Party, author of *Mein Kampf*
- Leon Blum: leader of the Popular Front government in France

AP® European History Themes

Interaction of Europe and the World

> The artistic movements described in this chapter were international in focus. Freudian psychology and the Bauhaus movement had great influence in the United States and elsewhere. American artists and writers flocked to Europe, particularly to Paris, in the 1920s and 1930s. The U.S. took the lead in the new cinema, making films in New York and Los Angeles.

> The U.S. played an important role in reducing the burden of reparations on Germany with the Dawes Plan.

> The Great Depression reflected the intersecting economic ties between Europe and the U.S. When the market crashed in 1929 in the U.S., American investors called in the loans they had made to Europeans and the impact in Europe was swift and severe. World output of goods declined by some 38 percent in the first few years of the Depression.

> Franklin Delano Roosevelt's (U.S. president, 1933–1945) New Deal was only partly successful as a response to the Great Depression. While certain projects such as the Works Progress Administration (WPA) and the national Social Security system, both established in 1935, were popular and enduring legacies of the New Deal, it wasn't until World War II that the United States was fully catapulted out of the depression.

Poverty and Prosperity

> When the French sent troops into the Ruhr (1923–1925), the German economy was paralyzed. The situation was saved when a new chancellor, Gustav Stresemann, agreed to pay reparations if France agreed to compromise on the amount. Germany returned to prosperity with remarkable speed and was able to pay a good part of its reparation bills by 1928.

> The Great Depression (1929–1939), which began in the United States mostly because of speculation in the stock market, hit Europe hard, causing high unemployment, spiraling deflation, and loss of productivity. Governments were not very effective in dealing with the crisis, and in many cases made it worse by imposing protectionist tariffs and cutting spending instead of increasing it to stimulate the economies. Britain went off the gold standard to drop the value of its currency.

> The Scandinavian response was the most successful of the industrialized nations. Sweden increased spending on social welfare programs and used large deficits to fund public works to keep people employed.

> During the 1930s, Britain and Germany saw unemployment skyrocket, with poverty, ill health, and hopelessness in millions of homes and a dramatic decline in birthrates.

Objective Knowledge and Subjective Visions

> **AP® Tip** Europe in the 1920s and 1930s was a fountain of new ideas in literature, philosophy, and the arts, which came to play an important role in the profound struggle between a new political idea (fascism) and the older ideas of constitutionalism and Marxism. This made the period phenomenally fertile but also very destabilizing. You will probably have looked at some of these artworks or read some of the poetry or novels; use what you are learning in history to contextualize your experience of the arts, and vice versa. It is a good idea to bring such insights into an AP essay, particularly if modernist primary sources appear in a document-based question.

> New ideas in philosophy, physics, and psychology developed before the Great War had significant impact afterwards. Many people abandoned or revised the rational worldview and the belief in progress created by the Scientific Revolution, the Enlightenment, and the Industrial Revolution. The table below summarizes some of the major ideas to influence science and philosophy during this period.

> Modernism, a general term for experimentation and new modes of expression, dominated the arts. Artists created new genres to convey the complex desires, memories, and ideas of the inner person.

> An international artistic culture came into being. Picasso was the model of the modern artist: famous, innovative, prolific, and politically engaged.

> Atonal and twelve-tone music found little popularity with concertgoers.

> Freudian theory was initially met with great resistance but over time had a huge influence not only on the field of psychology but also in the arts. The notion that human behavior was a response to deeply unconscious feelings and drives underlay much of Surrealism.

> The movies, at first silent and short, were created in the 1890s. The United States dominated the film industry as Hollywood stars became hugely popular. By the 1930s, movies were part of the weekly life of most Europeans and Americans.

> In 1920, the first radio broadcast was heard all over Europe, and national broadcasting networks were quickly established, mostly under state ownership. Radio rapidly became popular as entertainment, but also a powerful tool for propaganda for both dictators and democratic leaders.

> Movies, too, served as propaganda. Lenin and Hitler promoted the film industry and encouraged great directors like Sergei Eisenstein in Russia (*Potemkin*) and Leni Riefenstahl (*Triumph of the Will*) in Germany.

> The decades after World War I saw a revival of fundamental Christian thought. Søren Kierkegaard, a rediscovered nineteenth century Danish philosopher, called for a "leap of faith." He believed that even if God is unknowable and his existence cannot be proven, faith in God's power and majesty can remain. Karl Barth similarly called for an emotional and trusting acceptance of God's grace, regardless of reason and logic.

> Catholic existentialists argued that the Catholic Church offered a way out of the conundrums of the modern world. Many prominent English poets and novelists turned toward Catholicism.

Ideas and Literature			
Field	Leading Figures	Select Major Works	Key Ideas
Psychology	Sigmund Freud (Austrian)	*Civilization and Its Discontents* (1930)	Concept of self is divided into id (unconscious desires), ego (rational self), and superego (conscience), which are constantly at odds. Denying the id makes living in communities possible, but ultimately leads to unhappiness and dissatisfaction
Literature	Virginia Woolf (British)	Jacob's Room (1922)	Stream of consciousness, captures inner voice.
	James Joyce (Irish)	Ulysses (1922)	Stream of consciousness, abandons traditional plot and language to mirror the riddle of modern life.

Ideas and Literature			
Field	Leading Figures	Select Major Works	Key Ideas
Literature	Franz Kafka (Czech)	*The Metamorphosis* (1915), *The Trial* (1925)	Existential angst of ordinary people.
	T. S. Eliot (American)	*The Waste Land* (1922)	Widespread desolation and despair after WWI.
	George Orwell (British)	*The Road to Wigan Pier* (1937)	Socialism, well implemented, could end unemployment crises.
Visual Arts	Claude Monet (French)	*Water Lilies series* (early 20th cent.)	Impressionism—Conveying fleeting moments of light and color.
	Vincent Van Gogh (Dutch)	*The Starry Night* (1889)	Expressionism—Use of vivid colors and new techniques to illuminate inner feelings.
	Pablo Picasso (Spanish)		Cubism—Subjects broken into overlapping planes and geometric shapes.
	Salvador Dali (Spanish)	*Metamorphosis of Narcissus* (1937)	Surrealism—Portrays inner world of dreams, symbols, fantasies.
	Hugo Ball (German)	"Karawane" (1916)	Dadaism—Attacks all conventional art forms and delights in the outrageous and absurd.
Architecture	Le Corbusier (Swiss)	Towards New Architecture (1923)	Functionalism—Form follows function, eliminate unnecessary ornamentation.
	Walter Gropius (German)	Bauhaus School in Dessau Germany (1925)	Bauhaus—German school of art and architecture, valued sleek, functional design.
	Ludwig Mies van der Rohe (German)	Lake Shore Apartments, Chicago (1948)	Epitome of modern, international architecture style.
Music	Igor Stravinski (Russian)	*The Rite of Spring* (1913)	Expressionism—Rejection of nineteenth-century romanticism, using intense rhythms and dissonance.
	Alban Berg (Austrian)	*Wozzeck* (1925)	Atonality—Half spoken, half sung, often harsh and unmelodic.
	Arnold Schönberg (Austrian)		Twelve-tone scale—No musical key; notes seemed unrelated, but had mathematical patterns called "tone rows."

States and Other Institutions of Power

> Most Germans hated the 1919 Treaty of Versailles, especially the bill for reparations, set for $33 billion, which they had to pay or face occupation. The first postwar international crisis occurred when the Germans couldn't meet a reparations payment in 1922; the French occupied the Ruhr, an industrial area of western Germany. Moderates won out in both countries, and the crisis was resolved. The reorganization of reparations under the American Dawes Plan (1924) reduced Germany's annual payments but created a dangerous financial system. Germany received private loans from the United States in order to pay reparations to France and Britain, which they then used to repay the large war debts they owed to the United States. This was later to intensify the impact of the U.S. stock marked crash of 1929 in Europe.

> In 1925, Germany, France, and other states signed the Treaty of Locarno, accepting the borders created by the Treaty of Versailles. Germany made similar agreements with Czechoslovakia and Poland and joined the League of Nations. Fifteen nations (including the United States) signed the Kellogg-Briand Pact in 1928, agreeing to avoid war and solve international disputes peacefully. The pact fostered optimism at the time of its signing but did little to halt World War II eleven years later.

> France rebuilt quickly after the war, and the Great Depression arrived later there than in more heavily industrialized countries. There were frequent changes of government and a growing Fascist movement in France when the Great Depression hit. Communists, socialists, and others allied in the Popular Front in order to combat the growth in fascism at home and abroad. They won the election of 1936.

> In Britain, the postwar period saw high unemployment. The moderately socialist Labour Party replaced the Liberal Party as the second largest party that helped to maintain the greater social equality achieved during the war and to ensure social harmony. There was an unsuccessful general strike in 1926.

Individual and Society

> During the 1920s, mass culture deeply penetrated ordinary life. Inexpensive manufactured goods sold in department stores, and energetically advertised, created mass consumerism.

> The somewhat stereotyped image of the "new woman" emerged during the 1920s. Women had gained economic independence and voting rights, and the emergence of a consumer society allowed them greater personal freedom. The "new woman" image was used as a marketing tool in this consumer society.

> Radio and the cinema provided inexpensive entertainment and transformed cultural life on a mass scale never hitherto seen. Radio and film stars became celebrated figures, often on an international scale.

> Many of the innovators in the arts and science were German-speaking Jews, such as Kafka, Einstein, Freud, and Schönberg. Nazi and fascist denunciations of the new arts and science as degenerate or "Jewish science" were colored by the ethnic origin of these towering figures.

National and European Identity

> The new German republic survived an attempted coup d'état in Bavaria in 1923 by a small, extremely nationalist, anti-Semitic party: the National Socialists, or Nazis. Its leader, Adolf Hitler, came to national attention during his trial and with the subsequent 1924 publication of *Mein Kampf*, outlining his racist views and plans for the expansion of Germany.

> In 1922, the Irish Republic was created, although the northern province remained part of the United Kingdom.

> Spain was torn by a brutal civil war from 1936 to 1939, when nationalists and conservatives under the leadership of Francisco Franco challenged the Popular Front government that had been democratically elected in Spain. Fascist Italy and Germany helped the rebels, while Communist Russia helped the Republicans. The Republic lost and was replaced by an authoritarian dictatorship under Franco.

> The new artistic, literary, and musical movements were disturbing to ordinary people. Fascists and Nazis, who defined them as degenerate, fiercely denounced them. Many of the modernist artists, architects, filmmakers, and writers were forced into exile during the Nazi period.

McKay Chapter 26 Focus Questions

1. How did intellectual developments reflect the general crisis in Western thought?

2. How did modernism revolutionize Western culture?

3. How did consumer society change everyday life?

4. What obstacles to lasting peace did European leaders face?

5. What were the causes and consequences of the Great Depression?

NOTES:

CHAPTER 27
Dictatorships and the Second World War, 1919–1945

Areas of Focus: Italy, Germany, the U.S.S.R., the Pacific

Main Events: fascism, Nazism, Stalinism, World War II

Key Figures:

- Adolf Hitler: "Der Führer," the leader of Nazi Germany
- Heinrich Himmler: head of the S.S. in Nazi Germany
- Joseph Goebbels: Nazi propaganda chief
- Neville Chamberlain: British prime minister who followed a policy of appeasement
- Benito Mussolini: "Il Duce," leader of Fascist Italy
- Giacomo Matteotti: Socialist deputy murdered by fascists
- Joseph Stalin: dictator of Communist Russia
- Primo Levi: Italian Jewish chemist; wrote about his experiences in the Holocaust
- Winston Churchill: prime minister of the U.K. during World War II
- Emperor Hirohito: ruler of Japan
- Marshall Pétain: ruler of Vichy government in S. France
- Dwight David Eisenhower: U.S. general, commander of the Allied Forces

AP® European History Themes
Interaction of Europe and the World

> World War II had a huge impact on Asia. The Japanese so-called "Co-Prosperity Sphere" meant brutal occupation of most of Asia (eastern China, Burma, Thailand, Indochina, Indonesia, Malaya, Manchuria, the Philippines, Korea) by the Japanese. The Japanese conquest of China, particularly in the port of Nanking in 1937, was marked by particular brutality.

> Italy invaded Ethiopia in 1935, met with fierce resistance but nevertheless took possession of the country in 1936. The League of Nations failed to act to prevent this act of aggression; similarly it proved incapable of preventing Japan from taking Manchuria in 1931.

> The U.S. was brought into the war by the Japanese bombing of the American naval base at Pearl Harbor in Hawaii on December 7, 1941.

> Refugees from Nazi Germany, Fascist Italy, and Franco's Spain—many of the Jewish—came to the U.S., and in fewer numbers to Mexico and other countries in Latin America. After the war, there were hundreds of thousands of displaced persons, many of whom sought refuge in the U.S. or Israel.

> Although allied with Germany and Italy in the Axis Front in 1940, the Japanese gave Jewish refugees from Europe a safe haven in Shanghai.

> In 1942, one of the most important battlefronts was North Africa. After the Allies defeated Rommel's Afrika Corps at El Alamein, they were able to launch an invasion of Italy the next spring. This battle was important in turning the tide against the previously victorious German army.

> The war in Asia ended with the dropping of two atomic bombs on Japan in August 1945; the only time in world history that atomic weapons have been used. Their use, with their devastating death tolls and blanket destruction of the two cities, Hiroshima and Nagasaki, have been the source of debate ever since. Some have argued that their use on the Japanese reflected American racial prejudices about Asians or that it was militarily unnecessary; others counter that the island-hopping strategy of the Allies was proving too costly in terms of American lives and too slow.

> Many countries around the world had fascist movements or substantial segments of the population supporting the fascists in Italy and Germany.

Poverty and Prosperity

> In the U.S.S.R, Lenin's New Economic Policy (NEP) allowed some capitalistic profit making but kept major industries, banks, and utilities nationalized. Stalin's five-year plans set high targets for heavy industry and agriculture, to spectacular result, restoring production to prewar levels. Collectivization created large farms more efficient in the use of machinery, animals, and labor, but it was strongly resisted by peasants.

> In 1932 the Soviet government forced the Ukraine collectives to deliver grain at excessively high levels, resulting in starvation of the peasants; six million Ukrainians died.

> The Italian Fascists allowed big business to regulate itself, compromised with the elites who controlled the economy, and did not implement land reform.

> The depression hit Germany hard, and was a major factor behind Nazi ascension to power. It had little impact in Russia.

> The Nazi government initiated huge public works projects and in 1936 began to rearm, both of which reduced unemployment and modestly improved the standard of living, fulfilling Hitler's promise of "work and bread."

Objective Knowledge and Subjective Visions

> The Nazis burned books written by Jews, socialists, and democrats; rewrote school and university curricula to teach Nazi "science;" and prohibited Modernism in the arts.

> Both authoritarian and totalitarian states censored the press and repressed intellectuals and artists; many went into exile. Totalitarian regimes also used the media for propaganda.

> The arts became ideological tools of the totalitarian states. Under Stalin, socialist realism glorified the workers, Russia, and the Communist Party; while in Nazi Germany, the arts glorified Hitler, German heroes like Siegfried, and the idealized Aryan.

> In the U.S.S.R. and Germany, approved artists were invited into the ruling elites, while the dissidents were persecuted. Both states made particularly effective use of the radio. The images of the dictators were everywhere.

> The papacy signed the Lateran Agreement with Mussolini's government in 1929, which made the Vatican independent of Italy and restored relations between church and state.

> Russian communism was ideologically opposed to the Orthodox Church and actively repressed it. Churches were converted to "museums of atheism."

> Some members of the Protestant and Catholic churches in Nazi Germany were active in opposing the Nazi state, but these efforts were aimed mainly at preserving religious life, not overthrowing Hitler.

States and Other Institutions of Power

> The 1920s and 1930s saw the waning of European democracy, replaced in one country after another by authoritarian or Fascist dictatorships. Democracy survived only in Britain, France, Scandinavia, the Netherlands, Czechoslovakia, and Switzerland. Both authoritarian and totalitarian regimes rejected the entire liberal agenda of democracy, parliamentary governments, and individual liberties. Authoritarian governments in eastern and central Europe were conservative and relied on traditional sources of authority like the military.

> A new form of dictatorship was created in Germany, Russia, and Italy to a lesser degree—the totalitarian state—which aimed to control all economic, social, intellectual, and cultural aspects of society. Totalitarian dictators ruled with particular brutality but also with remarkable effectiveness.

> After Lenin's death in 1924, Stalin, whose program was "socialism in one country," defeated Trotsky and his ideas of "permanent revolution." Stalin rose to power with cunning, skill, and charisma. By 1927 he had effectively become a dictator who was ready to revolutionize Russia from above. He built the new socialist Soviet Union by terrorizing the masses and executing dissenters like the "Old Bolsheviks."

> Italian leader Benito Mussolini's fascism was a combination of revolutionary nationalism, anti-Marxism, and conservatism. In 1920, Mussolini and a few fellow veterans formed the Black Shirts, a Fascist militia that raided and threatened Socialist Party headquarters, newspaper offices, and union halls; finally pushing the Socialists out of northern Italy. After a march on Rome in 1922 threatened the king, Mussolini was appointed prime minister. The Fascist Party won a parliamentary majority in 1924 and created a one-party state with government by decree, strict censorship, abolition of independent labor unions, propaganda to win over the masses, and repression of opposition. Italian fascism was never fully totalitarian or a very thorough police state. The old power structure was not replaced, and the king, albeit weak, remained on the throne throughout.

> **AP® Tip** Although there were many similarities between Fascist and Communist states in practice—their intrusions into private life, masterful use of propaganda, brutal suppression of dissidents, and in the case of Nazi Germany and Stalinist Russia, the murder of millions—there were important differences. Communists saw war and violence as *a means to an end,* whereas Fascists saw them as ends themselves; Communists believed that when socialism was fully established, the state would wither away, while Fascists believed that the state was the essential element of any nation and must remain all-powerful; Communists were generally internationalists (Stalin may have been an exception), while Fascists were nationalists; Communists sought a just society that provided real freedom, but Fascists sought to create powerful nations and rejected freedom completely.

> Nazism shared some of the characteristics of fascism, but it was more radical and interventionist. It was distinguished by a complete control of all aspects of society; virulent, vicious anti-Semitism; and aggressive expansionism. Its political success was because of three main factors: the dynamic leadership of Adolf Hitler, an Austrian war veteran and charismatic speaker who blamed both communism and large-scale capitalism on the Jews; its promises of comradeship and change; and the crisis of the Great Depression. In 1932, when businesses went bankrupt and many Germans were unemployed, the Nazis became the largest party in the Reichstag.

> Hitler and his National Socialists, or Nazis, quickly established a totalitarian dictatorship. Shortly after his appointment as chancellor in January 1933, Hitler was granted emergency dictatorial powers in the Enabling Act. He immediately banned all independent organizations including unions and other political parties. Nazi party members took over government bureaucracies and transformed every aspect of public life. The Gestapo (Hitler's secret state police) and the elite SS (Hitler's personal guards) ferreted out and interned in concentration camps tens of thousands of political enemies. Jews lost their government jobs in 1933, their citizenship with the Nuremburg Laws in 1935, and then their private businesses. Other victims of Hitler's ethnic cleansing plan were Gypsies (Roma and Sinti), Jehovah's Witnesses, and homosexuals.

❭ In March 1939, Hitler invaded and occupied the rest of Czechoslovakia. The U.S.S.R. and Germany signed a nonaggression pact in August 1939, with secret protocols to divide up Poland and Baltic states. Hitler then ordered the invasion of Poland on September 1, 1939. In response Britain and France declared war. World War II, which would ultimately claim more than 50 million lives, had begun.

❭ The German *blitzkrieg,* or "lightning war," was hugely successful. By 1940, virtually every European country had been defeated or was a German ally. Spain, Switzerland, Turkey, and Sweden were officially neutral. For one year, Britain stood alone against Germany and survived the attempt to subdue it by air. Then in 1941 the United States and the U.S.S.R. were both attacked (by Japan and Germany respectively) and joined the war. Britain, Russia, and the United States were allies but didn't share ideologies. They agreed to accept only unconditional surrender from the Axis powers.

❭ Effective mobilization for war, nationalism, and the sacrifices of many people made possible the Allied victory in World War II. The United States had exceptional industrial might, out-producing its enemies and indeed the rest of the world by 1943. Britain played a crucial role as the strategic center for the Allied war on the continent. The U.S.S.R. moved its industrial plant and a large percentage of its population east of the Urals.

❭ The turning point in the war in Europe came in 1943. The Germans met with catastrophic defeat at Stalingrad in the Soviet Union, which took the offensive; the United States and Britain, having ousted German troops from North Africa, invaded Sicily. The Italians deposed Mussolini and surrendered. On June 6, 1944, in history's greatest naval invasion, two million Allied soldiers landed on the beaches of Normandy, France. British and American forces marching eastward from France met Soviet troops liberating Eastern Europe on the Elbe in April, 1945. Hitler committed suicide, and on May 8, 1945, Germany quickly surrendered, leaving the Allies to focus the remainder of their energies on the war in the Pacific.

❭ As in Nazi Germany and Fascist Italy, the Japanese government was highly nationalistic, militaristic, and committed to expansion based on racial theories of Asian superiority. Propagandists promoted a "Greater East Asia Co-Prosperity Sphere," but in reality power remained in the hands of Japan's military. By 1942, Japan had conquered a vast empire in the Pacific and threatened Australia. The outcome of the war in the Pacific was determined by great naval battles such as the Coral Sea, Midway, and Leyte Gulf. The Allied tactic of island-hopping to defeat Japan by retaking its colonial holdings was expensive in terms of lives.

❭ On August 6, 1945, the United States dropped its newly developed atomic bomb on Hiroshima and three days later on Nagasaki, killing and maiming a few hundred thousand people in a single moment. The Japanese surrendered a few days later. The war was over.

Individual and Society

❭ Under the Communists in Russia, a new class system privileged the industrial and political managerial elite; contrary to the egalitarian ideals of socialism, this elite earned significantly higher wages than unskilled workers and farmers. Women's lives were radically transformed with full equal rights, including divorce and abortion. Some women did hard physical work, and others pursued higher education and became doctors and engineers. Although women did make significant advances, they often earned less than their male counterparts.

❭ In Fascist Italy and Nazi Germany, women lost rights and were returned to traditional roles.

❭ In Germany, the mentally ill, handicapped, and other "undesirables" were euthanized or sterilized to purify the race. The Nazi regime justified this 'purification' process by using the pseudoscience of eugenics.

❭ In all three totalitarian states, youth groups were created to inculcate loyalty to the cause.

❭ Civilians in Europe and Japan were the victims of unprecedented bombing raids that destroyed entire cities, killed millions, and rendered many more homeless. Notable raids include the 1940 German air raid attacks on Britain (Battle of Britain); the Allied destruction of Dresden, Hamburg, and Berlin; and the atomic bombing of Hiroshima and Nagasaki, Japan.

National and European Identity

> World War II saw the emergence of the U.S. as one of the two great powers in the world, the other being the Soviet Union. European states were weakened by the war and lost their dominant position on the world stage.

> Fascist ideology rejected democracy and the validity of the individual in favor of the state. Its slogan was "everything in the state, nothing outside the state, nothing against the state."

> For Nazism, the fundamental basis of ideology was race rather than state. The image of an ideal German was deeply infused with Aryan (German) mythology, anti-Semitism, and contempt for other "inferior" races.

> A major Nazi goal was territorial expansion for living space (*lebensraum*) in the east for the racially superior Germans. Voiding provisions of the Treaty of Versailles, Germany withdrew from the League of Nations, established a military draft, rearmed, and remilitarized the Rhineland. All the while France and Britain practiced appeasement policies to avoid war. In 1936, Italy and Germany formed the Rome-Berlin Axis, soon joined by Japan. Hitler achieved his goal of a Greater Germany in 1938 by invading and annexing Austria unopposed (the Anschluss), and—as the result of an act of appeasement—winning control of the Sudetenland (a German part of Czechoslovakia) at the Munich Conference.

> In the German-controlled areas of conquered Europe, Nordic peoples—deemed racially close to the Germans—received preferential treatment, while Slavic peoples were considered subhuman slave laborers to serve the "master race." Slavs, Gypsies, and Jews were put to work for Germans under the harsh supervision of the SS.

> The Nazis wanted to make Germany free of Jews. Dehumanizing treatment led about half of the German Jews to flee Germany, especially after the pogrom called *Kristallnacht* in November 1938. Jews in German-controlled lands, and especially in occupied eastern Europe, were moved into ghettoes or slave labor camps and millions were murdered, first by shooting by *Einsatzgruppen,* then in extermination camps run by the SS. Some six million Jews were killed by the end of the war in 1945.

McKay Chapter 27 Focus Questions

1. How were Fascist and Communist totalitarian dictatorships similar and different?

2. How did Stalin and the Communist Party build a totalitarian state in the Soviet Union?

3. What kind of government did Mussolini establish in Italy?

4. What policies did Nazi Germany pursue, and how did they lead to World War II?

5. How did Germany and Japan conquer enormous empires during World War II, and how did the Allies defeat them?

NOTES:

CHAPTER 28
Cold War Conflict and Consensus, 1945–1965

Areas of Focus: Germany, Russia, France, eastern Europe

Main Events: division of Germany, de-Stalinization in Russia, western European economic miracle, decolonization, the consumer revolution

Key Figures:

- FDR, Jr., Stalin, Churchill: the Big Three who negotiated the post-war settlement at conferences in Teheran, Yalta, Potsdam
- Charles de Gaulle: first President of the Fifth Republic of France; negotiated Algerian independence
- Harry Truman: U.S. President; followed a policy of containment of communism, issued Truman Doctrine
- Dwight David Eisenhower: U.S. president during the Korean War
- John F. Kennedy: U.S. president during the Cuban Missile Crisis
- Ludwig Erhard: chancellor of West Germany; advocate of liberal capitalism, Christian Democrat
- Jean Monet and Robert Schuman: economists; created the idea of the European Coal and Steel Community
- Nikita Khrushchev: Soviet premier who pursued an aggressive foreign policy abroad but also destalinization at home; sent up Sputnik, first man-made satellite to orbit the earth
- Leonid Brezhnev: Soviet Premier after Khrushchev; slowed the destalinization process
- Josef Broz, a.k.a. Tito: ran independent Communist state in Yugoslavia
- Mahatma Gandhi: pacifist; advocated satyagraha, passive resistance and civil disobedience, led India to independence
- Franz Fanon: French psychiatrist; author of *The Wretch of the Earth,* which denounced imperialism and neocolonialism and called for revolution
- Patrice Lumumba: first president of the independent Congo; assassinated after a CIA-aided coup
- Gamel Abdel Nasser: president of Egypt; nationalized the Suez Canal in 1956

AP® European History Themes
Interaction of Europe and the World

> Decolonization began shortly after the end of the war. In India, long-standing opposition to British rule, energized by the pacifist leadership of Mahatma Gandhi, led Britain to partition Muslim and Hindu India and grant independence in 1947. A similar solution was used to resolve the tensions between Zionist Jews and Arabs in Palestine; a UN partition plan created Israel in 1948 and was immediately followed by a war from which Israel emerged victorious and enlarged. Many Jewish survivors of World War II immigrated to Palestine. In 1956, Israel, England and France went to war with Egypt, taking the Suez Canal, but U.S. President Eisenhower forced them to give it back.

❯ The Indian independence movement was led by Mahatma Gandhi, whose doctrine of non-violence and civil disobedience was inspiring to many around the globe. His ideas had great influence on the U.S. civil rights movement of the 1950s and 1960s.

❯ The French lost Indochina (now Vietnam, Laos, and Cambodia) in 1954 after military defeat led by the forces of Communist nationalist Ho Chi Minh.

❯ Elsewhere in Africa and Asia, most French and English colonies became independent without much violence and retained substantial economic and cultural ties with their colonial overlords. Three notably violent exceptions were in Indonesia, Algeria, and the Congo. In the Congo, the U.S. CIA helped oust Patrice Lumumba, a charismatic but Communist-leaning leader who was then assassinated. In Algeria, the French fought a long and nasty war against the FLN (Front for National Liberation), which won independence in 1962. Indonesia similarly experienced a long war against its Dutch overlord.

❯ Asia was where the Cold War heated up. In China, the Nationalists led by Jiang Jieshi (Chiang Kai-shek) were defeated in 1949 by the Communists, who quickly established a one-party state and implemented radical programs empowering the peasants. Mao Zedong created a new type of communism, although the state was as repressive as its Soviet counterpart.

❯ In Korea, three years of indecisive warfare between the North Koreans (backed by Communist China) and the South Koreans (supported by U.S. troops) ended in 1953, resulting in a negotiated division of Korea that continues to this day.

❯ Newly independent states were wooed by the superpowers, and most allied with one or the other. Each side used covert actions to undermine governments on the other side. Some states, India most noticeably, formed a nonaligned bloc. Many leaders, as well as scholars like Franz Fanon, argued that the U.S. and Europe had replaced colonialism with neocolonialism in which Western economic and political dominance continued in new forms.

Poverty and Prosperity

❯ West Germany and other countries instituted guest worker programs to supplement their labor forces in boom times, attracting millions of people from poorer countries. Many thousands of Turks settled in West Germany.

❯ European federalists began to imagine economic cooperation as the way to restore Europe's leadership in world affairs and prevent another war. In 1951, six states—France, Belgium, West Germany, Italy, Luxembourg, and the Netherlands—created the European Steel and Coal Community, a single market with no tariffs or quotas.

❯ Virtually full employment and rising wages bolstered the growth of the consumer economy in western Europe in the 1950s and 1960s. The number of cars in western Europe grew nine-fold by 1965. The ready availability of inexpensive consumer goods in the west became part of Cold War ideological competition.

❯ In the Eastern bloc, leaders were critical of the western-style consumer culture, but the availability of consumer goods lagged, leading to complaints and disillusionment.

Objective Knowledge and Subjective Visions

❯ During the war, inventions like radar and the nuclear bomb were crucial. Afterwards, "Big Science" came to be organized in public and private large bureaucracies employed in the Cold War arms and space races. The U.S.S.R. was the first to put a satellite (Sputnik) into orbit in 1957 and a man into orbit four years later. The United States was the first to put a human on the moon in 1969. Big science also benefited ordinary people, with transistors invented for computers, creating the consumer electronics industry, and research providing the means for the green revolution that increased agricultural yield. The discovery of the double helix, the mechanism for genetic transmission, transformed science, psychology, and medicine.

> In the Soviet Union, intellectuals such as the novelists Boris Pasternak *(Doctor Zhivago)* and Alexander Solzhenitsyn *(One Day in the Life of Ivan Denisovich)* indicted Stalinism.

> American jazz and rock 'n' roll found a ready audience among European youth, aided by the invention of the long-playing record album (LP) and 45 rpm singles.

> In eastern Europe and the U.S.S.R., the Communists attempted to eradicate all religious practices. Religiosity became a form of anticommunism.

> Mao Zedong created a new type of communism in which the peasants were considered the primary class. Although the programs he instituted in the 1950s, such the Great Leap Forward, proved disastrous and caused famine and great suffering, the regime remained strong. Maoist ideas attracted some seeking an alternative to the Soviet system.

States and Other Institutions of Power

➡️ **AP® Tip** If you are answering an essay question on the AP European History Exam about the Cold War or the postwar period of the 1950s and 1960s, be sure to focus your essay on Europe, rather than on American developments and attitudes.

> The defeated Axis powers of World War II were occupied by the victors. At conferences in Teheran (1943), Yalta (1945), and Potsdam (1945), the Allies decided the shape of postwar Europe. They divided Germany, its capital city of Berlin, and Austria into four zones of occupation.

> Thousands of Nazis were tried and convicted, and many others "denazified." The Allies jointly put the Nazi leaders that had not fled or committed suicide on trial at Nuremberg for war crimes and crimes against humanity; twelve were given the death penalty.

> With Europe weakened by war, the two dominant world powers, the United States and the U.S.S.R., each with a string of allies, engaged in a fierce ideological, economic, political, and cultural struggle called the Cold War. During World War II, eastern Europe was liberated by the U.S.S.R., which insisted on control of these states after the war as a buffer zone. In 1946, former British Prime Minister Winston Churchill lamented the "iron curtain" dividing Europe.

> Europe was the focal point of Soviet-American tensions. The popularity of Communist parties in France and Italy and the civil wars in Greece and China raised fears of the spread of communism. These fears led the United States to issue the Truman Doctrine in 1947, promising American military and economic aid to groups resisting communism.

> In occupied Germany, cooperation among the four powers quickly diminished. When England, France, and the United States announced a common currency for their zones in 1948, the U.S.S.R. cut off traffic through its zone to West Berlin. A yearlong Allied airlift forced the Soviets to relent. The next year, the occupation ended as East and West Germany became independent states.

> In western Europe, constitutional governments replaced wartime regimes, with republics created in France, Italy, Austria, and West Germany. Governments, whether of the left (the Labour Party in England) or the center (Christian Democrats in France, West Germany, and Italy) expanded social welfare programs. The Christian Democrats, anti-communist and moderate, dominated western European politics for some twenty years.

> Eastern European states became one-party dictatorships after Stalin purged non-communists from coalition governments. In 1955, the U.S.S.R. organized the Warsaw Pact, a military pact of Russia and its satellites, as a counterpoint to NATO. Only Yugoslavia, free of Soviet troops, remained outside the Soviet orbit. Its war hero, Josef Broz "Tito," successfully stood up to Stalin in 1948; until its dissolution in the 1980s, Yugoslavia was unique—a European Communist state independent of the U.S.S.R.

> After Stalin's death in 1953, his successors, realizing reforms would be necessary, restricted the secret police and closed many of the labor camps. Premier Nikita Khrushchev revealed Stalin's crimes to the Party Congress in 1956, initiating a de-Stalinization or liberalization. This meant a loosening of the tight control the Russian state had had.

> Khrushchev initially moved Soviet foreign policy toward "peaceful coexistence" with the West, but not liberalization in the Soviet satellites. He toppled reforming governments in Poland and Hungary in 1956. The crushing of the Hungarian revolution by Soviet tanks led to widespread disillusionment with communism. In 1962, Khrushchev tried to place nuclear missiles in newly Communist Cuba, but he was forced to withdraw them by U.S. President Kennedy.

> In 1961, East Germany—with Soviet backing—built a wall in Berlin and along its borders with West Germany. This wall, designed to prevent East Germans from escaping, became a symbol of Cold War tensions.

> Khrushchev was succeeded in 1964 by Leonid Brezhnev, whose policies restricted the destalinization process began by Khrushchev and led to economic stagnation.

Individual and Society

> Europe was devastated by World War II. Cities from London to Dresden to Leningrad were in ruins. Some 50 million people died, including large numbers of civilians, and a similar number were left homeless. Many of these lived in displaced persons camps run by the United Nations.

> During the 1950s and 1960s, social mobility increased and traditional class barriers blurred. Family connections and inherited property became less important. Many industrial workers became better educated and moved into white-collar (service or office) jobs. As the standard of living rose, poorer people could afford what had been luxuries for the rich, such as cars and household gadgets, month-long vacations, and travel. The middle class became dominated by corporate and government managers.

> The emancipation of women in the twentieth century is one of its most important developments. The strong demand for labor in the postwar economic boom, the short- age of men due to war death tolls, and the decline in birthrates allowed women to enter the workforce in momentous numbers, many in white-collar jobs, especially in the Communist Soviet Union and eastern Europe.

> The high birthrate in the decade after World War II led to an unusually high proportion of the population that was young. With economic prosperity and a more open class structure, a distinct youth culture and rebellious "counterculture" emerged with its own consumer goods marketed specifically to the new youth culture. This culture had its own idols and its own music—rock 'n' roll—all of which worried the older generations and led to a "generation gap."

National and European Identity

> Western Europe recovered remarkably quickly from the devastation of World War II. This "economic miracle" involved government focus on economic growth, the adoption of Keynesian economics, help from the Marshall Plan (1947), and a mixture of government intervention and free-market capitalism. The infusion of huge sums of American money into the European economy was a key factor in the restoration of western Europe states to economic growth and political stability. Extensive welfare programs such as Britain's "cradle to grave" model became the norm in western Europe.

> Eastern Europe stagnated economically in spite of COMECON, the Soviet economic program for its satellites. East Germany, Romania, and Hungary, which fought the U.S.S.R. in the war, paid it reparations in the form of factories and machines. The Soviet satellite states nationalized industries and instituted collectivization of agriculture and Soviet-style five-year plans.

> After the success of the European Steel and Coal Community, Europeans expanded it in 1957 into the European Economic Community, or Common Market, an economic union with free movement of

peoples and goods. The Common Market was a huge success and added other member countries over the years, rivaling the United States as an economic power.

> Soviet and eastern European artists and writers were required to conform to socialist realism and represent the ideals of their party. The U.S.S.R. and its satellites were dappled with idealized paintings and monumental sculptures trying to build a consensus for communism.

> U.S. foreign policy was containment (the Truman Doctrine), preventing the further spread of communism but accepting existing Communist states. Most western European countries joined the United States in a military alliance, the North Atlantic Treaty Organization (NATO), in 1949; those under Soviet control joined the Warsaw Pact (1955). The United Nations replaced the League of Nations and was often the venue for the display of Cold War tensions.

> Within the U.S.S.R., World War II had created a strong nationalistic bond between government and people. After the war, dissidents and Jews were targeted, rigid political authoritarianism returned, and the five-year plans that emphasized heavy industry at the expense of consumer goods were reinstituted. In 1953, a workers' rebellion in East Germany was crushed by force.

> National identities became more fluid. Millions of people from former colonies moved to the colonizing power, forming significant minority populations.

McKay Chapter 28 Focus Questions

1. Why was World War II followed so quickly by the Cold War?

2. What were the sources of postwar recovery and stability in western Europe?

3. What was the pattern of postwar development in the Soviet bloc?

4. What led to decolonization after World War II, and how did the Cold War influence the process?

5. How did changes in social relations contribute to European stability on both sides of the iron curtain?

NOTES:

CHAPTER 29
Challenging the Postwar Order, 1960–1991

Areas of Focus: Eastern Europe, Russia, western Europe, the United States

Main Events: Vietnam War, German unification, 1989 revolutions, fall of the Communist system, end of the U.S.S.R., radical youth groups and counterculture movement, feminist movement

Key Figures:

■ Willy Brandt: Social Democratic Chancellor of Germany; initiated the "opening to the East"

■ Mikhail Gorbachev: last Soviet Premier; initiated major reforms of *glasnost* and *perestroika*

■ Boris Yeltsin: first leader of the Russian Soviet Republic, the Russian Federation that replaced the U.S.S.R.

■ Margaret Thatcher: Conservative Prime Minister of the U.K.; anti-union, closed down unprofitable coal mines, instituted neoliberal policies

■ Helmut Kohl: last Chancellor of West Germany; oversaw the unification of Germany

■ Pope John Paul II: Polish archbishop elected pope; supporter of Solidarity

■ François Mitterrand: Socialist, President of France

■ Jean-Marie Le Pen: founder of rightwing, anti-immigration National Front party in France

■ Ronald Reagan: U.S. President; instituted neoliberal policies in the U.S.

■ Anwar-al-Sadat and Yitzhak Rabin: Egyptian President and Israeli Prime Minister who signed the Camp David Accords

■ Alexander Dubček: leader of the Prague Spring–"Socialism with a Human Face," in Czechoslovakia

■ Lech Walesa: leader of Solidarity movement in Poland, later President

■ Pavel Havel: Czech playwright, president of the Czechoslovak Republic; led "Velvet Revolution" against the Communist regime

AP® European History Themes
Interaction of Europe and the World

❯ When Vietnamese nationalists and Communists forced the French out in 1954, Vietnam was divided into two states, which led to civil war and American military involvement on behalf of the anticommunist South Vietnamese government. By the mid-1960s the war had escalated to a half million U.S. soldiers fighting abroad. Costly in lives as well as money, the long Vietnam War alienated many U.S. allies, sparked fierce protests at home and abroad, and ended in U.S. withdrawal in 1973 and Vietnam's subsequent unification as a Communist state.

❯ Similarly, the expansion of the Vietnam War into Cambodia, which had terrible consequences for the Cambodians, was widely criticized.

❯ In the U.S., several student protesters were shot and killed at Kent State in Ohio.

> The 1960s, 1970s, and 1980s were tumultuous years around the globe, where numerous left-wing governments were toppled or weakened by CIA or other U.S. interventions. Similarly, the U.S. government supported the reformers in the U.S.S.R.

> In the Middle East, there were three Arab-Israeli wars of notes: 1867, (the Six-Day War), when Israel took the Sinai Peninsula, the Golan Heights, the West Bank, and Jerusalem. It gave back the Sinai to Egypt in exchange for recognition in the late 1970s, but still occupies the other areas, although a form of a Palestinian State has come into being. The 1973 Yom Kippur War was more or less a draw. The 1982 invasion of Lebanon proved to be a mistake, as it allowed for brutal massacres of one group of Lebanese against others. The situation has not much changed to this day. Within Europe, Germany was for a long time Israel's most staunch ally; many other Europeans criticized the occupation of Palestine.

> In protest of the 1973 aid given to the Israelis by the U.S, OPEC (the Organization of Petroleum Exporting Countries) began an embargo on exports to the U.S. The price of gasoline and other petroleum products skyrocketed, leading to stagflation and sluggish economies in the U.S. and Europe.

> In China, when Mao died and his coterie has been replaced, the government adopted a pro-capitalism stance on the economy while maintaining a one-party, authoritarian and repressive state. In 1989, a peaceful protest in Tiananmen Square asking for political freedom was crushed by tanks. China has pursued this dual policy ever since. The fall of the U.S.S.R. after initiating political reform was seen as a dangerous model.

Poverty and Prosperity

> By the 1970s, eastern European economic successes brought about under Communist leadership policies–collectivization of agriculture, nationalization of industry and business, increased class mobility, and substantial welfare benefits—became known as "real existing socialism" or "developed socialism." While some consumer goods became common, such as the television, others were hard to come by, causing resentment and frustration among citizens of the Soviet bloc.

> After some twenty years of prosperity, the European economy experienced simultaneous inflation and stagnation (stagflation) in the 1970s, sparked by the sudden, sharp increase in the cost of oil and uncertainty in the international monetary system. Unemployment rose to its highest level since the Great Depression, and living standards declined. In the late 1970s, conservatives won office and enacted neoliberal policies. Margaret Thatcher, prime minister of Great Britain for eleven years, replaced much of the welfare system, privatized industries, and reduced taxes. The results were high unemployment, widening gaps between rich and poor, and riots, but also the creation of new groups of property owners. In Germany, similar cuts in taxes and government spending prompted economic growth.

> Heavy industry lost economic ground to high-tech industries like computing and biotechnology, and to service industries like medicine, banking, and finance. This shift brought about what scholars now refer to as the "postindustrial society" or "information age."

> After the fall of communism, the standard of living and quality of life in the former Communist states severely declined as industries were privatized and unemployment and prices soared.

Objective Knowledge and Subjective Visions

> The feminist movement was sparked by *The Second Sex* (1949) by Simone de Beauvoir. This book inspired feminists like Betty Friedan, author of *The Feminine Mystique* (1963) and cofounder of the National Organization for Women in the United States.

> American biologist Rachel Carson's 1962 book *Silent Spring* was read widely across Europe and helped to spark the early environmental movement.

> *Samizdat*, underground literature critical of communism, blossomed in East Bloc countries during the 1960s. Distribution of this literature helped to build support for the growing countercultural

movement in the East Bloc. Intellectuals challenged the conformity, Americanization, and vulgarity of the new consumer society, and many lamented the loss of traditional foods, values, and lifestyles.

❯ Intellectuals on the right and left sought new ideologies to replace those of the Cold War. The "New Left" criticized both Stalinism and corporate capitalism, exploring how to create socialism without oppression. Neoliberals argued for a modern form of laissez-faire capitalism to free up economic life, reduce and regulate taxes, and increase private profits, their means to achieve economic growth.

❯ The Second Vatican Council in the early 1960s aimed to democratize and open the church. The Latin mass was replaced by the vernacular in an attempt to broaden church appeal.

❯ The council's efforts did little to counteract secularization. Church attendance fell virtually everywhere in western and central Europe, though it was less pronounced in Catholic areas such as Poland.

States and Other Institutions of Power

❯ During the 1960s and early 1970s, the left, such as the Labour Party in Britain and the Social Democrats in Germany, generally dominated European politics. Willy Brandt, the chancellor of West Germany, initiated détente, a compromise with the Communist east. He signed a treaty of reconciliation with Poland in 1970, apologized for German crimes during World War II, and opened direct negotiations with East Germany. This Ostpolitik policy eased tensions and allowed greater contact between the two Germanies.

❯ In eastern Europe in the 1960s and 1970s, continuing economic shortages prompted changes — decentralization, provision of consumer goods, and cultural freedom—with mixed success. The most important movement for change was "socialism with a human face" in Czechoslovakia, seen in the "Prague Spring" of 1968. Led by Alexander Dubcek, this period of political and cultural freedom was ended by Warsaw Pact forces, after which Soviet leader Leonid Brezhnev announced the Brezhnev Doctrine, asserting the right of the Soviet Union to intervene in the internal affairs of the satellite states. The U.S.S.R. also invaded Afghanistan in 1979 to support its local Communist regime, embroiling it in a long and costly war.

❯ In the late 1960s and 1970s, environmentalists formed Green parties and later had some electoral success, particularly in Germany. At the same time, far-right parties opposing increased immigration, such as the French National Front, led by Le Pen, and the Austrian Freedom Party, grew in size and importance during the 1970s and1980s.

❯ The tumultuous year 1968 saw significant left-wing and student protests against the Vietnam War throughout the world. Local issues also fed into the discontent. In May 1968, students infused with New Left ideals, and supported by workers on strike, fought with police in a short-lived Paris insurrection, bringing the French economy to a standstill. President Charles de Gaulle surrounded Paris with troops, made promises to the workers that ended the strike, and brought the conservatives to victory in the next election. The student movement declined in the 1970s.

❯ Radical youth groups from West Germany (the Red Army Faction) and Italy (the Red Brigades) tried to achieve change through sabotage, kidnapping, and murder. Most of these terrorists were incarcerated and their goals unachieved. Separatist movements in Spain (Basque ETA) and Northern Ireland (IRA) also used violent tactics.

❯ Conservatives dominated in western Europe (except in France) in the late 1970s and 1980s. They followed neoliberal policies like cutting spending, privatizing industries, and modifying the welfare state.

❯ The first successful challenge to Communist rule in eastern Europe was won by striking dockworkers at Gdansk in Poland, who organized a national labor union demanding political and labor rights, which then grew into a political party led by Lech Walesa. With the support of the first Polish pope, John Paul II, Solidarity won concessions from the government, was legalized in 1988, and won an overwhelming victory in an open election. It quickly destroyed the Communist economy with neoliberal "shock therapy" policies.

> Within the U.S.S.R. there was significant apathy and growing frustration over the stagnant economy, the privileged Communist elite, and the lack of freedom. Growing demands for reform led in 1985 to the premiership of Mikhail Gorbachev, who instituted *glasnost* (a policy of government openness) and *perestroika* (economic reconstruction).

> *Glasnost* brought open criticism of the state-directed (command) economy, a floodgate of public discussion, and demands for democracy. Free elections were held in the U.S.S.R. in 1989, the first since 1917. Gorbachev also renounced the Brezhnev Doctrine, withdrew Russian troops from Afghanistan, and sought arms limitations treaties with the United States.

> At the same time, within the Soviet bloc, larger and larger peaceful demonstrations demanded greater freedom. When Hungary opened its borders to Germans wishing to flee to the West, the response was so great that the East German government opened the Berlin Wall in November 1989. It was torn down by jubilant Berliners on both sides, a moment of liberation celebrated around the globe. Similarly, popular demonstrations led to the end of communism in other satellite states. In Czechoslovakia, this process was so smooth it was called the Velvet Revolution. Only in Romania did the toppling of the Communist system involve violent revolution; there the Communist dictator Nicolae Ceausescu was executed.

> In 1990, the delegates of twenty-two European nations, the United States, and the Soviet Union signed the Paris Accord agreeing to scale down their armed forces and affirming all existing borders.

> Political instability followed the fall of communism in Russia. The Communist Party lost the election in 1990 and Boris Yeltsin, the leader of the Russian Federation Parliament, who won widespread popular support by stopping an attempted coup by hardliners, replaced Gorbachev. The Communist Party was outlawed in Russia, and the Soviet Union dissolved in 1991. The Baltic republics and Ukraine became independent states, although other former Soviet republics joined a new Commonwealth of Independent States.

> **AP® Tip** There's a certain American triumphalism that ought to be avoided in discussing the end of the Communist system in Russia and Eastern Europe. While Americans often credit U.S. president Ronald Reagan for its collapse, it was a much more complex phenomenon with deep roots in local histories and the limitations of the command economy.

Individual and Society

> The plethora of household gadgets and easy shopping in Western European supermarkets increased rather than lessened the domestic duties of women. Feminist movements grew stronger and better organized. Women in Catholic countries fought for divorce and abortion rights; elsewhere feminists focused on legal and employment equity.

> Family ties lessened as prosperity and the ease of movement offered by the European Community made it easier for young people to move away from their native areas.

> More people lived alone, the divorce rate was high, and family size shrank.

> The youth subculture, in addition to its political activism, fought for individual freedom on personal and sexual matters, stating that "the personal is the political." Their rock 'n' roll music, their highly spirited consumerism, their publicly acknowledged use of illegal drugs, and the sexual revolution, fueled by the safe, reliable, and inexpensive oral contraceptive ("the pill") that made it easier to separate sex from procreation, upset traditionalists.

National and European Identity

> The Common Market became the European Economic Community (EEC), with twelve member states.

> The counterculture rejected the artistic canon and advocated pop and performance art. Rock music became international, with English bands like the Rolling Stones and the Beatles wildly adored around the globe, bringing east and west Europe closer.

❯ In 1975, the Helsinki Accords—aimed at reducing Cold War tensions and guaranteeing human and political rights—were signed by thirty-five nations, including all of the states in Europe, the Soviet Union, and the United States.

❯ In October 1990, Germany was reunified under West German leadership, disappointing those who sought a "third way" between oppressive communism and ruthless capitalism.

❯ Germany once again became the dominant continental state.

McKay Chapter 29 Focus Questions

1. Why did the postwar consensus of the 1950s break down?

2. What were the consequences of economic decline in the 1970s?

3. What led to the decline of Soviet power in the East Bloc?

4. Why did revolutions sweep through the East Block in 1989, and what were the immediate consequences?

NOTES:

CHAPTER 30
Life in an Age of Globalization, 1990 to the Present

Areas of Focus: European Union, Eastern Europe, Russia, United States, Iraq and Afghanistan

Main Events: Maastricht Treaty (formation of the EU), Russian revival, Bosnian War, globalization

Key Figures:

- Boris Yeltsin: president of the Russian Federation; instituted "shock therapy" and privatization of Russian industries

- Vladimir Putin: popular successor to Yeltsin, elected president of Russia three times; established semi-authoritarian rule

- Slobodan Miloševic: Serbian nationalist; chief figure in the civil wars among the former member states of Yugoslavia

- Edward Snowden: American former CIA operative; leaked to world press secret surveillance of U.S. intelligence agencies

- Saddam Hussein: president of Iraq overthrown in the U.S. war on Iraq after the 2001 attack on the World Trade Center and the Pentagon

- Osama bin Laden: Saudi Arabian leader of the radical Islamic group al-Qaeda; engineered the 9/11 attacks

- David Cameron: Conservative prime minister of Britain; resigned after Brexit vote

- Angela Merkel: Christian Democratic chancellor of Germany

- George W. Bush: U.S. president; went to war with Iraq and Afghanistan

- Barack Hussein Obama: first African-American president of the U.S.

AP® European History Themes
Interaction of Europe and the World

> Generally throughout the Muslim world, growing political Islam reflected continuing resentment of perceived foreign control and secularization. It became more radical, seeking to reinforce traditional religious beliefs but also to make social and economic reform, In Egypt; the Muslim Brotherhood had widespread appeal.

> In the wake of the terrorist attacks on New York and Washington D.C. on September 11, 2001, U.S. President Bush went to war with Iraq—with British collaboration—claiming its dictator Saddam Hussein had weapons of mass destruction. While this claim was not substantiated, the war toppled the regime, leading to political stability and rapid economic and social decline because of ethnic and religious tensions and terrorist violence.

> Afghanistan proved an important focus of conflict. In the 1980s, Muslim guerillas fought Soviet troops and ultimately forced the U.S.S.R. to withdrew its troops. The Taliban, a radical Muslim army, then dominated most of the country. The U.S. sent troops under President Bush, installed a friendly government, and pushed the Taliban back, although they continued to offer resistance.

> The Arab Spring of 1911 brought down long-standing rulers in Egypt (Hosni Mubarak) and Libya (Musummar Gaddafi); a civil war broke out in Syria where Bashar al-Assad has managed to hold on. After an initial flurry of mass enthusiasm for political democracy, the movements faltered, and the civil war in Syria brought in Russia in support of Assad and the U.S. in support of the rebels. As the reform movements in the Arab world faltered, the Islamic State (ISIS or ISIL) emerged to establish a new caliphate to unify Muslims. Islamic state soldiers were effective militarily and took key cities in Iraq and Syria.

> Dependency on fossil fuels was an important factor in the U.S. wars in the Middle East and Russian interventions in Georgia and Chechnya. Europe's dependency on Russian natural gas made it possible for Russia to assert its international power.

Poverty and Prosperity

> The transition from the Communist command economy to market capitalism proved easier in Hungary, the Czech Republic, and Poland—all of which had made economic reforms before 1989 and had stronger entrepreneurial traditions than Romania and Bulgaria did.

> Virtually everywhere in the former Communist states, ordinary people suffered from high inflation that devalued pensions and savings, unemployment, and uncertainty as the guaranteed employment and social benefits of the Communist states disappeared. The young and the elite thrived, and capital cities catered to the wealthy, while provincial cities declined and gangsterism grew, particularly in Russia.

> In 2002, the euro—the common currency adopted by most EU members—transformed European trade and travel.

> A recession that began in the United States in 2008 spread across the world, a sign of the interconnectedness of the global economy. First Ireland and then other countries were severely hit. By 2010, Spain, Portugal, and Greece were on the verge of bankruptcy.

> Austerity measures imposed by wealthy EU states as a condition for needed financial aid proved highly unpopular at home, and by 2013, several countries in southern Europe debated the question of pulling out of the euro.

> The process of globalization—brought about by factors like the ever-increasing speed of communication resulting from the Internet and the easy availability of personal computers, the ability to hire technically proficient people from anywhere in the world (outsourcing), and the growth of the multinational corporations—transformed the world economy and Europe's role in it starting in the 1990s.

> Globalization revealed the underdevelopment of Mediterranean Europe and the dangers of overreliance on industry but helped London transition to a global center. Conglomerates like the German firm Siemens have vast holdings in many economic arenas. Because of globalization, global recessions were triggered by local events, like the Asian banking crisis of 1997, the collapse of Iceland's currency and banking in 2008, and the U.S. housing market collapse in 2008. Recovery from this global recession was slow and weak.

> Outsourcing of jobs to the still-industrializing world accelerated the decline of the industrial sector of employment in Europe. Many previously employed in well-paying industry jobs faced unemployment and had to take service jobs, some of which were poorly paid.

Objective Knowledge and Subjective Visions

❯ Intellectuals and ordinary Europeans often expressed anti-Americanism. Others delineated a new global role for Europe as standard-bearer of human rights.

❯ Multicultural authors, mostly immigrants or first-generation Europeans, explored their engagement with European culture and their transitions in the second generation.

❯ New forms of popular music like rai developed from the multicultural mix and created new international superstars such as the Algerian Cheb Khaled.

❯ Film has also been an important venue for exploring European multiculturalism. Films such as the British *Bend It Like Beckham* (2002) and French *The Class* (2008) portray the challenges caused by cross-cultural interaction in the new European society

❯ Staff of the French satirical magazine *Charlie Hebdo* was savagely attacked in early 2015 after publishing cartoons about the Prophet Mohammed. This led to much debate about the proper role of a free press and satire.

States and Other Institutions of Power

❯ In Russia, Yeltsin applied neoliberal shock therapy in 1992 and privatized industries. Instead of prompting rapid economic growth and spreading prosperity, the elite of the old Communist system turned previous state monopolies into private ones, and high inflation, huge decline in production, and hardship on ordinary citizens lasted nearly a decade.

❯ Criminal elements took control over Russia's valuable oil and natural resources. Democracy seemed to many to be a hollow cover for corruption and decline. The next president, Vladimir Putin, a former secret police officer, restored order by re-instituting authoritarian rule and repressing independent media and political opposition. He asserted Russia's role on the international stage, increased military spending, and challenged the United States. Putin also engaged in a long brutal war against the tiny state of Chechnya that had declared its independence and intervened in Georgia. Under Putin, high prices for oil and expansion of Russia's energy market share led to sustained economic growth. Putin stepped down as president after his term ended in 2008, but became prime minister. He was re-elected President in 2012.

❯ The expansion of the EU to include the former Soviet satellites slowed the pace of political unification and led to a new EU constitution in the Treaty of Lisbon (2009). A continuing issue is the much-resisted application of Turkey, a large Muslim state, to EU membership.

❯ Climate change and environmental concerns became ever more important as globalization of the economy increased the use of energy and coal emissions in expanding economies like China. The EU is at the forefront of efforts to contain climate change, develop alternative sources of energy, protect water resources, and to take preventive measures against future rises in sea levels.

❯ **AP® Tip** In a way, Europe is returning full circle to where it was at the start of this course—many small states unified by a central structure. In the Middle Ages, the structure was the Holy Roman Empire, and now it is the EU. Both versions of Europe wrestled with two sets of identities at the same time: strong local bonds but also participation in an international culture. But as the EU was slowly creating an effective government, what is happening now is quite unlike the Holy Roman Empire: there is a remarkable willingness to abandon old hostilities and fears, bringing west, north, east, and south Europe together for the first time. However, economic troubles and political restiveness in the 2010s suggest that significant tensions between local and European interests remain. In 2016, the British voted for a referendum to withdraw from the E.U., sending shockwaves across Europe.

Individual and Society

❯ Economic hardship in post-communist Russia devalued the working classes and had a huge impact on health. Life expectancy of males sharply declined.

❯ The digital revolution—the easy availability of ever more sophisticated, compact, and affordable systems of entertainment and communication, and the remarkable speed of information gathering on the Internet—transformed every aspect of life. The spread of the Internet and of social media created new ways for people to access information, communicate, and connect to one another.

❯ The deindustrialization of Europe changed its social structure. While the managerial and technical elite did well, the standard of living of the middle class declined. A poorly paid underclass of unskilled laborers was made up of recent immigrants, often nonwhites.

❯ European birthrates continued to decline, prompting general concern over declining and aging national populations. Immigration from poorer nations in Asia, Africa, and the Middle East sharply increased the percentage of Europe's population that was nonwhite.

National and European Identity

❯ Most Europeans were critical or cautious of U.S. foreign policy. Only Britain was a supporter of the war with Iraq and sent troops to the Middle East.

❯ Some, often conservative, intellectuals urged Europe to assert its identity in fear of Euro-Islam, which was going to increase in size and undermine European values of individualism, secularism, and tolerance, because Muslim immigrants would never assimilate.

❯ Others, however, argued that Europe needs immigrant labor and that multiculturalism will invigorate European culture. Muslim immigrants will acculturate as previous groups had and ought to be integrated in order to prevent radicalization and alienation.

⟶ **AP® Tip** Europe had been virtually all white and mostly Christian until the late twentieth century. This new immigration is forcing Europeans to wrestle with issues of race and identity, complicated by threats to ethnic identities from the "wired" global culture and the slow development of a Europe-wide identity. The question "What does it mean to be a European?" is a difficult one to answer.

❯ Europe moved toward political unity with the Maastricht Treaty of 1991, which created a multinational currency, defense, and foreign policy. The European Community became the European Union (EU), with twenty-seven members by 2010. Free movement of peoples, services, capital, and goods, and common standards made the EU powerful though all members did not accept the new currency.

❯ Nationalism and ethnic tensions flared up in the former Eastern bloc countries after the fall of communism, particularly in Yugoslavia. When Croatia became independent in 1991, Serbian president Slobodan Milosevic invaded to take back as much territory as he could. Bosnia-Herzegovina broke away the next year, leading to a brutal civil war between Bosnian Serbs and Bosniaks (Muslims). Some 300,000 Bosniaks were slaughtered in "ethnic cleansing," the first mass killings in Europe since the Holocaust.

❯ The United States, the UN, the EU, and NATO at various points intervened in Bosnia; ultimately a complicated accord ended the violence. When Serbia used force to prevent Kosovo from gaining independence, NATO bombed Serbia to force it to withdraw. In 2001, Slobodan Milosevic was turned over to the war crimes tribunal in the Netherlands for his role in the "ethnic cleansing." Kosovo declared its independence from Serbia in 2008 after ten years of civil war, but tensions remain.

❯ The close foreign policy relationship of western Europeans and the United States began to break down in the 1990s, as the EU asserted its independence and NATO expanded to become a virtually

Europe-wide alliance. Europeans, except for the British, generally took dim views of the U.S. wars in Iraq and Afghanistan that began in 2003 in response to the al-Qaeda attacks in New York and Washington of September11, 2001. Although initially enthusiastic over the toppling of Iraqi president Saddam Hussein, most EU states doubted the legitimacy of the "war on terror" and worried that the United States had violated international law and tolerated human rights abuses.

> By the 1990s, immigration had become a hot political issue and had given rise to new parties and movements, particularly successful in France and Austria. The issue became more complicated when Islamic terrorism came to haunt Europe with bombings in Madrid in 2004 and London in 2005 and in Paris in 2015 committed by Muslim residents, some of who were born citizens of the countries.

> Muslim youths rioted in France in 2005 and several times thereafter. These riots challenged the idea that Muslim immigrants could be well integrated into European societies.

> European anti-Americanism abated somewhat with widespread enthusiasm over the election of Barack Obama as U.S. president in 2008.

> As the EU expanded, conservatives and nationalists chafed at times over "Eurocrats" in EU headquarters dictating policies. The unpopularity of the EU structure had led to defeat of a draft constitution in 2004. In the 2010s, British Conservative prime minister David Cameron pledged an "in or out" vote on EU membership. When the supporters of withdrawal from the EU, the so-called Brexit, won in 2016, He resigned, and Theresa May became Prime Minister. An economic crisis that threatened the common currency in the 2010s added to renewed uncertainty over the EU's future.

> Illegal immigration became easier when the EU abolished border controls between member states. The rapid rise in the percentage of foreign-born residents, evident in ethnically and racially mixed national sports teams and multicultural foods, has created a crisis of identity for some Europeans and led to some tensions as well as celebrations of a new multicultural Europe.

> The integration of the more than 15 million Muslims within the EU became a fraught issue in many countries as Europeans debated the degree to which these immigrants would embrace European values. Muslim youths born in France but with little hope of good employment, decent housing, and cultural acceptance, rioted on the outskirts of Paris in 2005 and 2009. Some Europeans had difficulties accepting the religiosity of many resident Muslims and were disturbed by women wearing the traditional veil. At the same time, some devout Muslims had difficulty accepting secular Western culture. Some commentators have emphasized that Islam is not new to Europe but has been a vital part of European society for many centuries.

McKay Chapter 30 Focus Questions

1. How did life change in Russia and the former East Lock countries after 1989?

2. How did globalization affect European life and society?

3. What are the main causes and effect of growing ethnic diversity in contemporary Europe?

4. What challenges will Europeans face in the coming decades?

NOTES:

SECTION 2: Prep Guide

Preparing for the AP® Exam

This section includes two complete AP® European History practice exams. You should take the tests toward the end of your AP® course and evaluate your weaknesses and strengths. If you can do well on these practice tests, we are confident you will do well on the AP® Exam in May.

As mentioned in the preface, this guide does not include answers to the exam questions. This is because some teachers like to use these practice exams for credit. Your teacher has access to the practice exam answers (for essays: what good answers will include), and can provide them to you, depending on his or her plans for utilizing this book in class. If your teacher gives you the answer key and allows you to practice the exams on your own, do not just get your score and leave it at that. Take the time to look over each question carefully and read the explanations of what makes a good essay response. Make a list of what you got wrong. Are there topics in which you were particularly weak as indicated by a high proportion of wrong answers? Are there certain types of questions that you often got wrong? Did you struggle with your essays? Once you have a better sense of what you need to work on, you can prepare better for the actual AP® Exam. Do not be shy about asking your teacher, too; he or she is likely to be able to make recommendations about where to focus your energies.

Registering for the Exam

Most likely your school will be taking care of this for you, but if not, make sure that you register in time, sometime during the month of February. If you are homeschooled, you need to contact AP® Services at the College Board by March 1 to find out the name of an AP® coordinator near you; you will have two weeks to make contact and locate a school near you where you can take the examination. If you qualify for extra time or are a student with a disability, make sure that all your paperwork is in order and that the AP® coordinator at your school is aware of your special needs. The coordinator will have to submit an SSD form by mid-February if documentation is needed or early March if it is not. Check the AP® Web site early for exact dates.

If your family is struggling to pay the full examination fee, it can be reduced by the College Board through your school, so look into this early. Not only does the College Board provide a subsidy, but many states also help underwrite the cost of exams for low-income students. Qualification information is available on the College Board Web site (http://apcentral.collegeboard.com) in February, through your school's AP® coordinator, or via your state's department of education Web site. There is also a useful downloadable Bulletin for AP® Students and Parents at the site. If you have questions, e-mail apexams@info.collegeboard.org or call AP® Services at 609-771-7300 or 888-225-5427.

Familiarizing Yourself with the Exam

If your teacher has not given you AP® Exam questions or old AP® Exams as practice, you should look closely at these two practice tests in this book. You can also go to the AP® Web site (http://apcentral.collegeboard.com) and review the many past exams that have been posted there.

The AP® European History Exam is three hours and fifteen minutes long and consists of two section. The first section of the exam consists of two parts. Part A will be multiple-choice and Part B will be short-answer questions. You will have 55 minutes to complete 55 multiple-choice questions in Part A. Each question contains four answer options. Part A will account for 40% of your total score. Part B will consist of four short-answer questions; you will be required to answer the first two questions, but will then be able to choose between #3 or #4 as your third question to answer. You will have 40 minutes for Part B, which will account for 20% of your score. The second section of the exam will also have two parts. Part A will be one document-based question. It will include seven documents followed by an essay question and will account for 25% of your score. You will have 60 minutes to complete Part A. It is recommended that you spend the first 15 minutes of that time reading the documents and planning your essay. Part B will be the long-essay question. You will be offered three long-essay questions but only answer one. Part B will account for 15% of your grade and you will have 40 minutes to complete it.

Setting Up a Review Schedule

Your teacher will almost certainly organize review sessions or review in class, but often that is insufficient to feel really ready for the exam. You might want to reread the textbook to prepare, but for most students, that's impossible because of time constraints. Thus, a study guide like this one is an excellent way to prepare, as it crystallizes the information in the textbook and allows you to hear a fresh voice. See those Guided Reading Questions in the Section 1 of this guide—they are a helpful review.

You should schedule three weeks of review time in order to prepare for the exam, but in most cases, your teacher will still be trying to teach the rest of the course in April. For this reason, you will have to begin reviewing while you are still learning new material. What is the best way to do this?

Ideally, take the three weeks leading up to the exam and read one chapter of the study guide a night, which, if you remain focused, should be about a half-hour's work. Since there are twenty-three chapters, this works out to a little over three weeks of review. If this plan doesn't work for you, try to set up a schedule before the end of April in which you complete two or three chapters a night. On the exam, time periods 3 to 6 each comprise 20 percent of the multiple-choice questions, while periods 1 and 2 combined make up the remaining 20 percent, so you can't afford to neglect any part of the year's curriculum during your preparation.

The time before the AP® Exams is often very hectic for students. If you are on an athletic team, you may have playoffs or championship games, and the workload in all your classes may be getting intense as the year is coming to its conclusion. You do not want to let your other responsibilities get in the way of earning a 5 on the exam, so an absolute key to success is time management. While this is always useful, it is crucial in the period before AP® Exams. Otherwise, you will not prepare much and have to rely on your innate abilities and your memory. In most cases, such "preparation" will not bring you to a score higher than 3. If you want the 5, you will need to spend the week or two before the AP® Exam preparing for the test instead of socializing or focusing on your other activities.

Is it worth it? Absolutely! In almost every college, a score of 5, and in some places a 4, will bring you three or more credits. Even if you do not receive college credit, you might be placed directly into advanced-level history courses. *Since you are very likely taking this exam as a sophomore, garnering a good score is something you can include on your college applications. It will help set you apart as a good college candidate.*

The AP® Exam is physically grueling—about an hour's worth of multiple-choice questions and two hours of writing. If you are not used to writing by hand, be sure to practice in the weeks before the exam, otherwise your hand might cramp up or get tired. Be sure to eat well, stay away from junk food, and get enough sleep the night before the exam so that your body will be an ally and not a detriment to you. Be sure to have a good and healthy breakfast before the exam so your energies will not flag in the last hour. Do not drink too many liquids; you don't want to lose valuable exam time making frequent bathroom visits. Take a snack in with you to the exam for the break if that's allowed, wear comfortable clothes and shoes, and bring a sweater or jacket in case the room is cold. You do not want anything to interfere with your ability to concentrate on the exam. Most importantly, bring a watch! *You will not be able to use your cell phone to help you with timing.* You need a good, reliable timepiece that will accurately tell you how much time is left. *Do not assume there will be a clock in the room.*

Your examination proctor will certainly remind you of this, but in any case, leave all cell phones and other electronic devices outside the examination room. If you are involved in a breach of security, your examination will likely be canceled, and there could be other consequences at your school. It's simply not worth it to take such a chance.

How the Exams Are Scored

It helps to know how the exams are scored so that you can understand how to earn the highest score. The multiple-choice question answers are scored electronically, but the essays and short answer questions are read by people.

In June more than 1,000 readers—university professors and high school AP® European History teachers—meet for a week in a central location to read and score the essays and short answer questions. Readers are organized into groups of eight at a table, chaired by a table leader who is responsible for quality control.

The exams are scored in June, and you can access your scores online on an assigned date in July.

You should not need this, but just in case: if the exam proves to be a disaster—which it certainly should not—you can cancel the score in writing by mail or fax to AP® Services by June 15, before you get your score. You can also have AP® Services withhold a score from being sent to a college.

AP® European History Exam Strategies

If you are well prepared, you will be successful on the AP® Exam; however, there are key test-taking skills that will all but guarantee that you get the score that your level of mastery should bring you.

The single most common problem is not reading the question carefully or ignoring parts of a question. For the essays, read the question carefully, think about what the question is asking, and answer every part. Students sometimes answer the question they know or the one they wish had been asked, rather than the one that has been asked; this is particularly true on the essays but can be true on multiple-choice questions, too. Do not rush and assume you understand the question before you read it carefully.

Types of Multiple-Choice Questions

There are seven types of multiple-choice questions that appear on the AP Exam. All questions will be grouped in sets of 2-5 questions and will refer to a provided stimulus, such as a primary or secondary text, a map, photograph, or work of art. The questions will test your ability to interpret the stimulus and relate it to your own knowledge of European history. The questions below are included as examples of how multiple choice questions test your historical thinking skills.

Causation

Causation questions will ask you to look at the relationship between causes—either short term or long term—and effects.

Example:

"The Petrograd Council of Workmen's and Soldiers' Delegates considers this to be the program of the new authority:
First–The offer of an immediate democratic peace.
Second–The immediate handing over of large proprietorial lands to the peasants.
Third–The transmission of all authority to the Council of Workmen's and Soldiers' Delegates.
Fourth–The honest convocation of a Constitutional Assembly.
The national revolutionary army must not permit uncertain military detachments to leave the front for Petrograd. They should use persuasion, but where this fails they must oppose any such action on the part of these detachments by force without mercy.
Soldiers! For peace, for bread, for land, and for the power of the people!"

Records of the Great War, Vol. V, ed. Charles F. Horne

Which of the following was the most immediate cause of the success of the Bolshevik Revolution in 1918?

    (a) The organization of the Comintern
    (b) The failure of the Czar Nicholas II to attempt political reforms
    (c) The fall of Stalingrad to German armies
    (d) The hardships faced in Russia due to World War I

Answer: D

Chronological Reasoning

Chronological reasoning questions will test your understanding of changes and continuities within or between time periods.

Example:

"From this it follows that women, by nature indolent and unable to keep secrets, are little suited to government, particularly if one also considers that they are subject to their emotions and consequently little susceptible to reason and justice, attributes which should exclude them from all public office. This is not to say that a few might be found so free of these faults as to make them admissible to public service. There are few general rules for which no exceptions can be found. This era bears witness to several women whose deeds cannot be praised enough. But it is true that their weakness denies them the masculine vigor necessary to public administration, and it is almost impossible for them to govern without a base exploitation of their sex, or without acts of injustice and cruelty arising from the disorderly ascendancy of their emotions."

Cardinal Richelieu, Political Testament, 1691

Which of the following was an important continuity in European history from the 15th to the 17th century illustrated in this excerpt?

    (a) Opportunities in public service were growing steadily by the 17th century
    (b) Women were typically excluded from public service due to gender
    (c) Aristocratic women were more likely to be given opportunities in public service
    (d) Women gained opportunities as education became more available

Answer: B

Comparison

Comparison questions ask you to compare related historical developments and processes across geography, chronology, or different societies, or within one society.

Example:

"Required as we are, universally, to support and obey the laws, nature and reason entitle us to demand, that in the making of the laws, the universal voice shall be implicitly listened to.
We perform the duties of freemen; we must have the privileges of freemen.
WE DEMAND UNIVERSAL SUFFRAGE.
The suffrage to be exempt from the corruption of the wealthy, and the violence of the powerful, must be secret.
The assertion of our right necessarily involves the power of its uncontrolled exercise.
WE DEMAND THE BALLOT.
The connection between the representatives and the people, to be beneficial must be intimate.
The legislative and constituent powers, for correction and for instruction, ought to be brought into frequent contact."

The Chartist Movement, The People's Petition, 1838

Which of the following groups would most likely support the ideas expressed by the Chartist Movement?

(a) Jacobin controlled Committee of Public Safety in Paris 1793
(b) Members of the National Assembly who met at Versailles in 1789
(c) Leaders at the Congress of Vienna in 1815
(d) Philosophers who supported the ideas of Charles Fourier

Answer: B

Contextualization

Contextualization questions test your ability to recognize how historical phenomena or processes connect to broader regional, national, or global processes.

Example:

"Rousseau declares that a woman should never, for a moment, feel herself independent, that she should be governed by fear to exercise her natural cunning, and made a coquettish slave in order to render her a more alluring object of desire, a sweeter companion to man, whenever he chooses to relax himself. He carries the arguments, which he pretends to draw from the indications of nature, still further, and insinuates that truth and fortitude, the corner stones of all human virtue, should be cultivated with certain restrictions, because, with respect to the female character, obedience is the grand lesson which ought to be impressed with unrelenting rigour.

... That women at present are by ignorance rendered foolish or vicious is, I think, not to be disputed; and that the most salutary effects tending to improve mankind might be expected from a REVOLUTION in female manners, appears, at least with a face of probability, to rise out of the observation."

Mary Wollstonecraft, *A Vindication of the Rights of Woman with Strictures on Political and Moral Subjects,* London, 1792

The excerpt from Mary Wollstonecraft is best understood in which of the following contexts?

(a) Rise of feminism related to women's actions in the French Revolution
(b) Influence of Utopian Socialism on education of women
(c) Divisions between British political parties on women's suffrage in 19th century
(d) Rising fears that women's suffrage would lead to support for Marxist movements

Answer: A

Historical Argumentation

Historical argumentation questions require you to identify the answer choice that best supports a conclusion or assertion from a historical argument.

Example:

"We all know that the two World Wars through which we have passed arose out of the vain passion of Germany to play a dominating part in the world. In this last struggle crimes and massacres have been committed for which there is no parallel since the Mongol invasion of the 13th century, no equal at any time in human history. The guilty must be punished. Germany must be deprived of the power to rearm and make another aggressive war. But when all this has been done, as it will be done, as it is being done, there must be an end to retribution. There must be what Mr Gladstone many years ago called a "blessed act of oblivion". We must all turn our backs upon the horrors of the past and look to the future. We cannot afford to drag forward across the years to come hatreds and revenges which have sprung from the injuries of the past. If Europe is to be saved from infinite misery, and indeed from final doom, there must be this act of faith in the European family, this act of oblivion against all crimes and follies of the past. ..."

Winston Churchill, Speech delivered at the University of Zurich, 19 September 1946

Which of the following best supports the argument made by Winston Churchill regarding the actions taken toward Germany after World War II?

   (a) The agreements made at the Potsdam Conference effectively determined the means to limit the power of Germany after World War II.

   (b) Most Europeans were opposed to moving towards a unified Europe after World War II.

   (c) European leaders in the victorious nations following World War II were motivated by a desire to reunite Germany.

   (d) The chain of events leading to World War II were related to the failures of European diplomacy following World War I.

Answer: D

Historical Interpretation

     Historical interpretation questions ask you to critique various historical interpretations of a specific event.

Example:

     ". . . both sides of human consciousness–the side turned to the world and that turned inward– lay, as it were, beneath a common veil, dreaming or half awake. The veil was woven of faith, childlike prejudices, and illusion; seen through it, world and history appeared in strange hues; man recognized himself only as a member of a race, a nation, a party, a corporation, a family, or in some other general category. It was in Italy that this veil first melted into thin air, and awakened an objective perception and treatment of the state and all things of this world in general; but by its side, and with full power, there also arose the subjective; man becomes a self-aware individual and recognises himself as such."

          Jacob Burckhardt, *The Civilization of the Renaissance in Italy,* 1860, translated 1878

Which of the following evidence would counter the view of the Renaissance expressed by Jakob Burckhardt?

   (a) The existence of an urban, elite class of rulers as patrons in Italian city-states.

   (b) The influence of Greek texts through extended trade networks in the Mediterranean.

   (c) The invention and dissemination of the printing press in Northern Europe.

   (d) The expansion of papal power and patronage of the arts through the Catholic Church.

Answer: C

Use of Evidence

In this question, students are expected to analyze one type of historical evidence: audience, purpose, point of view, format, or argument.

Example:

     "On the contrary, new barriers need to be erected against the exploitation of the proletarian woman. Her rights as wife and mother need to be restored and permanently secured. Her final aim is not the free competition with the man, but the achievement of the political rule of the proletariat. The proletarian woman fights hand in hand with the man of her class against capitalist society. To be sure, she also agrees with the demands of the bourgeois women's movement, but she regards the fulfillment of these demands simply as a means to enable that movement to enter the battle, equipped with the same weapons, alongside the proletariat."

          Clara Zetkin. Speech at the Party Congress of the
       Social Democratic Party of Germany, Gotha, October 16th, 1896

In the excerpt above, Zetkin's main purpose is to argue that

   (a) negative consequences for women result from women fighting for equality with men in the workplace.

   (b) the lack of women's rights results from the weakness of Proletarian women in the work force.

(c) women in Europe should abandon the fight for women's rights and instead focus on the Marxist fight against capitalism.

(d) because proletarian women agree with demands of bourgeois women, they should unite to demand equal rights for all women.

Answer: C

Strategies for Multiple-Choice Questions (MCQ)

1. **Pace yourself.** You are expected to answer the questions in one minute per question, so do not spend a long time on any one question. If you are struggling to select the correct answer, leave it and return to it at the end of the allotted time. On the other hand, do not rush. Get to know how long a minute is. Time yourself often so you know the rhythm of the exam.

2. **Make sure that you fill in your answers accurately and in a timely fashion.** If you skip a question, be sure that you skip an answer on the answer sheet. Periodically check that you are filling in the circles on the correct line. You do not want to find at the end of the exam that you have filled in the wrong circles for your answers, as you may not have time to correct the errors. If you like working questions in your test booklet and THEN bubbling in the answers, make sure you leave plenty of time to do so. Once time is called, you will not be able to fill in the bubbles. Anything in your multiple-choice test booklet will not be scored.

3. **About guessing:** until 2011, there was a penalty of one-quarter of a point off for each wrong answer, but this has been eliminated for AP® Exams in all subjects. As there is no longer a guessing penalty, answer every question, even with a wild guess. You have nothing to lose and a 25 percent chance of getting the answer right.

4. **Some questions will be straightforward and easy,** so don't assume that they are trying to trick you. The fifty-five questions will vary in difficulty; a number of them are easy and will be answered correctly by the vast majority of students. Similarly, there will be a few multiple-choice questions that are really tough, and only a small percentage of students will get them right.

5. **The higher you score on the multiple-choice section,** the greater the likelihood of a high score on the exam. Remember, the multiple-choice section counts for 40% of your final score.

6. **Read each question and its answer choices carefully** and be sure to notice if the question is an "except" question. Use the process of elimination as you read the choices (you can write on the exam booklet), crossing out the choices you know for sure are wrong. General rules of thumb: absolute answers — "all of the above" or "none of the above" — are usually wrong. Remember, the correct answer for a multiple-choice question should be the best answer of the four options. Typically, one potential answer will be clearly and definitively wrong, two might be correct or partially true, while the remaining one is the most accurate or complete answer to the question.

Strategies for Short-Answer Questions (SAQ)

Each short answer question will be graded on a scale of 0-3. You will be required to answer SAQ#1 and SAQ#2, but then you will have the choice of whether to answer SAQ#3 or SAQ#4. It does not matter which one you choose to complete. In total, you will answer three SAQs on the AP® exam. the SAQ section will test particular skills. The first question will primarily assess your ability to analyze secondary sources by responding to a historian's argument on a topic from 1600 to 2001. The second SAQ will assess either the skill of causation OR continuity and change over time in relation to a primary source (written or visual). You will have a choice between two final short-answer questions—one will deal with periods 1-2 and the other periods 3-4. Both of these choices will deal with either causation or change and continuity over time (but not the same skill as assessed in the second SAQ). Some of the SAQs will be based on a stimulus, but not all of them will be. To answer each of the questions you will need to be able to interpret the stimulus but also to incorporate prior knowledge of European history. Not surprisingly, the stimulus is intended to stimulate your thought memory and thought processes; you will not be able to infer from it all the information you will need to answer the question.

You will be provided with an answer sheet for each Short Answer Question. Your answer sheet will contain a box. You must write your answer within the box and you cannot use additional space. This will force you to keep your answer succinct.

Strategies for the Document-Based Question (DBQ)

The DBQ tests your abilities with multiple skills: analyzing primary sources, contextualization, and argument development. It requires that you develop an argument based on primary documents, cite the documents specifically as evidence, extend your analysis of the documents by analyzing the author's point of view or purpose, and incorporate relevant context and evidence from beyond the documents.

While this may sound like a tall order you should remember many successful essays will be able to accomplish some but not all of the tasks mentioned above. Furthermore, readers understand that you are under time pressure and are trained to regard your essay as a first draft. Consequently, neither grammatical errors nor occasional factual errors will detract from your score.

DBQ Scoring

The basic premise of scoring is that there are specific and identifiable skills that can be articulated as demonstrations of competence in DBQ essay writing. The maximum score you can receive on a DBQ will be seven points.

1. **Thesis (1 point).** One point will be awarded for a thesis that makes a historically defensible claim, consists of one or more sentences, and is located in the first or final paragraph of the essay.

2. **Evidence & Reasoning (3 points).** Students will receive one point for utilizing the content of at least three documents to address the topic or question. An additional point will be awarded if students use the content of at least six documents to support the topic or question. And a third point will be awarded if students use historical reasoning to explain relationships between the pieces of evidence provided in the response and explain how they corroborate, quantify, or modify the an argument that addresses the entirety of the question. Students will only receive a third point if they meet all the criteria of the second evidence point.

3. **Document Analysis (1 point).** One point will be awarded if students use four documents, and explain each document's point of view, purpose, historical situation, and/or how the audience is relevant to the argument.

4. **Contextualization (1 point).** Students must utilize information not contained in the documents to explain relevant historical events or processes. "Contextualization" in this case refers to an explanation of a larger historic process or development which sets the context for the argument of the essay. Setting the historical context for merely a single document will not be sufficient. It is recommended that you include this in the introduction, in the same paragraph as the thesis, or in the conclusion.

5. **Evidence Beyond the Documents (1 point).** Students will receive one point for using at least one additional piece of evidence beyond those found in the documents provided.

Other DBQ Essay-Writing Tips

1. **Pay attention to the wording of the question.** It is crucial that your essay directly responds to the prompt. If the question asks for a comparison, for example, you must show similarities and differences. If the questions asks you to address causes, you must address causes and/or effects. Note also that if the prompt includes pluralized words (eg., causes, responses, results, relationships), you must discuss more than one.

2. **Do not repeat the historical background.** Each DBQ begins with a question, followed by a paragraph called historical background, which is designed to give you key information you need to understand and analyze the documents. You may use or refer to it, of course, but do not waste your time repeating it. The readers already know it well.

3. **There are no intentionally misleading or trick documents.** You should use every document. Even though you are allowed to use only six out of seven, using all seven provides you with some insurance in case you misinterpret one of the documents. Think of this like a jigsaw puzzle: every document has a place in the narrative you are creating.

4. **Do not simply paraphrase or summarize a document.** In fact, given the time constraints, it is not recommended that you provide lengthy quotations from any of the documents. The point is to show that you can use the documents to support a historical argument; not merely that you know what they say. If you use quotations, keep them brief, and make sure you provide a context for such quotations in your own words.

Be sure to examine the DBQs, the essays, and the generic rubrics available to you on the College Board Web site for students, www.collegeboard.com/testing. While you will not be provided with a copy of the rubric as you take the test, the essential requirements of the DBQ will be provided to you at the beginning of the question.

Strategies for the Long-Essay Question (LEQ)

There will be three long-essay questions on your test and you will choose one. Each will test the same historical thinking skill: comparison, causation, continuity and change over time. While each essay choice will address the same skill, they may refer to different regions and/or time periods.

LEQ Scoring

The LEQ will be scored on a 0-6 scale.

1. **Thesis (1 point).** One point will be awarded for a thesis that presents a defensible claim and addresses all parts of the question (e.g., change *and* continuity, similarities *and* differences, causes *and/or* effects, or why a particular event or time period should or should not be characterized as a turning point). The thesis may be one or multiple sentences and may appear in the first paragraph or in the conclusion.

2. **Evidence and Reasoning (3 points).** This portion of the LEQ rubric will award one point for providing accurate and specific examples of historical evidence that is related to the topic of the question. A second point will be awarded if the student effectively uses the given evidence to support an argument in response to the prompt. Finally, a third evidence point will be given for using historical reasoning in a way that illustrates the relationship between different pieces of evidence that shows corroboration, qualification, or modification of an argument that addresses the entire prompt.

3. **Contextualization (2 points).** One point will be given for accurately describing a broader historical context that is directly related to the topic of the prompt. It is highly recommended that contextualization be included in the introduction to the essay before the thesis. This point can not be awarded for evidence used in other parts of the essay. A second point will be awarded for contextualization that goes farther to explain the influence of the historical context on the specific topic addressed in the prompt. Again, there is no "double dipping:" evidence used to gain the 1-3 points for Evidence and Reasoning can not be used to award these points.

Interpreting Your Results on a Practice Exam

1. First, look at the multiple-choice score. It is a fair indicator of what your overall score will be. How many out of fifty-five did you get right?

2. Check to see if you got too many wrong answers for the goal you have set for yourself. Examine the ones you got wrong to see if you got them wrong because you did not know the answer or because you guessed poorly. Look at those questions closely to see what you might have missed that would have helped you make a better choice.

3. Examine your essay scores. What strengths and weaknesses do you find? If you did not do as well as you would have liked, try to focus on whatever problems you had in writing the essays. Was it your thesis statement, use of evidence, errors, or lack of organization? Once you identify your difficulties, you can focus your attention on addressing them.

4. Set a realistic goal for yourself. 60% of your score will be based on your written responses so it pays to write well. The more you can strive to become a well-rounded student, the more likely it is that you will be able to earn a 5 on the AP® Exam.

5. Make it happen!

NOTES:

PRACTICE EXAM 1

EUROPEAN HISTORY SECTION I

Total time: 1 hour, 35 minutes

Part A: Multiple-Choice Questions

Time: 55 minutes

Questions 1-3 refer to the passage below.

"Finally the Great Artisan ordained that man, to whom He could give nothing belonging only to himself, should share in common whatever properties had been peculiar to each of the other creatures. He received man, therefore, as a creature of undetermined nature, and placing him in the middle of the universe, said this to him: 'Neither an established place, nor a form belonging to you alone, nor any special function have We given to you, O Adam, and for this reason, that you may have and possess, according to your desire and judgment, whatever place, whatever form, and whatever functions you shall desire. The nature of other creatures, which has been determined, is confined within the bounds prescribed by Us. You, who are confined by no limits, shall determine for yourself your own nature, in accordance with your own free will . . .'"

Giovanni Pico della Mirandola, Italian nobleman and philosopher, *Oration on the Dignity of Man,* 1486

1. Mirandola most directly reflected the beliefs of

   a. Secularists
   b. Realists
   c. Modernists
   d. Humanists

2. Which of the following most accurately describes who would have read Mirandola's work?

   a. Members of mass-based political parties who sought political change
   b. Peasants and serfs who sought to understand economic influences in agriculture
   c. Princes and commercial elites who were often patrons of the arts
   d. Absolute monarchs who often sought to limit the power of the nobility

3. Which of the following most likely helped spread Mirandola's ideas?

   a. The printing press
   b. The clergy
   c. The enlightened monarchs
   d. The innovations in banking

Questions 4-6 refer to the painting below by Benozzo Gozzoli, c. 1459.

Frescoes of the Chapel of the Magi, by Benozzo di Lese di Sandro known as Benozzo Gozzoli, 15th Century, 1459-1460
Electra/UIG/REX/Shutterstock
© 2017 Bedford/St. Martin's
Distributed by Bedford/St. Martin's/Macmillan Higher Education strictly for use with its products; not for redistribution.

4. All of the following are characteristics of Renaissance art EXCEPT

  a. an emphasis on nature
  b. an emphasis on the individual
  c. influences from African art styles
  d. influences from Greek and Roman art styles

5. Which of the following most directly inspired the painting above?

  a. Romanticism, which emphasized emotion and the supernatural
  b. Classicism, which promoted a revival in ancient texts
  c. Secularism, which emphasized political authority
  d. Absolutism, which celebrated the power of the state

6. Which later movement most directly challenged the artistic movement represented by the painting?

  a. Humanism, which focused on humans being the measure of all things
  b. Cubism, which rested on subjective interpretations of reality by the individual artist or writer
  c. Baroque, which glorified state power
  d. Mannerism, which employed distortion, drama, and illusion

Questions 7-9 refer to the graph below, showing the increase in population in Europe, 1650-1850.

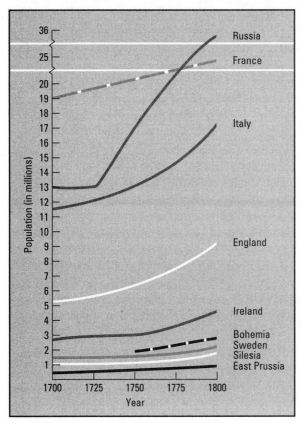

Figure 17.2, The Increase in Population in Europe, 1650-1850
Data from Massimo Livi Bacci, The Population of Europe [Wiley-Blackwell, 2000], p. 8.
Chapter 17, *A History of Western Society,* Eleventh Edition
© 2017 Bedford/St. Martin's

7. What conclusion can be drawn about the rise in population in Europe during the eighteenth century?

   a. The biggest increases were in industrializing areas
   b. The biggest increases were in mostly agricultural countries
   c. Northern Europe had the highest rate of increase
   d. Southern Europe had the highest rate of increase

8. Which of the following best describes the reason for the rise in population depicted in the graph?

   a. Population grew due to raised productivity and increased supply of food and other products
   b. New efficient methods of transportation and other innovations created new industries
   c. Developments in price regulation led to a rise in population to pre-Great Plague levels
   d. Economic alliances such as the Common Market spurred economic recovery and development

9. Which of the following best accounts for the rise in population shown in Russia?

   a. The Russians implemented the New Economic Policy, which assisted in food distribution.
   b. During the eighteenth century, the Russians shifted from binding serfdom to a free peasantry, which increased the standard of living.
   c. Peter the Great "westernized" the Russian state and society, leading to reforms continued by Catherine the Great.
   d. Russians implemented plans of *perestroika* and *glasnost,* designed to make Russia economically better, leading to greater access to commodities.

Questions 10-12 refer to the graph below, showing exports of English manufactured goods, 1700-1774.

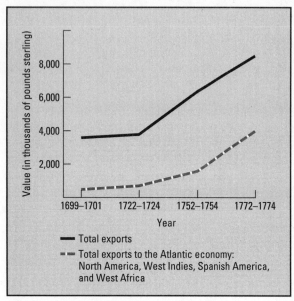

Figure 17.3, Exports of English Manufactured Goods, 1700-1774
Data from R. Davis, "English Foreign Trade, 1700-1774," *Economic History Review*, 2d ser., 15 [1962]: 302-303.
Chapter 17, *A History of Western Society*, Eleventh Edition
© 2017 Bedford/St. Martin's
Distributed by Bedford/St. Martin's/Macmillan Higher Education strictly for use with its products; not for redistribution.

10. Which of the following accounts for the rise in exports to the Atlantic economy?

    a. Communication and transportation technologies allowed for the creation of European empires
    b. New technologies, such as the railroad, created global economic networks
    c. Volatile business cycles led to the creation of tariffs on foreign goods
    d. Europeans expanded the slave trade in response to the establishment of a plantation economy in the Americas

11. How did the exports depicted on the graph affect Europe's economy?

    a. Overseas products contributed to the development of a consumer culture in Europe
    b. The exporting of goods diminished commercial and industrial enterprises in Europe
    c. Demand for English exports reduced the demand for a slave-labor system in Europe
    d. European countries rejected mercantilism as a successful economic system

12. Which of the following developments was most directly a result of the changes depicted in the graph?

    a. The development of advanced weaponry led to the military dominance of Asia and Africa over Europe in the late nineteenth century.
    b. The search from raw materials and markets for manufactured goods led Europeans to colonize Africa in the late nineteenth century.
    c. Independence for Africans and Asians occurred rapidly in the aftermath of World War I.
    d. The League of Nations encouraged the abolishment of the mandate system to encourage African colonial independence during the early twentieth century.

Questions 13-16 refer to the frontispiece below from Thomas Hobbe's *Leviathan* (1651).

Title page of *Leviathan* by Thomas Hobbes (London, 1651).
Images Group/REX/Shutterstock
© 2017 Bedford/St. Martin's
Distributed by Bedford/St. Martin's/Macmillan Higher Education strictly for use with its products; not for redistribution.

13. Which of the following political philosophies is best depicted in the image above?

    a. The establishment of a republican form of government
    b. The complete control of Parliament over the monarch
    c. The creation of an universal Christian empire
    d. The support of a monarch's power over Parliament

14. Thomas Hobbes wrote *Leviathan* in response to which event?

    a. The Glorious Revolution
    b. The French Revolution
    c. The English Civil War
    d. The Thirty Years' War

15. Which of the following was most directly a result of the beliefs illustrated in the image?

   a. Absolute monarchies grew throughout western Europe, limiting the nobility's participation in governance

   b. Central and eastern European countries experienced republican revolutions, challenging the power of the monarchy

   c. Challenges to absolutism grew throughout western Europe, asserting the rights of legislative bodies

   d. Central and eastern European countries experienced successful peasant rebellions, leading to the abolishment of serfdom

16. Which economic system is most directly reflected in the beliefs illustrated in the image?

   a. Mercantilism, which emphasized the need to increase one's economic power over others by gaining a greater share of the existing sources of wealth

   b. Capitalism, which focused on individual investment of capital and wealth

   c. Socialism, which argued for state ownership of property and economic planning to promote equality

   d. Communism, which inspired working-class movements and revolutions

Questions 17-19 refer to the two maps below, showing the Industrial Revolution in Great Britain and on the continent, ca. 1850.

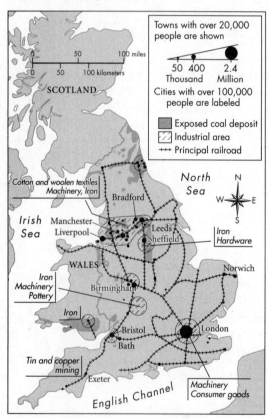

Map 20.1, The Industrial Revolution in Great Britain, ca. 1850
Chapter 20, *A History of Western Society*, Eleventh Edition
© 2017 Bedford/St. Martin's
Distributed by Bedford/St. Martin's/Macmillan Higher Education strictly for use with its products; not for redistribution.

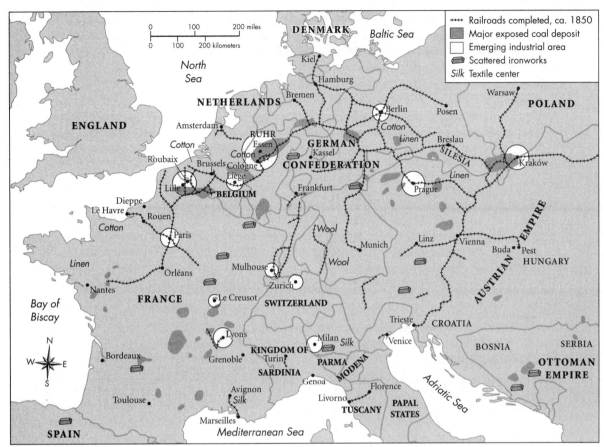

Map 20.2, Continental Industrialization, ca. 1850
Chapter 20, *A History of Western Society,* Eleventh Edition
© 2017 Bedford/St. Martin's
Distributed by Bedford/St. Martin's/Macmillan Higher Education strictly for use with its products; not for redistribution.

17. Which of the following statements is an accurate conclusion based on a comparison of these maps showing England (left) and the European continent in about 1850 (above)?

    a. England had more industrialized areas than the continent because of England's abundance of natural resources.
    b. England had a greater population than the German Confederation and France combined, due to the development of vaccinations in the eighteenth and nineteenth centuries.
    c. The continent had more ironworks per capita than England because of laissez-faire capitalism.
    d. England had a more efficient and interconnected railroad system than the continent did because of nineteenth century liberal political ideologies.

18. Which of the following historical developments best explains the growth of railroads depicted in the maps above?

    a. France moved toward industrialization at a more gradual pace than Great Britain
    b. The government in Prussia did not support developments in industrialization
    c. Continental Europe lacked natural resources to support industrialization
    d. The Industrial Revolution began in continental Europe and spread to Great Britain

19. Which of the following statements best describes the population development depicted on the map?

    a. With migration from urban to rural areas, agricultural communities experienced overcrowding.
    b. Uneven price increases along with low wages led to a decreased standard of living for some.
    c. Industrialization, along with the commercialization of agriculture, promoted population growth.
    d. Population growth developed due to new medical technologies and theories, and led to prolonged life.

Questions 20-22 refer to the table below, showing per capital levels of industrialization, ca. 1750-1913.

	1750	1800	1830	1860	1880	1900	1913
Great Britan	10	16	25	64	87	100	115
Belgium	9	10	14	28	43	56	88
United States	4	9	14	21	38	69	126
France	9	9	12	20	28	39	59
Germany	8	8	9	15	25	52	85
Austria–Hungary	7	7	8	11	15	23	32
Italy	8	8	8	10	12	17	26
Russia	6	6	7	8	10	15	20
China	8	6	6	4	4	3	3
India	7	6	6	3	2	1	2

Table 20.1, Per Capita Levels of Industrialization, ca. 1750-1913
P. Bairoch, "International Industrialization Levels from 1750 to 1980," *Journal of European Economic History* 11 (Spring 1982):
294, U.S. Journals at Cambridge University Press.
Chapter 20, *A History of Western Society,* Twelfth Edition

20. The table above illustrates

    a. the gap between Great Britain's textile production and that of other countries due to mercantilist practices in Europe

    b. that Great Britain's per capita income increased four times by 1860 because of liberal, bourgeois economic policies

    c. that the United States had the fastest rate of increase in per capita industrialization in the nineteenth century due to the lack of industrial development in Continental Europe

    d. that Germany was an industrial competitive force during the early nineteenth century in part due to trade unions

21. Which development described below is best reflected in the chart above on Europe?

    a. Green parties in western and central Europe challenged consumerism and cautioned against globalization.

    b. New technologies enhanced traditional military strategies and led to massive troop losses during World War I

    c. European states began to develop mercantilist policies, which exploited colonies throughout the world.

    d. Serfdom was codified in eastern Europe, resulting in the nobility dominating economic life on large estates.

22. Which statement best describes the differences in industrial development throughout Europe?

    a. Napoleon's government-supported industrial development allowed France to become a leading industrial power.

    b. The English Civil War led to political division and upheaval, resulting in a lag in industrial development.

    c. Lack of resources, dominance of landed elites, and inadequate government sponsorship led to eastern Europe's lag in industrialization.

    d. Bismarck's rejection of industrial development contributed to slow industrial growth in Germany.

Questions 23-25 refer to the cartoon below.

Leopold, King of the Congo, in his national dress
Granger, NYC – All rights reserved.
Chapter 24, *A History of Western Society*, Twelfth Edition
© 2017 Bedford/St. Martin's
Distributed by Bedford/St. Martin's/Macmillan Higher Education strictly for use with its products; not for redistribution.

23. The 1908 cartoon above, *Leopold, King of the Congo, in his national dress,* depicts

    a. the end of colonial rule in the Congo
    b. growing scrutiny of imperialism in Europe by Europeans
    c. the bitterness of African nobles toward Western colonists
    d. the brutality of native Africans toward whites

24. Which of the following was a significant motivation of European imperialism, which led to developments like the one depicted above?

    a. Europeans justified imperialism through an ideology of cultural and racial superiority.
    b. Europeans justified imperialism through modernization movements to implement new technology.
    c. Europeans justified imperialism through mercantilist economic policies.
    d. Europeans justified imperialism through concerns about sustainable development and globalization.

25. Which of the following developments occurred as a result of the actions depicted in the cartoon above?

    a. Indigenous, nationalist movements led to independence in Africa and Asia during the mid-to-late twentieth century.
    b. The League of Nations dismantled the mandate system, which had created further imperial control in Africa and Asia.
    c. Competition for trade led to conflicts and rivalries among European imperial empires in Africa and Asia.
    d. The exchange of new plants, animals, and diseases facilitated European destruction of indigenous peoples.

Questions 26-29 refer to the passage below.

"21. Thus those indulgence preachers are in error who say that a man is absolved from every penalty and saved by papal indulgences. . . .

26. The pope does very well when he grants remission to souls in purgatory, not by the power of the keys, which he does not have, but by way of intercession for them.

27. They preach only human doctrines who say that as soon as the money clinks into the money chest, the soul flies out of purgatory.

28. It is certain that when money clinks in the money chest, greed and avarice can be increased; but when the church intercedes, the result is in the hands of God alone."

Martin Luther, theologian, *95 Theses*, 1517

26. The passage above reflects which of the following historical developments?

    a. The rational analysis of religious practices led to natural religion and demand for religious toleration

    b. New relativism in values led to modernism in intellectual and cultural life

    c. Reformers criticized Catholic abuses and established new interpretations of Christian doctrine

    d. Reform in the Catholic Church found expression in the Second Vatican Council, which redefined church dogma

27. Which of the following most directly influenced the beliefs reflected in the statement above?

    a. Monarchs and princes, who initiated religious reforms in an effort to exercise greater control over religious life, such as Henry VIII in England

    b. Christian humanists, who employed Renaissance learning in the service of religious reform

    c. Jesuits, who focused on religious reform within the Catholic Church

    d. The Habsburgs, who sought to restore Catholic unity across Europe during the Thirty Years' War

28. Which of the following was most directly a result of the ideas reflected in the statements above?

    a. Christianity established increased religious uniformity in the face of reform movements throughout Europe.

    b. Christianity was strengthened through the establishment of Catholic control throughout the entirety of the Holy Roman Empire.

    c. Religious reform increased state control of religious institutions and provided justifications to challenge state authority.

    d. Religion became an increasingly public matter, developing into public conversions and punishment for religious opposition.

29. Which of the following describes the impact of the *95 Theses* on politics?

    a. Conflicts among religious groups were limited by the power of absolute monarchs in the sixteenth century

    b. Conflicts among religious groups led to wars between Catholics and Protestants

    c. Conflicts among religious groups led to the development of two world wars

    d. Conflicts among religious groups led to churches gaining power of monarchies

Questions 30-33 refer to the passage below.

"But no sooner had I embarked on this project than I noticed that while I was trying in this way to think everything to be false it had to be the case that I, who was thinking this, was something. And observing that this truth I am thinking, therefore I exist was so firm and sure that not even the most extravagant suppositions of the sceptics could shake it, I decided that I could accept it without scruple as the first principle of the philosophy I was seeking."

René Descartes, french philosopher,
Discourse on the Method of Rightly Conducting One's Reason and of Seeking Truth in the Sciences, 1637

30. The excerpt above describes which type of reasoning?

   a. Reasoning that believes in the existence of a creator on the basis of reason but rejected belief in a supernatural deity who interacts with humankind
   b. Reasoning that takes specific information and makes a broader generalization that is considered probable
   c. Reasoning that starts out with a general statement, or hypothesis, and examines the possibilities to reach a specific, logical conclusion
   d. Reasoning that emphasizes the subjective component of knowledge

31. Which of the following statements best reflects the impact of the ideas described above?

   a. New ideas in science based on experimentation and mathematics challenged classical views of the cosmos and nature
   b. New movements explored subconscious and subjective states and satirized Western society and its values
   c. New ideas reinforced ecclesiastical authorities and classical cosmology as a means of understanding the world
   d. New movements in psychology emphasized the role of the irrational and the struggle between the conscious and subconscious

32. Which of the following was most directly a continuation of the changes brought about by the ideas described in the above passage?

   a. Romanticism
   b. Postmodernism
   c. Positivism
   d. Impressionism

33. Which statement best describes a result of the ideas expressed in the above passage?

   a. Religious uniformity developed throughout the Holy Roman Empire to oppose these ideas.
   b. Intellectuals such as Voltaire and Diderot began to apply the principles of the scientific revolution to society and human institutions.
   c. A human-centered naturalism that considered individuals and everyday life appropriate objects of artistic representation.
   d. The pursuit of discovery led to the development of the printing press in order to disseminate ideas.

Questions 34-36 refer to the passage below.

"And now we perceive, with thankful acknowledgment of God's aid, that our endeavors have attained their proposed end, inasmuch as the better and the greater part of our subjects of the said R.P.R. [*Religion prétendue réformée*—"the religion called the Reformed"] have embraced the Catholic faith. And since by this fact the execution of the Edict of Nantes and of all that has ever been ordained in favor of the said R.P.R. has been rendered nugatory, we have determined that we can do nothing better, in order wholly to obliterate the memory of the troubles, the confusion, and the evils which the progress of this false religion has caused in this (289) kingdom, and which furnished occasion for the said edict and for so many previous and subsequent edicts and declarations, than entirely to revoke the said Edict of Nantes, with the special articles granted as a sequel to it, as well as all that has since been done in favor of the said religion."

Louis XIV, King of France, The Revocation of the Edict of Nantes, 1685

34. Why had the Edict of Nantes previously been issued by the French government?

    a. To convert all the people of France to Catholicism
    b. To allow religious pluralism to maintain domestic peace
    c. To persecute nobles who led the French Wars of Religion
    d. To prevent John Calvin's ideas from spreading into France

35. Why did Louis XIV revoke the Edict of Nantes?

    a. He wanted to extend religious control over France
    b. He wanted to develop religious toleration in France
    c. He wanted to suppress the radicals of the French Revolution
    d. He wanted to support the power of the Holy Roman Emperor

36. Which of the following was most directly a response to Louis XIV's actions?

    a. Political revolutions developed in France, inspired by Enlightenment ideals
    b. The nobility established an oligarchy of landed gentry to promote trade and traditional rights
    c. Romanticism emerged as an artistic statement against the power of an absolute monarchy
    d. Mass-based political parties emerged as vehicles for social, economic, and political reform

Questions 37-39 refer to the passage below.

"Like all other contracts, wages should be left to the fair and free competition of the market, and should never be controlled by the interference of the legislature. The clear and direct tendency of the poor laws is in direct opposition to these obvious principles: it is not, as the legislature benevolently intended, to amend the condition of the poor, but to deteriorate the condition of both poor and rich; instead of making the poor rich, they are calculated to make the rich poor;. . ."

David Ricardo, British political economist, *Iron Law of Wages*, 1817

37. Which of the following eighteenth or nineteenth century economic philosophies is best reflected in the above statement?

   a. The belief in state ownership of property and economic planning to promote equality
   b. The belief that the only way to increase one's economic power over others was to gain a greater share of the existing sources of wealth
   c. The belief in working-class movements and revolutions to overthrow the capitalist system
   d. The belief in the authority of natural law and the market

38. All of the following developments were responses to David Ricardo's ideas EXCEPT

   a. labor unions
   b. utopian communities
   c. the Cult of Domesticity
   d. demands for universal suffrage

39. Which of these is the most direct effect of the Industrial Revolution on society?

   a. Agrarian landed elites established serfdom to maintain control over the poor in eastern Europe, while peasants became free in western Europe.
   b. Socio-economic changes led to development of self-conscious social classes, such as the proletariat and the bourgeoisie.
   c. New modes of marriage, partnership, motherhood, divorce, and reproduction gave women more options in their personal lives.
   d. Governments created large-scale guest-worker programs to support labor-force participation.

Questions 40-42 refer to the painting below, *Metamorphosis of Narcissus* (1937) by Salvador Dalí.

Salvador Dalí, *Metamorphosis of Narcissus*
Granger Collection, New York © 2013 Artists Rights Society (ARS), New York
Chapter 26, *A History of Western Society,* Twelfth Edition
© 2017 Bedford/St. Martin's
Distributed by Bedford/St. Martin's/Macmillan Higher Education strictly for use with its products; not for redistribution.

40. This painting was created in response to

    a. The development of fascism in France

    b. The communist revolution in Russia

    c. Unstable conditions in Europe after World War I

    d. The creation of the "Iron Curtain" in Europe

41. Which European thinkers reflected similar themes in their writings?

    a. Freud and Nietzsche

    b. Locke and Rousseau

    c. Luther and Calvin

    d. Wollstonecraft and de Beauvoir

42. What artistic values are best represented by this painting?

    a. Romantic artists emphasized emotion, nature, individuality, and the supernatural in their works.

    b. New movements in the visual arts explored subconscious and subjective states, satirizing Western society and its values.

    c. Baroque artists employed distortion, drama, and illusion in their works, which were often commissioned by the government.

    d. Man-centered naturalism considered individuals and everyday life appropriate objects of artistic representation.

Questions 43-44 refer to the engraving below, *Concordia (Harmony),* **c. 1589,
by Crispijn van de Passe the Elder.**

Concordia (Harmony)
Mary Evans/The Image Works
Chapter 13, *A History of Western Society,* Twelfth Edition
© 2017 Bedford/St. Martin's
Distributed by Bedford/St. Martin's/Macmillan Higher Education strictly for use with its products; not for redistribution.

43. Which of the following statements about family in the sixteenth century is best reflected in the image?

    a. New modes of marriage, motherhood and reproduction gave women more options in their personal lives.

    b. Bourgeois families became focused on the nuclear family and the "cult of domesticity," with distinct gender roles for men and women.

    c. The middle-class notion of companionate marriage began to be adopted by the working classes.

    d. Rural and urban households worked as units, with men and women engaged in separate but complementary tasks.

44. Which of the following statements about leisure time in the sixteenth century is best reflected in the image?

    a. Leisure time became increasingly centered on small groups, concurrent with the development of activities and spaces to use that time.

    b. Leisure activities continued to be organized according to the religious calendar and agricultural cycle.

    c. Mass production increased disposable income and created a consumer culture, which used leisure time to purchase goods with great domestic comfort.

    d. Industrialization and mass marketing increased demand for consumer goods, including processed food, clothing and leisure.

Questions 45-48 refer to the passage below.

"A great question is pending before the supreme tribunal of France. Will the Jews be citizens or not? . . . In general, civil rights are entirely independent from religious principles. And all men of whatever religion, whatever sect they belong to, whatever creed they practice, provided that their creed, their sect, their religion does not offend the principles of a pure and severe morality, all these men, we say, equally able to serve the fatherland, defend its interests, contribute to its splendor, should all equally have the title and the rights of citizen. . . . In general, civil rights are entirely independent from religious principles. And all men of whatever religion, whatever sect they belong to, whatever creed they practice, provided that their creed, their sect, their religion does not offend the principles of a pure and severe morality, all these men, we say, equally able to serve the fatherland, defend its interests, contribute to its splendor, should all equally have the title and the rights of citizen. . . ."

A Petition of French Jews of Paris, Alsace and Lorraine to the National Assembly, 1790

45. The passage above was written in response to which event in France?

   a. The first phase of the French Revolution, which established a constitutional monarchy
   b. The radical phase of the French Revolution, which created a republic
   c. The conservative phase of the French Revolution, which re-established the Catholic Church
   d. Napoleon's control over France, which created an empire across Europe

46. Which movement most directly inspired the sentiments expressed above?

   a. Enlightenment
   b. Reformation
   c. Romanticism
   d. Realism

47. Which of the following statements would most likely support the sentiments expressed above?

   a. Nationalism encouraged loyalty to the nation in a variety of ways, including racialism
   b. By 1800, most governments had extended toleration to Christian minorities and, in some states, civil equality to Jews
   c. Germany sought to establish a "new racial order" in Europe
   d. Some states, such as Spain and Portugal, sought to create religious uniformity

48. Which of the following is most directly a continuation of the perspectives described above?

   a. Religious conflicts became the basis for challenging the monarch's control of religious institutions
   b. Zionism was welcomed within European countries to celebrate Jewish heritage
   c. Nationalism developed as a form of anti-Semitism in the nineteenth century
   d. Jews worked as "guest workers" throughout Europe during the 1950s and 1960s

Questions 49-52 refer to the poem below.

At dawn the ridge emerges massed and dun
In the wild purple of the glowering sun,
Smouldering through spouts of drifting smoke that shroud
The menacing scarred slope; and, one by one,
Tanks creep and topple forward to the wire.
The barrage roars and lifts. Then, clumsily bowed
With bombs and guns and shovels and battle-gear,
Men jostle and climb to meet the bristling fire.
Lines of grey, muttering faces, masked with fear,
They leave their trenches, going over the top,
While time ticks blank and busy on their wrists,
And hope, with furtive eyes and grappling fists,
Flounders in the mud. O Jesu, make it stop!

Siegfried Sassoon, "Attack," 1918

49. The poem reflects which of the following developments?

   a. Religious conflicts, economic issues, and political control contributed to brutal and destructive wars
   b. A coalition of European powers sought to restore a balance of power by waging war against Napoleon
   c. The emergence of fascism, extreme nationalism, and racist ideologies resulted in the catastrophe of world war
   d. Nationalism, military plans, the alliance system and imperial competition turned a regional dispute into world war

50. Which of the following literary movements is reflected in this poem?

   a. Materialist themes emerged in literature, as writers depicted the lives of ordinary people
   b. A "lost generation" of writers emerges, who explored the subconscious and satirized Western values
   c. Romantic writers responded to the Industrial Revolution and political revolutions
   d. Humanist writers promoted a revival in classical literature and valued secularism and individualism

51. Which of the following actions would be a continuation of the developments reflected in the poem?

   a. Military technologies made possible industrialized warfare, genocide, nuclear proliferation, and the risk of global nuclear war.
   b. European national rivalries and strategic concerns fostered imperial expansion and competition for colonies.
   c. Rivalries between Britain and France led to global wars in both Europe and in the colonies, with Britain supplanting France as the greatest European power.
   d. The competition for trade led to conflicts and rivalries among European powers.

52. The themes expressed in the poem most directly challenge which ideology?

   a. The emphasis on emotions developed in Romanticism
   b. The focus on everyday life and social problems in Realism
   c. The development of natural laws in the Scientific Revolution and Enlightenment
   d. The concepts of experimentation and self-expression in Modernism

Questions 53-55 are based on the passage below.

"You have told us that we do not know the One who gives us life and being, who is Lord of the heavens and of the earth. You also say that those we worship are not gods. This way of speaking is entirely new to us, and very scandalous. We are frightened by this way of speaking because our forebears who engendered and governed us never said anything like this. On the contrary, they left us this our custom of worshiping our gods, in which they believed and which they worshiped all the time that they lived here on earth. They taught us how to honor them. And they taught us all the ceremonies and sacrifices that we make. They told us that through them [our gods] we live and are, and that we were beholden to them, to be theirs and to serve countless centuries before the sun began to shine and before there was daytime. They said that these gods that we worship give us everything we need for our physical existence: maize, beans, chia seeds, etc. We appeal to them for the rain to make the things of the earth grow."

Passage from "Tenochtitlán Leaders Respond to Spanish Missionaries," 1524

53. The passage above was written in response to

    a. Growing nationalist movements that challenged European imperialism
    b. The desire for Europeans to spread the Christian faith to indigenous civilizations
    c. Religious pluralism, which challenged the concept of a unified Europe
    d. Increased immigration into Europe, which altered Europe's religious makeup

54. Which of the following was most directly a result of the interactions described above?

    a. The subjugation and destruction of people, particularly in the Americas
    b. Successful uprisings in decolonization of European empires
    c. The rejection of mercantilist economic policies throughout Europe
    d. Cooperation between European countries to develop technology and communication

55. In what way was imperialism in the nineteenth century different from colonization in the sixteenth century?

    a. A desire to access raw materials and establish trade networks
    b. A focus on direct political and cultural control of indigenous people
    c. A belief in racial and ethnic superiority
    d. A focus on competition between European countries

Part B: Short-Answer Questions

Time: 40 minutes

Please answer the following two questions.

1. Use the passages below and your knowledge of European history to answer all parts of the question that follow.

> "During the period 1790-1830 factory production increased rapidly. A greater proportion of the people came to benefit from it both as producers and as consumers. The fall in the price of textiles reduced the price of clothing. . . . Miscellaneous commodities, ranging from clocks to . . . handkerchiefs . . . and after 1820 such things as tea and coffee and sugar fell in price substantially. The growth of trade-unions . . . savings banks, popular newspapers and pamphlets, schools . . . all give evidence of the existence of a large class raised well above the level of mere subsistence."
>
> T.S. Ashton, "The Standard Life of Workers in England. 1790-1830," published in 1949

> "By the later eighteenth century, . . . it has recently been argued that in general the ideology of the law served to constrain authority not to rely on coercive power. Nevertheless, the period between the French Revolution and the later 1820s should be seen as one of severe repression of workers' rights reflected in the Combination Acts and the use of the military to suppress popular disturbances, with 12,000 troops used against the Luddites in 1812. From the mid-1830s to 1850, the general trend is one of easing of repression and major advances for working-class organizations. . . ."
>
> N.F.R. Crafts, "Some Dimensions of the 'Quality of Life' during the British Industrial Revolution," published in 1997

    a. Briefly explain one difference between Ashton's argument and Crafts's argument.
    b. Briefly explain one piece of evidence from 1790-1820 not mentioned in the excerpts above that supports Ashton's argument.
    c. Briefly explain one piece of evidence from 1790-1820 not mentioned in the excerpts above that supports Crafts's argument.

2. Use the cartoon and your knowledge of European history to answer all parts of the question that follow.

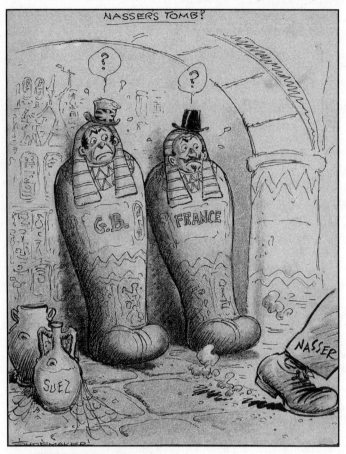

Nasser's Tomb? (1957) Chicago's American
politicalcartoon.com
© 2017 Bedford/St. Martin's
Distributed by Bedford/St. Martin's/Macmillan Higher Education strictly for use with its products; not for redistribution.

    a. Describe one image in this cartoon that represents continuity with traditional European conceptions of Egypt before 1950.

    b. Describe one image in this cartoon that represents a change in traditional European conceptions of Egypt before 1950.

    c. Briefly explain one historical example from Europe in 1950-1979 that supports the artists' argument in this cartoon.

Please choose between question #3 or #4 for your final SAQ question.

3. Please answer all parts of the question.

    a. Identify one political cause for the Protestant Reformation in Europe.

    b. Identify one religious cause for the Protestant Reformation in Europe.

    c. Identify one political or religious effect on Europe between 1517 and 1648.

4. a. Identify and explain one economic cause of the collapse of the Soviet Union

    b. Identify and explain one political cause of the collapse of the Soviet Union.

    c. Identify and explain one political or economic effect of the collapse of the Soviet Union.

EUROPEAN HISTORY SECTION II

Total ime: 1 hour, 40 minutes

Question 1 (Document-Based Question)
Time: 60 minutes

**It is suggested that you spend 15 minutes reading the documents
and 45 minutes writing your response.
Note: You may begin writing your response before the reading period is over.**

Directions: Question 1 is based on the accompanying documents. The documents have been edited for the purpose of this exercise.

In your response you should do the following:

- **Thesis:** Present a thesis that makes a historically defensible claim and responds to all parts of the question. The thesis must consist of one or more sentences located in one place, either in the introduction or the conclusion.

- **Evidence and Reasoning:** Develop and support a cohesive argument that recognizes and accounts for historical complexity by explicitly illustrating relationships among historical evidence such as contradiction, corroboration, and/or qualification. Utilize the content of at least six of the documents to support the stated thesis or a relevant argument.

- **Document Analysis:** Explain the significance of the author's point of view, author's purpose, historical context, and/or audience for at least four documents.

- **Contextualization:** Situate the argument by explaining the influence of the broader historical events, developments, or processes immediately relevant to the question.

- **Evidence Beyond the Documents:** Provide additional specific evidence beyond those found in the documents to support or qualify the argument.

1. Compare perspectives of absolutism in England and France during the seventeenth century.

Document 1

Source: Various eyewitnesses to the conclusion of the trial of Charles I, published 1650.

Now . . . this court is in judgment and conscience satisfied that he (the said Charles Stuart) is guilty of levying war against the said Parliament and people, and [of] maintaining and continuing the same, for which . . . he stands accused. . . . This court is fully satisfied in their judgments and consciences that he hath been and is guilty of the wicked designs and endeavors in the said charge set forth; and that the said war hath been levied, maintained, and continued by him as aforesaid . . . and that he hath been and is the occasioner, author, and continuer of the said unnatural, cruel, and bloody wars, and therein guilty of High Treason and of the murders, rapines, burnings, spoils, desolations, damage, and mischief to this nation acted and committed in the said war and occasioned thereby. For all which treasons and crimes this court doth adjudge that he, the said Charles Stuart, as a tyrant, traitor, murderer, and public enemy to the good people of this nation, shall be put to death by the severing of his head from his body.

Document 2

Source: King Charles His Speech Made upon the Scaffold at Whitehall Gate, Immediately before His Execution, on Tuesday the 30. of Jan. 1648.

[As for the people,] truly I desire their liberty and freedom as much as anybody whomsoever; but I must tell you that their liberty and freedom consist in having of government. . . . It is not for having share in government, sirs; that is nothing pertaining to them; a subject and a sovereign are clear different things. . . . I tell you (and I pray God it be not laid to your charge) that I am the martyr of the people. . . . And to the executioner he said, 'I shall say but very short prayers, and when I thrust out my hands. . . .' The bishop: 'You are exchanged from a temporal to an eternal crown,—a good exchange.' After a very short pause, his Majesty stretching forth his hands, the executioner at one blow severed his head from his body; which, being held up and showed to the people, was with his body put into a coffin covered with black velvet and carried into his lodging. His blood was taken up by divers persons for different ends: by some as trophies of their villainy; by others as relics of a martyr; and in some had had the same effect, by the blessing of God, which was often found in his sacred touch when living.

Document 3

Source: Reaction from the King of France to the execution of Charles I, 1649.

At length, with kisses and greetings beginning their betrayal, they invited his Majesty to a personal treaty. To show his passionate desire for peace, he bent over backwards, going beyond all former rulers in generous concessions [giving in and making promises]. Yet even when he had given in beyond their hope and expectation, and surrendered his most unquestionable rights and privileges into their hands, with hate as relentless as the grave, deep and bottomless as hell, they abruptly broke off. By force of arms they dragged him to court. Subordinates took it upon themselves to judge their king. They called him to an account, he who owed an account to none but God alone. They disrespectfully criticized him with the unjust shame of tyrant, traitor and murderer. Having behaved with scorn and contempt, after a short time, in triumph they took him to the scaffold. Making his sorrow worse, they had prepared the scaffold at the entrance to his royal palace. In the sight of his subjects they committed a most brutal murder upon his sacred person, by severing his royal head from his body, by the hands of the common hangman.

Document 4

Source: Portrait of Louis XIV, by Hyacinthe Rigaud, 1701.

Hyacinthe Rigaud, portrait of Louis XIV, 1701.
Louis XIV in Royal Costume, 1701 (oil on canvas)/Rigaud, Hyacinthe Francois (1659-1743)/
Louvre, Paris, France/Bridgeman Images.
Chapter 15, *A History of Western Society*, Twelfth Edition

Document 5

Source: Charles II, King of England 1660-1685, Speech to Parliament, 1660.

Never King valu'd himself more upon the Affections of his People than I do; Nor do I know a better Way to make myself sure of your Affections, than by being just and kind to you all: And, whilst I am so, I pray let the World see, that I am possess'd of your Affections. . . . I am so confident of your Affections, that I will not move you in any thing that immediately relates to myself: And yet I must tell you, That I am not richer, that is, I have not so much Money in my Purse, as when I came to you. The truth is, I have liv'd principally ever since upon what I brought with me, which was indeed your Money; you sent it to me, and I thank you for it. . . . Nor have I been able to give my Brothers one Shilling since I came into England, nor to keep any Table in my House but where I eat myself. And that which troubles me most, is, to see many of you come to me at Whitehall, and to think you must go somewhere else to seek a Dinner. I do not mention this to you, as any thing that troubles me: Do but take care of the Publick, and for what is necessary for the Peace and Quiet of the Kingdom, and take your own Time for my own Particular, which I am sure you will provide for with as much Affection and Frankness as I can desire.

Document 6

Source: John Locke, *Second Treatise on Civil Government,* 1689.

If we ask 'What security, what fence, do we have to protect us from the violence and oppression of this absolute ruler?', the very question is ·found to be· almost intolerable. They are ready to tell you that even to ask about safety ·from the monarch· is an offence that deserves to be punished by death. Between subjects, they will grant, there must be measures, laws and judges to produce mutual peace and security: but the ruler ought to be absolute, and is above all such considerations; because he has power to do more hurt and wrong, it is right when he does it! To ask how you may be guarded from harm coming from the direction where the strongest hand is available to do it is to use the voice of faction and rebellion; as if when men left the state of nature and entered into society they agreed that all but one of them should be under the restraint of laws, and that that one should keep all the liberty of the state of nature, increased by power, and made licentious by impunity. This implies that men are so foolish that they would take care to avoid harms from polecats or foxes, but think it is safety to be eaten by lions.

Document 7

Source: Louis XIV, King of France, Letter to Count Tallard, Ambassador to Great Britain, 1698.

The more anxious the English are to restrict his [the king's] authority the more they must fear a new war which would give him more extensive power than the kings of England have ever enjoyed. If the resources of that kingdom were as great as formerly, the nation might have no reason to be afraid of recommencing a war. But in the present state of England, this war could not recommence without recourse being had to extraordinary measures to levy the taxes and to such taxes as the nation has never yet allowed to be imposed upon it. If it once consented it would no longer be necessary for the kings of England to summon parliaments; and I am persuaded that considerations so powerful will restrain the English, especially when they see that they have no interest in disturbing the peace.

Question 2 or 3 or 4 (Long Essay Question)

Suggested writing time: 40 minutes

Directions: Choose EITHER question 2 OR question 3 OR question 4.

In your response you should do the following.

- **Thesis:** Respond to the question with an evaluative thesis that makes a historically defensible claim.

- **Contextualization:** Explain a broader historical context immediately relevant to the question.

- **Evidence and Reasoning:**
  - Use specific and relevant examples of historical evidence in support of argument.
  - Explain how the evidence corroborates, qualifies, or modifies your argument.

2. Characterize the extent to which religion influenced politics in the time period 1517-1648.

3. Characterize the extent to which religion influenced politics in the time period 1815-1914.

4. Characterize the extent to which religion influenced politics in the time period 1945-2001.

NOTES:

EUROPEAN HISTORY SECTION I

Total time: 1 hour, 35 minutes

Part A: Multiple-Choice Questions

Time: 55 minutes

Questions 1-3 refer to the chart below, showing the decline of death rates in England and Wales, Germany, France, and Sweden from 1840-1913.

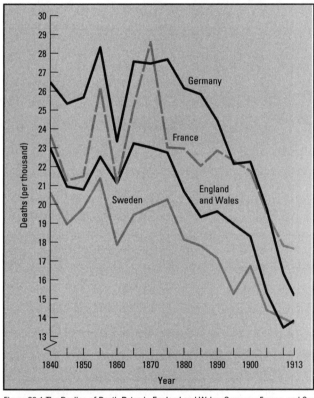

Figure 22.1 The Decline of Death Rates in England and Wales, Germany, France, and Sweden, 1840-1913
Chapter 22, *A History of Western Society,* Eleventh Edition
© 2017 Bedford/St. Martin's
Distributed by Bedford/St. Martin's/Macmillan Higher Education strictly for use with its products; not for redistribution.

1. All of the following factors helped contribute to the trend exhibited by the chart above EXCEPT
   a. a rising standard of living
   b. improvements in public health
   c. medical advances
   d. the miasmatic theory of disease

2. Which of the following best explains the decline of death rates shown in the chart above?
   a. A decline in infant mortality
   b. A decline in global conflicts
   c. An increase in nuclear technology
   d. An increase in migration to the cities

3. Which of the following best represents a continuation of the trend shown in the chart above?

    a. Development of vaccinations

    b. New medical theories and technologies

    c. Warfare and genocide against ethnic minorities

    d. The rise of consumerism

Questions 4-7 refers to the photo below of the Bauhaus School in Dessau, Germany.

The Bauhaus School in Dessau, Germany, designed by Walter Gropius opened in 1926.
imageBROKER/imageBROKER/Superstock
Chapter 26, *A History of Western Society,* Twelfth Edition
© 2017 Bedford/St. Martin's
Distributed by Bedford/St. Martin's/Macmillan Higher Education strictly for use with its products; not for redistribution.

4. The Bauhaus school of design, represented by the photograph above,

    a. represents the type of architecture commissioned by the Nazi government in Germany

    b. was an elite institution separating out art from traditional crafts

    c. promoted the idea that form should follow function

    d. was a celebration of nationalist history

5. Which of the following artistic developments is best represented in the photograph above?

    a. A celebration of nature and emotion as well as the supernatural

    b. A focus on classical Greek and Roman architecture

    c. A challenge to existing aesthetic standards through exploring subjective states

    d. An emphasis on religious themes and glorification of royal power

6. Which of the following intellectual movements is most directly affected by the architectural themes represented in the photograph above?

    a. Enlightenment

    b. Romanticism

    c. Realism

    d. Existentialism

7. Which of the following events most directly led to the changes represented in the photograph above?

    a. World War I because of the challenge to rational thinking

    b. The Cold War because of the emphasis on scientific realism

    c. World War II because of the rise of dictatorships

    d. The 1930s global Great Depression, which emphasized practical architecture

Questions 8-10 refer to the map below, showing European cities of 100,00 or more from 1800-1900.

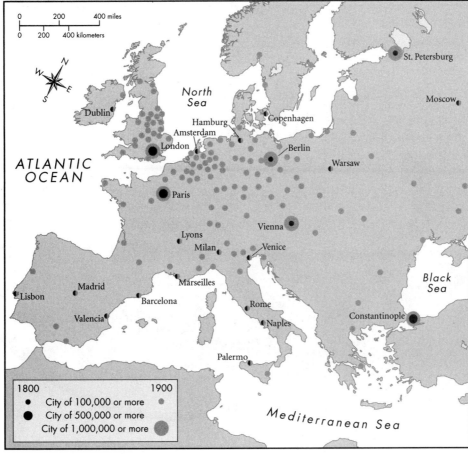

Map 22.1 European Cities of 100,000 or More, 1800-1900
Chapter 22, *A History of Western Society*, Eleventh Edition
© 2017 Bedford/St. Martin's
Distributed by Bedford/St. Martin's/Macmillan Higher Education strictly for use with its products; not for redistribution.

8. What conclusion can be drawn from the map above?
    a. There were more large cities in Great Britain in 1900 than in all of Europe in 1800
    b. Cities demonstrated slower growth at the end of the nineteenth century
    c. Many cities grew due to migration between European countries
    d. Most populous areas grew due to immigration from Europe's colonies

9. Which of these most directly accounts for the growth of cities illustrated above?
    a. Population recovered to its pre-Great Plague level and population pressures developed
    b. Europe's Agricultural Revolution produced more food using fewer workers, resulting in migration to urban areas
    c. Migration developed from rural areas to urban, industrialized regions, resulting in declines in rural areas
    d. Because of economic growth and nationalist movements, people from southern Europe, Asia, and Africa migrated to western and central Europe

10. What was a direct result of the growth of cities illustrated above?
    a. Green parties developed in western and central Europe, focusing on sustainable development.
    b. Government reforms focused on modernizing infrastructure, regulating public health and establishing modern police forces.
    c. Cottage industries expanded as increasing numbers of laborers in homes produced for markets.
    d. Merchant elites and craft guilds governed cities through trade regulation, agricultural developments and price controls.

Questions 11-13 refer to the map below, showing European investment to 1914.

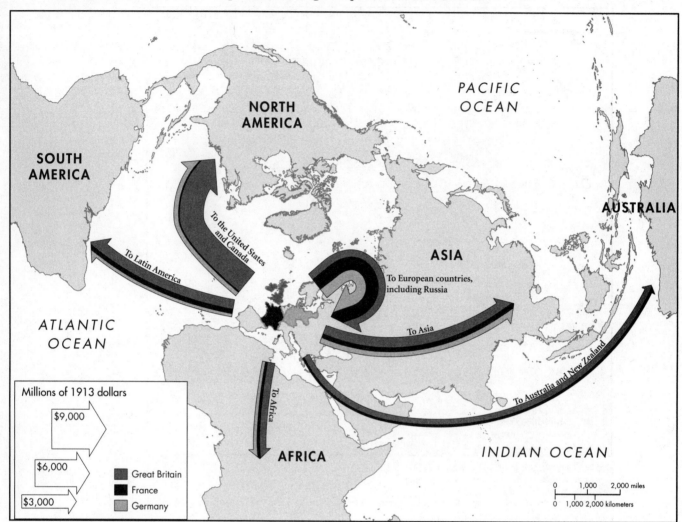

Map 24.1 European Investment to 1914
Chapter 24, *A History of Western Society,* Eleventh Edition
© 2017 Bedford/St. Martin's
Distributed by Bedford/St. Martin's/Macmillan Higher Education strictly for use with its products; not for redistribution.

11. This map indicates that the largest part of financial investment

    a. benefitted European nations equally, maintaining a balance of power
    b. aided native peoples in overthrowing colonial powers
    c. supported Bismarck's alliance system
    d. maintained European empires around the world

12. Which of the following most directly led to the developments illustrated in the map above?

    a. An emphasis on mercantilism promoted the acquisition of colonies overseas
    b. The search for raw materials and manufactured goods fostered imperial expansion
    c. The development of uprisings amongst enslaved people led to the collapse of colonies
    d. Decolonization led to the migration of Asians and Africans into Europe as "guest workers"

13. Which of the following was most directly a result of the developments illustrated in the map above?

    a. Imperial competition turned regional disputes into global conflict in the first half of the twentieth century.

b. Successful uprisings throughout Asia and Africa led to colonial independence in the first half of the twentieth century for the majority of colonial people.

c. Europeans subjugated and decimated indigenous populations throughout Asia and Africa primarily through disease.

d. European religious authorities during the twentieth century focused on spreading Christianity to counter Islam in Asia and Africa

Questions 14-16 refer to the chart below, showing emigration from Europe by decade from 1860-1940.

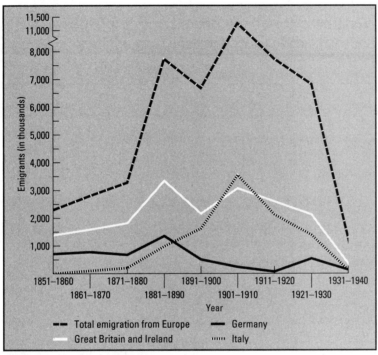

Figure 24.2 Emigration from Europe by Decade, 1860-1940
Chapter 24, *A History of Western Society,* Eleventh Edition
© 2017 Bedford/St. Martin's
Distributed by Bedford/St. Martin's/Macmillan Higher Education strictly for use with its products; not for redistribution.

14. Which pattern of migration is described accurately by this chart?

    a. Italians mostly left in the 1860s, just before unification was completed

    b. Religious wars between Catholics and Protestants led to mass emigration from Europe

    c. The United States received more than half of all immigrants from Europe in the nineteenth century because of emerging anti-semitism

    d. Germans emigrated in large numbers in the 1850s and again in the 1880s

15. Which of the following developments was LEAST likely to be a cause of the pattern of migration shown above?

    a. Poor economic conditions

    b. Religious conflicts

    c. Political revolutions

    d. Industrial modernization

16. What pattern of migration emerged after the developments shown above?

    a. The reduction of barriers to migration led to the arrival of new permanent residents from outside Europe.

    b. Missionaries, journalists, and intellectuals migrated to eastern and southern Asia to develop colonial administrations as part of European empires.

c. Influenced by political revolutions, Europeans migrated to newly developed empires, shifting the balance of power in Europe.

d. Migrants traveled outside of Europe to exchange commodities and convert indigenous populations to Christianity to further expand European empires.

Questions 17-20 refer to the map below, showing the partition of the Ottoman Empire from 1914-1923.

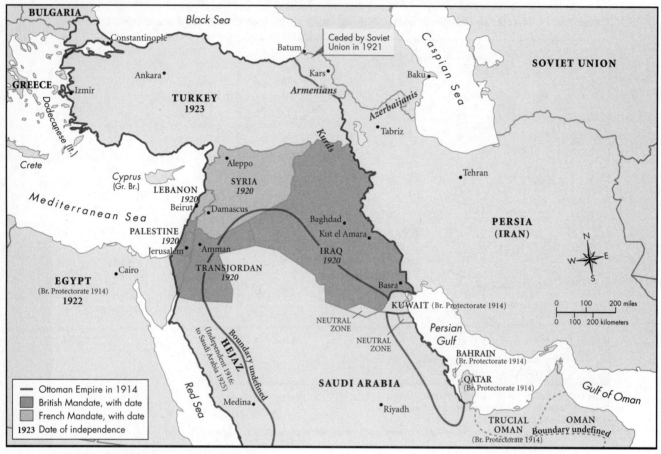

The partition of the Ottoman Empire, 1914-1923
Chapter 25, *A History of Western Society*, Eleventh Edition
© 2017 Bedford/St. Martin's
Distributed by Bedford/St. Martin's/Macmillan Higher Education strictly for use with its products; not for redistribution.

17. The map above illustrates which of the following effects of World War I?

    a. Promises made by German and Russian leaders to Arab nationalists during World War I
    b. Decisions developed by the League of Nations
    c. The fulfillment of self-determination expressed in Wilson's Fourteen Points
    d. Turkey's acceptance of the peace settlement made after World War I

18. Which of the following economic trends occurred as a result of the developments shown in the map above?

    a. Mercantilism was challenged by a new free market system
    b. Competition for raw materials led to the creation of European empires
    c. New technologies developed a global network
    d. Strategic interests developed in oil

19. Which of the following was a long-term result of the developments in the map above?
    a. The exchange of goods created economic opportunities for indigenous peoples
    b. Imperialism created diplomatic tensions among Europeans
    d. Increased immigration into Europe altered Europe's religious makeup
    d. Christian missionaries converted indigenous peoples

20. The developments on the map above are a continuation of what previous process in European history?
    a. Indigenous nationalist movements led to independence from imperial control
    b. Slave-labor systems expanded as demand for global products increased
    c. European empires focused on direct political control of colonies
    d. Diseases led to the decimation of indigenous populations

Questions 21-24 refer to the advertisement below for Volkswagon from 1938.

German advertisement for the Volkswagen, produced by the Nazi organisation KdF, 1938 (colour litho)/Axster-Heudtlass,
Werner von (1898-1949)/DEUTSCHES HISTORISCHES MUSEUM/Deutsches Historisches Museum, Berlin, Germany/Bridgeman Images.
Chapter 27, *A History of Western Society,* Twelfth Edition
© 2017 Bedford/St. Martin's
Distributed by Bedford/St. Martin's/Macmillan Higher Education strictly for use with its products; not for redistribution.

21. This advertisement reflects which of the following about Hitler?
    a. Hitler's exploitation of postwar instability
    b. Hitler's focus on the glorification of nationalism
    c. Hitler's policy of a "Final Solution" concerning Europe's Jewish population
    d. Hitler's use of terror and manipulation

22. Which of the following developments most directly influenced the rise of Hitler?
    a. European movements supporting universal male suffrage
    b. Liberalism which supported government intervention on behalf of the poor
    c. Nationalism which encouraged loyalty to the nation and an ethnic ideal
    d. Green parties which advocated sustainable development in the environment

23. Which of the following best reflects the economic ideal portrayed in the picture?
    a. Hitler took advantage of postwar economic growth
    b. Hitler developed a global economy
    c. Hitler subscribed to laissez-faire economic principles
    d. Hitler brought economic stability to Germany

24. Which of the following was most directly a legacy of the image above?
    a. The establishment of a welfare state in Europe
    b. The cultural importance of consumerism
    c. A critique of families and leisure time
    d. A decrease in the standard of living after World War II

Questions 25-27 refer to the photograph below, showing the student rebellion in Paris.

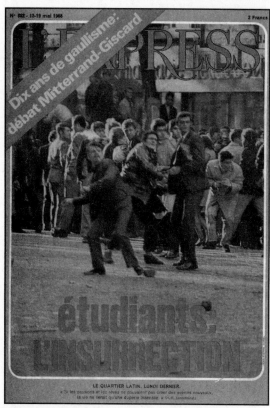

Student Rebellion in Paris
Mai 68/Photo © Collection Gregoire/Bridgeman Images
Chapter 29, *A History of Western Society,* Twelfth Edition
© 2017 Bedford/St. Martin's
Distributed by Bedford/St. Martin's/Macmillan Higher Education strictly for use with its products; not for redistribution.

25. The chief issue prompting these French student protests in the 1960s was
    a. the government's acceptance of Algerian independence
    b. lack of jobs for Muslim immigrants
    c. discrimination against women
    d. a desire for reforms in the university system

26. Which of the following best describes the scene depicted in the photograph above?
    a. Youth and intellectuals reacted against bourgeois materialism
    b. Young nationalists and separatists focused on ethnic cleansing
    c. Young workers established labor unions to promote social reform
    d. Youth leaders protested against compulsory public education

27. Which of these best reflects a demographic change in France after WWII that influenced the developments depicted in the photograph above?
    a. A reduction in infant mortality as a result of the commercialization of agriculture
    b. The Baby Boom, which was a reflection of post-war economic recovery
    c. Early practices of birth control as a result of changing marriage practices
    d. Inoculation, which resulted in the decline of smallpox mortality

Questions 28-31 refer to the map below, showing democratic movements in Eastern Europe.

Map 29.2 Democratic Movements in Eastern Europe, 1989
Chapter 29, *A History of Western Society,* Eleventh Edition
© 2017 Bedford/St. Martin's
Distributed by Bedford/St. Martin's/Macmillan Higher Education strictly for use with its products; not for redistribution.

28. The map above best refers to which of these developments in European history?

    a. Battle sites of the Napoleonic Wars

    b. Urban unrest in 1848

    c. Pro-democracy protests in 1989

    d. World War I battles

29. Which of the following most directly inspired the events depicted on the map above?

    a. The Russian Revolution

    b. The Rise of Dictators in Europe

    c. The establishment of NATO

    d. The collapse of the Soviet Union

30. Which of the following was most directly affected by the developments depicted above?

    a The League of Nations

    b. The European Union

    c. The European Coal and Steel Community

    d. The Vatican Council

31. Which of the following was a result of the events depicted in the map above?

    a. Nationalist and separatist movements led to ethnic cleansing in some regions
    b. Fascist dictatorships developed in some regions
    c. An "iron curtain" descended in some regions
    d. Decolonization led to the collapse of European empires in some regions

Questions 32-35 refer to the passage below.

"As every individual, therefore, endeavours as much as he can both to employ his capital in the support of domestic industry, and so to direct that industry that its produce may be of the greatest value; every individual necessarily labours to render the annual revenue of the society as great as he can. He generally, indeed, neither intends to promote the public interest, nor knows how much he is promoting it. By preferring the support of domestic to that of foreign industry, he intends only his own security; and by directing that industry in such a manner as its produce may be of the greatest value, he intends only his own gain, and he is in this, as in many other cases, led by an invisible hand to promote an end which was no part of his intention."

Adam Smith, Scottish economist and philosopher, *An Inquiry into the Nature and Causes of the Wealth of Nations,* 1776

32. The theory of economic liberalism, first articulated by Adam Smith, is concerned mostly with the needs of

    a. landlords, who were primarily nobility
    b. governments, specifically monarchs
    c. merchants, members of the middle class
    d. consumers, who purchased manufactured goods

33. The concepts described above were most directly a reaction against

    a. Laissez-faire capitalism
    b. Mercantilism
    c. Interventionist capitalism
    d. Communism

34. The concepts described above most directly led to

    a. a rise in classical economic liberalism
    b. Lenin's New Economic Policy
    c. the economic development of overseas colonies
    d. the growth of economic urban financial centers, such as Amsterdam

35. Which group was most significantly critical of the ideas described above?

    a. The bourgeoisie
    b. Supporters of a republic
    c. Marxists
    d. Manufacturers

Questions 36-39 refer to the passage below.

"When I arrived at the board or workings of the pit I found at one of the sideboards down a narrow passage a girl of fourteen years of age in boy's clothes, picking down the coal with the regular pick used by the men. She was half sitting half lying at her work, and said she found it tired her very much, and 'of course she didn't like it.' The place where she was at work was not 2 feet high. Further on were men lying on their sides and getting. No less than six girls out of eighteen men and children are employed in this pit.

Whilst I was in the pit the Rev Mr Bruce, of Wadsley, and the Rev Mr Nelson, of Rotherham, who accompanied me, and remained outside, saw another girl of ten years of age, also dressed in boy's clothes, who was employed in hurrying, and these gentlemen saw her at work. She was a nice-looking little child, but of course as black as a tinker, and with a little necklace round her throat.

In two other pits in the Huddersfield Union I have seen the same sight. In one near New Mills, the chain, passing high up between the legs of two of these girls, had worn large holes in their trousers; and any sight more disgustingly indecent or revolting can scarcely be imagined than these girls at work-no brothel can beat it."

From Great Britain, Parliamentary Papers, "Women Miners in the English Coal Pits," 1842

36. Which was a specific impact of industrialization on European society in the nineteenth century?

    a. A dramatic decrease in agricultural output, as farmers abandoned their land to work in factories

    b. Greater opportunities and rights for women

    c. The growth of trade unions

    d. Successful socialist revolutions in industrially advanced countries

37. Which of the following developments led to the conditions described above?

    a. The transition from an agricultural to an industrial economy

    b. Britain's parliamentary government discouraged commercial and industrial interests

    c. Socialists called for a fair distribution of society's resources.

    d. Radicals demanded full citizenship without regard to wealth and property

38. Which of the following developments emerged as a response to the conditions described above?

    a. Feminists pressed for economic rights and improved working conditions

    b. Conservatives developed a new ideology in support of traditional political authority

    c. Green parties emerged to develop sustainable environmental goals

    d. Communists led successful revolutions in England

39. Which of the following artistic movements developed in reaction to industrialization?

    a. Impressionism, which moved beyond the representational to the subjective, abstract, and expressive

    b. Romanticism, which focused on intuition and emotion

    c. Post-modern, which undermined confidence in science and human reason

    d. Baroque, which glorified the state

Questions 40-43 refer to the passage below.

"Of the Rights and Respective Duties of Husband and Wife:

Husband and wife mutually owe to each other fidelity, succor, and assistance.

The husband owes protection to his wife, the wife obedience to her husband. . . .

The wife can do no act in law without the authority of the husband, even where she shall be a public trader, or not in community, or separate in property."

The French Civil Code, 1804

40. Napoleon's Civil Code

    a. gave women full equality including the vote

    b. gave women equality before the law but not the vote

    c. made women legally subservient to their husbands or fathers

    d. gave legal equality to noble women but not to bourgeois women

41. The Civil Code was an example of

    a. Napoleon's challenge to Enlightenment principles
    b. Napoleon's development of domestic reforms
    c. Napoleon's focus on military tactics
    d. Napoleon's response to the Reign of Terror

42. This excerpt of the Civil Code is a continuation of which French Revolution ideology?

    a. An emphasis on equality and human rights
    b. An increase in popular participation of the people
    c. An emphasis on citizenship restricted to men
    d. An increase in legal rights for women

43. Which of the following nineteenth century groups reflected similar beliefs to the passage above?

    a. Feminists who championed rights for women
    b. Republicans who sought to create a representative government
    c. Nationalists who advocated for the creation of nation-states
    d. Supporters Cult of Domesticity who anchored men and women in separate spheres

Questions 44–47 refer to the passage below.

"... it is not by speeches and majority resolutions that the great questions of the time are decided– that was the big mistake of 1848 and 1849–but by iron and blood."

Otto von Bismarck, Chancellor of Prussia, "Blood and Iron" Speech, 1862

44. Bismarck delivered this speech in response to

    a. the rise of socialism
    b. parliamentary resistance to his military budgets
    c. Austria's aggressive statements provoking the Seven Weeks' War
    d. efforts to form the North German Federation

45. Which of the following political ideologies is most closely connected to the passage above?

    a. Development of the state is based on the consent of the governed
    b. Development of authoritarian dictatorships
    c. Development of a new conservatism that embraced nationalism
    d. Development of support for traditional political and religious authority

46. Which of the following was a result of the actions described above?

    a. Changes in the balance of power in Europe
    b. Establishment of the Concert of Europe
    c. Development of the League of Nations
    d. Creation of the United Nations

47. Which of the following actions did Bismarck take after the unification of Germany in 1871?

    a. He created a dual-monarchy between Prussia and Germany.
    b. He established the Congress of Vienna to suppress nationalist uprisings in Europe.
    c. He declared war on France.
    d. He developed a complex system of alliances.

Questions 48-51 refer to the passage below.

"I'm not able to take responsibility upon myself for doing everything in just five to seven days; this is a complex process. . . . And the party must keep control of this process, bringing the nation along with it in the construction of socialism. In this we see our duty, and in this we see our obligation, but it's impossible to do this in as short a time as you are suggesting, Cde. Brezhnev. . . . I am telling you that if you don't believe me. . . then you should take the measures that your Politburo believes are necessary."

> Alexander Dûbcek, leader of the Prague Spring, Document No. 81:
> Transcript of Leonid Brezhnev's Telephone Conversation with Alexander Dûbcek, August 13, 1968

48. Alexander Dûbek's establishment of "socialism with a human face" in Czechoslovakia

    a. was militarily and economically supported by the United States as part of the Truman Doctrine
    b. received the same military suppression as the Hungarian revolution by the Soviet Union
    c. sparked a similar movement in Poland during the 1960s
    d. led to the building of the Berlin Wall

49. The events described above were caused by which political development in the second half of the twentieth century?

    a. The Soviet Union sought hegemonic control over satellite nations
    b. The implementation of *perestroika* and *glasnost* in the Soviet Union
    c. The establishment of a common currency in Europe
    d. A totalitarian government was established to overcome massive economic depression

50. Which of the following political developments was a result of the ideas expressed above?

    a. Marshall Plan funds from the United States financed the rebuilding of the infrastructure of central and eastern Europe
    b. Authoritarian dictatorships emerged in central and eastern Europe after failures to establish democracies
    c. The rise of new nationalism in central and eastern Europe brought peaceful revolutions in most countries
    d. An "Iron Curtain" divided USSR and the West focused on deep-seated tensions and political conflict

51. Which of the following was a long-term result of the ideas expressed above?

    a. The Czechs and the Slovaks parted
    b. Yugoslavia was re-unified
    c. Germany became divided
    d. The Warsaw Pact emerged

Use the following excerpt to answer questions 52-55.

"On the basis of these reports, the Council, acting by a qualified majority on a recommendation from the Commission, shall assess:

–for each Member State, whether it fulfils the necessary conditions for the adoption of a single currency;
–whether a majority of the Member States fulfil the necessary conditions for the adoption of a single currency,
and recommend its findings to the Council, meeting in the composition of the Heads of State or of Government. The European Parliament shall be consulted and forward its opinion to the Council, meeting in the composition of the Heads of State or of Government."

> Treaty on European Union, Maastricht Treaty, 1991

52. The Maastricht Treaty of 1991

    a. ended World War II by accepting national borders
    b. promised European intervention to prevent human rights abuses
    c. specifically accepted eastern European countries into the European Union
    d. established a common currency for most European Union members

53. The Maastricht Treaty was most closely connected to which previous organization?

    a. The establishment of the European Coal and Steel Community
    b. The establishment of the United Nations
    c. The establishment of the League of Nations
    d. The establishment of the Concert of Europe

54. Which of the following was most likely an influence over the creation of the Maastricht Treaty?

    a. The desire for western Europe to compete with COMECON
    b. The desire for western Europe to compete with the Warsaw Pact
    c. The desire for Europe to create economic and political integration
    d. The desire for Europe to develop a process for decolonization

55. Which of the following was the greatest challenge to the ideals of the European Union?

    a. The collapse of the Berlin Wall and the dissolution of the Soviet Union
    b. Anti-immigrant and extreme nationalist political parties
    c. Military and political opposition from the United States
    d. Economic reforms such as *glasnost* and *perestroika*

Part B: Short-Answer Questions
Time: 40 minutes

1. Use the passages below and your knowledge of European history to answer all parts of the question that follow.

> "When the Berlin Wall fell on November 9, 1989 . . . The costs to women are hard to overlook: In the new Germany . . . It was women . . . who were expected to care for sick children or manage the "second shift" of housework, because they were the ones who were "given" the time to do so. Men were not seen as having any role in child- rearing. The turn to "mommy politics" that began in the early 1970s was also associated with noticeable increases in gender segregation on the job."
>
> Myra Marx Ferree, "The Rise and Fall of 'Mommy Politics': Feminism and Unification in (East) Germany," 1993

> "[During the 1970s, German Democratic Republican (GDR)] Party . . . undertook a comprehensive revision of the legal code to guarantee full statutory equality for women and instituted a series of laws and policies promoting women's education and training . . . Legislation assured women maternity leave and benefits with guaranteed reemployment, sick leave, and paid time off for child care and housework. Economic measures instituted a broad range of transfer payments subsidies and enforced equal pay for equal work. Political pressure and propaganda campaigns encouraged the integration of women into professions and skilled trades, and the full integration of women higher education."
>
> Dorothy J. Rosenberg,
> "Shock Therapy: GDR Women in Transition from a Socialist Welfar State to a Social Market Economy", 1991

    a. Briefly explain one difference between Ferree's argument and Rosenberg's argument.
    b. Briefly explain one piece of evidence from 1945-1991 not mentioned in the excerpts above that supports Ferree's argument.
    c. Briefly explain one piece of evidence from 1945-1991 not mentioned in the excerpts above that supports Rosenberg's argument.

2. a. Describe and explain one economic cause for imperialism in the late nineteenth century.
    b. Describe and explain one social/cultural cause for imperialism in the late nineteenth century.
    c. Describe either an economic or social/cultural effect of imperialism in the late nineteenth century.

Please choose between question #3 or #4 for your final SAQ question.

3. Use the image below and your knowledge of European history to answer all parts of the question that follow.

Raphael, *School of Athens* (1509-1511)
Images Group/REX/Shutterstock
© 2017 Bedford/St. Martin's
Distributed by Bedford/St. Martin's/Macmillan Higher Education strictly for use with its products; not for redistribution.

    a. Briefly identify and explain the humanist ideas expressed in this painting about ONE of the following.

       • Individualism
       • Classicism
       • Secularism

    b. Briefly explain how an historical example not found in the image reflects a continuation of the values of humanism in the time period 1648-1815.

    c. Briefly explain how an historical example not found in the image reflects a change in the values of humanism in the time period 1648-1815.

4. a. Briefly describe and explain a continuation regarding political unity from 1945-2001
   b. Briefly describe and explain a change regarding political unity from 1945-2001.
   c. Briefly describe and explain a change regarding economic unity from 1945-2001.

EUROPEAN HISTORY SECTION II

Total time: 1 hour, 40 minutes

Question 1 (Document-Based Question)
Time: 60 minutes

**It is suggested that you spend 15 minutes reading the documents
and 45 minutes writing your response.
Note: You may begin writing your response before the reading period is over.**

Directions: Question 1 is based on the accompanying documents. The documents have been edited for the purpose of this exercise.

In your response you should do the following:

■ **Thesis:** Present a thesis that makes a historically defensible claim and responds to all parts of the question. The thesis must consist of one or more sentences located in one place, either in the introduction or the conclusion.

■ **Evidence and Reasoning:** Develop and support a cohesive argument that recognizes and accounts for historical complexity by explicitly illustrating relationships among historical evidence such as contradiction, corroboration, and/or qualification.Utilize the content of at least six of the documents to support the stated thesis or a relevant argument.

■ **Document Analysis:** Explain the significance of the author's point of view, author's purpose, historical context, and/or audience for at least four documents.

■ **Contextualization:** Situate the argument by explaining the influence of the broader historical events, developments, or processes immediately relevant to the question.

■ **Evidence Beyond the Documents:** Provide additional specific evidence beyond those found in the documents to support or qualify the argument.

1. Analyze continuities and changes in views about the nature of women and their place in society from the late seventeenth to the early twentieth centuries.

Document 1

Source: Mary Cary, member of a religious sect during the English Civil War which believed mankind was living in the "end of days," excerpt from her book, *The New Jerusalem's Glory,* England, published in1656.

And if there be very few men that are thus furnished with the gift of the Spirit; how few are the women! Not but that there are many godly women, many who have indeed received the Spirit: but in how small a measure is it? How weak are they? And how unable to prophesie? For it is that that I am speaking of, which this text says they shall do; which yet we see not fulfilled. . . . But the time is coming when this promise shall be fulfilled, and the Saints shall be abundantly filled with the spirit; and not only men, but women shall prophesie; not only aged men, but young men; not only superiours, but inferiours; not only those that have University learning, but those that have it not; even servants and handmaids.

Document 2

Source: Mary Astell, unmarried English writer, Some Reflections Upon Marriage, 1700.

But how can a Woman scruple entire Subjection, how can she forbear to affirm the Worth and Excellency of the Superior Sex, if she at all considers it! Have not all the great Actions that have been performed in the World been done by Men? Have they not founded Empires and over-turned them? Do they not make Laws and continually repeal and amend them? Their vast Minds lay Kingdoms waste, no Bounds or Measures can be prescribed to their Desires. War and Peace depend on them; they . . . have the Wisdom and Courage to get over all . . . the petty Restraints which Honor and Conscience may lay in the way of their desired Grandeur. What is it they cannot do? They make Worlds and ruin them, form Systems of universal Nature, and dispute eternally about them; their Pen gives Worth to the most trifling Controversy. . . . It is a Woman's Happiness to hear, admire and praise them, especially if a little Ill nature keeps them at any time from bestowing the Applauses to each other! And if she aspires no further, she is thought to be in her proper Sphere of Action, she is as wise and as good as can be expected from her!

Document 3

Source: Lady Mary Wortley Montagu, author and wife of a Whig member of British Parliament, in a paper called The Nonsense of Common-Sense, January 24, 1738..

Among the most universal errors, I reckon that of treating the weaker sex with a contempt which has a very bad influence on their conduct. How many of them think it excuse enough to say they are women, to indulge any folly that comes into their heads! This renders them useless members of the commonwealth, and only burdensome to their own families. . . . What reason nature has given them is thrown away. . . .

A woman really virtuous, in the utmost extent of this expression, has virtue of a purer kind than any philosopher has ever shown. I have some thoughts of exhibiting a set of pictures of such meritorious ladies, where I shall say nothing of the fire of their eyes, or the pureness of their complexions, but give them such praises as befit a rational sensible being: virtues of choice, and not beauties of accident. . . . I would not have them place so much value on a quality that can be only useful to one, as to neglect that which may be of benefit to thousands, by precept or by example. There will be no occasion of amusing themselves with trifles, when they consider themselves capable of not only making the most amiable, but the most estimable, figures in life. Begin, then, ladies, by paying those authors with scorn and contempt who, with a sneer of affected admiration, would throw you below the dignity of the human species.

Document 4

Source: Portrait of Gabrielle Emilie Le Tonnelier de Breteui, Marquise de Châtelet, French mathematician, physicist, author, and companion of Voltaire, attributed to Maurice-Quentin de la Tour, ca. 1740.

Portrait of Gabrielle Emilie Le Tonnelier de Breteuil, Marquise de Châtelet
(Paris, 1706-Luneville, 1749), French mathematician, physics and writer. Oil on canvas
attributed to Maurice-Quentin de La Tour (1704-1788).
G. DAGLI ORTI /DEA/DeAgostini/Getty Images

Document 5

Source: Mary Wollstonecraft, English author, *A Vindication of the Rights of Women*, 1792.

My own sex, I hope, will excuse me, if I treat them like rational creatures, instead of flattering their fascinating graces, and viewing them as if they were in a state of perpetual childhood, unable to stand alone. I earnestly wish to point out in what true dignity and human happiness consists—I wish to persuade women to endeavor to acquire strength, both of mind and body, and to convince them that the soft phrases, susceptibility of heart, delicacy of sentiment, and refinement of taste, are almost synonymous with epithets of weakness, and that those beings who are only the objects of pity will soon become objects of contempt.

Dismissing those soft pretty feminine phrases, which the men condescendingly use to soften our slavish dependence, and despising that weak elegancy of mind, exquisite sensibility, and sweet docility of manners, supposed to be the sexual characteristics of the weaker vessel, I wish to shew that elegance is inferior to virtue, that the first object of laudable ambition is to obtain a character as a human being, regardless of the distinction of sex. . . . Why must the female mind be tainted by coquettish arts to gratify the sensualist and prevent love from subsiding into friendship, or compassionate tenderness, when there are not qualities on which friendship can be built? Let the honest heart shew itself, and reason teach passion to submit to necessity; or, let the dignified pursuit of virtue and knowledge raise the mind above those emotions.

Document 6

Source: Clara Zetkin, German socialist and suffragist, *A Socialist Solution to the Question of Women's Rights*, 1887.

Given the fact that many thousands of female workers are active in industry, it is vital for the trade unions to incorporate them into their movement. In individual industries where female labor plays an important role, any movement advocating better wages, shorter working hours, etc., would be doomed from the start because of the attitude of those women workers who are not organized. Battles which begin propitiously enough, ended up in failure because the employers were able to play off non-union female workers against those that are organized in unions. These non-union workers continued to work (or took up work) under any conditions, which transformed them from competitors in dirty work to scabs.

Certainly one of the reasons for these poor wages for women is the circumstances that female workers are practically unorganized. They lack the strength which comes with unity. They lack the courage, the feeling of power, the spirit of resistance, and the ability to resist which is produced by the strength of an organization in which the individual fights for everybody and everybody fights for the individual. Furthermore, they lack the enlightenment and the training which an organization provides.

Document 7

Source: Annie Steel, best-selling author of books about India, education, and women's issues, *The Complete Indian Housekeeper and Cook,* London, 1902.

It is not necessary, or in the least degree desirable, that an educated woman [in India] should waste the best years of her life in scolding and petty supervision. Life holds higher duties, and it is indubitable that friction and over-zeal is a sure sign of a bad housekeeper. . . .

The personal attention of the mistress is quite as much needed here as at home. . . . The first duty of the woman of the house is, of course, to be able to give intelligible orders to her servants, therefore it is necessary she should learn to speak Hindustani. . . .The next duty is obviously to insist on her orders being carried out. . . . The secret lies in making rules and keeping to them. The Indian servant is a child in everything save age, and should be treated as a child, that is to say, kindly but with the greatest firmness. . . . A good mistress in India will try to set a good example to her servants, in routine, method and tidiness. . . . An untidy woman invariably has untidy, weak , and idle servants.

NOTES:

Question 2 or 3 or 4 (Long Essay Question)

Suggested writing time: 40 minutes

Directions: Choose EITHER question 2 OR question 3 OR question 4.

In your response you should do the following:

- ■ **Thesis:** Respond to the question with an evaluative thesis that makes a historically defensible claim.

- ■ **Contextualization:** Explain a broader historical context immediately relevant to the question.

- ■ **Evidence and Reasoning:**
  - Use specific and relevant examples of historical evidence in support of argument.
  - Explain how the evidence corroborates, qualifies, or modifies your argument.

2. Discuss and analyze the extent to which humanism was a cause of the Protestant Reformation (1517–1555).

3. Discuss and analyze the extent to which imperialism was a cause of World War I.

4. Discuss and analyze the extent to which nationalism caused an end to the Soviet Union in 1991.

NOTES: